DRAMA IN WORSHIP

by
Lawrence Waddy

PAULIST PRESS
New York, N.Y./Ramsey, N.J./Toronto

Library of Congress
Catalog Card Number: 78-58952

ISBN: 0-8091-2107-7

Published by Paulist Press
Editorial Office: 1865 Broadway, New York, N.Y. 10023
Business Office: 545 Island Road, Ramsey, N.J. 07446

Printed and bound in the
United States of America

CONTENTS

LEADER'S HANDBOOK

Drama as a joyful experience . . .
Drama as a teaching medium, involving those who are taught . . .
Drama as fellowship, relaxing barriers . . .
Drama as reverent worship . . .
Because they have discovered some or all of these things, more and more churches are using drama as an important part of their program, in the church itself and in halls and classrooms.

The very encouraging response to THE BIBLE AS DRAMA, published by the Paulist Press in 1975, has led me to prepare this new collection of plays and scenes. The earlier book contains ninety Biblical scenes, whereas most of the scenes in this collection have a modern setting. All are designed for only one purpose: to help make worship more meaningful, and to illuminate the word of God.

In some cases this can better be achieved in a scene with a modern context. For example, THE EMPIRE (see page 164) is a play illustrating Jesus' command to a deaf and dumb man: 'Be opened!' Elise Morgan is the kind of person we have all met: bottled-up, lonely, repressed, in spite of all her ability and success. Denise Gibson in THE PERFECT HOUSE has a good deal in common with King Solomon, and Dene Peck in THE CHAMPION is a modern version of Samson; but in each case the modern setting ties the story in with things which ordinary people see on television every day.

The framework used is the three year cycle of scripture readings in the new Catholic Lectionary. This is very similar to lectionaries now being used by many other Christian Churches: the Episcopal Church, some Lutheran bodies, the United Methodist, some Christian (Disciples) Churches, and some Presbyterians. It would not be difficult to adapt the settings of the scenes to fit any of these lectionaries.

At the end of the book you will find a Drama Calendar. Its aim is to provide choices for each season of the year, linked to the scriptures in the Lectionary. In this way you can plan a coordinated drama program to fit into, and enrich, each year's worship.

Some of the scenes are appropriate on almost any Sunday of the year, such as WHO IS MY NEIGHBOR? and MARTIN THE COBBLER. You should feel free to work out your own timetable, to suit your special needs; but the Calendar is there as a guide.

1

1. Forming a Drama Company

How is all this to be put into practice? It is not as difficult as you might think. The circumstances are not the same in any two churches, but here is some general advice.

Most churches have a choir, as a matter of course, to lead the congregation in praising God through music. Very few have regular drama groups, to lead in the teaching of God's word. To me it seems as important to have the one as the other. Why not try it, and see?

The first requirement is a director. He or she must have some experience, but the main qualities needed are enthusiasm, love, and common sense. It is important for the director to have the confidence of the clergy of the church, so that he will work loyally inside the framework of worship. Better no drama group at all than one which seeks its own glorification at the expense of balanced and reverent services.

Then the director sets about finding a nucleus of members. My advice is to start on a small scale with adults. Find at least three, and not more than eight, who can be relied on to meet regularly. You should require that they stick faithfully to the schedule of rehearsals, but do not demand an unrealistic amount of time.

Next, with this nucleus READ a number of plays. This will establish friendships, test abilities, and break down constraints. Also, the members will gain a general view of the group's purpose, if they read a few plays before starting to concentrate on one.

After this, settle on a play or scene, to fit one of the upcoming Sundays. Plan with the clergy how it is to be fitted into the services. Should it be in place of a Gradual, leading into the Gospel? Or is it to be linked closely to the sermon? If you have begun to meet in August or September (a good idea, with time to prepare for the new Church year) you might choose TO ENTER INTO LIFE CRIPPLED, or HONOR YOUR FATHER, or TAKE-OVER; or you may prefer to begin with a scene from THE BIBLE AS DRAMA.

A short scene should only require four or five rehearsals. Be especially careful to anticipate technical problems for this first presentation, such as the question of audibility.

If your first effort earns approval, prepare a series of scenes. And ask for volunteers to increase your numbers, until you have a company of between twelve and twenty adults. You will now come to know whether you should undertake only the shorter, simpler scenes, or whether you can include more demanding texts like THE PERFECT HOUSE or THE CHAMPION. Furthermore, with each presentation you will learn more about the technical needs of your building. Confidence, and the feeling of fulfillment which comes from doing a good job for the church, should raise the morale of your company to a high level.

You will need the help of younger actors. If they are introduced when the standards have already been set, they will easily fit in. They can add a great deal, and contribute skill and color. By introducing them among adults, you prevent the congregation from thinking that drama is just a way of occupying children, as opposed to a form of witness and teaching to be taken seriously.

2. Two Specimen Plays

Let us analyze the production of two plays, one short and simple, the other more complex.

GLAD TO SEE YOU BACK is a five-minute play. The challenge is in the hands of two actresses, since Henry's part is short and straight. Marie and Delia have to grow into their characters, and they will find opportunity for development and interpretation even in this short scene. The director probably starts off with a good idea of how he wishes these parts to be played. He will allow the two actresses to share their ideas, and the result will be partly his and partly theirs, although he must have the last word.

Looking at the scene in Marie's office carefully, we can see that her voice and manner change at a definite moment. In her first four lines, she is friendly and matter-of-fact, professional. She is trying to find out what Delia's trouble is—for Delia, quiet and tense, shows at once that her ordinary words cover deep emotions. The cues should be taken up quickly in this early dialogue, especially Marie's.

Then Marie has an important line; "I—oh, I remember. But—." For the first time, she pauses before this line. She must show that she is taken by surprise, and trying to think back to yesterday's encounter, which meant nothing to her at the time.

A moment later there is a pair of vital lines. Delia says, "No. You said you were glad to see me back," and Marie replies, "Yes, Delia. I believe I did say that." I suggest that these two lines be spoken unemotionally, and yet convey deep feeling. Delia is repeating the words which have been in her mind ever since they were spoken. Marie understands this now, and is recalling that the words were in fact purely automatic.

Practice these two lines until you are sure that they are making a full impact. We liked Marie from the start. Now we identify with her, and feel how greatly stirred she is by Delia's trust. But Marie never, throughout the scene, allows her emotions to be fully shown.

3

While Delia is telling the story of her sister, she is the emotional center of the scene. Marie is reacting to what she is told, and we feel her choosing her words with care and concern. She realizes that she has stepped unawares into a relationship which matters immensely. The next key moment comes with Delia's words, "She was fifteen, Mrs. Edwards." Practice this line, and Marie's reply, until the balance is right. Delia is not far from breaking down, but still just in control. Marie, without over-dramatizing the line, "Oh, Delia! I'm so sorry," shows us how deeply she is affected.

So far we have discussed words only. But words convey a different meaning spoken from a distance, or accompanied by physical contact. I envisage Marie behind a desk at the beginning of the scene, leaving Delia both closer to the audience and in the limelight. Marie should come forward at whatever moment you find to be most effective. It could be either at the words, "Oh, Delia! I'm so sorry," or on her next line, when she reacts to Delia's tears. Notice that in a scene which has no dramatic actions, a small thing like a box of tissues becomes important. How will you use it?

A final moment of great significance comes with Delia's last speech, and Marie's reply. Delia says, "I enjoyed your class last year," and Marie answers, "I'm glad" — and she IS glad. In a small way, and also without realizing it, Delia has given back to her teacher the same kind of lift which she had received in the corridor a day earlier.

Marie had then used the word 'glad' perfunctorily, and it proved to have great meaning for Delia. Now she uses it again, and means it; but this time Delia is not aware of it.

Two more observations about this play. First, rehearse the crowd of students in the corridor. Crowd scenes are never easy, and can be painfully clumsy. Spend time coaching the students to make their lines sound natural, while Henry and Marie are speaking their opening words. Overlapping crowd voices, not too loud, are a matter of careful discipline.

Secondly, think where you will set this play in the service. Best of all, I think, just before the Gospel. Then the marvelous words, "Who touched me?" should have a greater impact on the audience than ever before.

3. The Perfect House

This is a longer play, and appears to demand a large stage and a complicated set. But the words and characters must conquer the imagination of the audience. The bulletin should explain that the

4

setting is the Gibsons' lavish home. Most people will respond to this challenge, and conjure up the setting in their minds. If your congregation is already used to the idea of drama in the church, this presentation should not prove too hard for them or for the actors.

You need only a suggestion of the room's furniture: a telephone on a table, a good light-colored rug, and an armchair—these are required by the text—and anything else which may be helpful in building the atmosphere. A good settee, upstage center, may pull the room together.

Amadeo is slow-moving, easy-going, and gently humorous, in sharp contrast to Denise. Whatever she says or does, we feel her intensity and compulsion, as well as her great ability. You can express this in her dress, her hairstyle, her movements, and her speech. There should be a clear contrast in the pace and expression of these two actors' early lines.

The contrast between Denise and Bob is, in a way, the same. Bob should, for preference, be a big, fine-looking man; a man's man, silver-haired, with a deep voice and relaxed manner. But we know that he is not relaxed in relation to Denise. From his first entrance we feel an undercurrent of worry about her, about the house, and about the party. He knows that her compulsiveness is dangerous, and that there will be a reaction after the first excitement. Bob loves Denise, and she him; but the house is already a barrier threatening them, although they have not spoken of it.

This comes out, of course, in the final scene, but it is implicit in the scene with Lester, the architect. One of Denise's key speeches begins with the words, "I could stop the clock forever at this moment." She must convince the audience that this comes from her heart, even though it is true that she agrees at the end of the play that it is a "silly house"—so that we know she has been unsure about it. The actress playing Denise has to soak herself in Denise's feeling about the house, and bring this out in her own way.

As for Bob, he brushes aside Lester's comments about the finished house. "I'm an outdoor nut," he says—which is an admission that the house is going to be hard to live in. But he is loyal to Denise in talking to their friend. "It's her big day," he tells Lester. "If it fulfills what she wants, that's fine by me." We like Bob for this, but we feel uncomfortable and apprehensive with him.

The first part of the play, up to Lester's departure, has established what the characters think about the party (the Amadeo scene) and the house (the Lester scene). By this time, the house should be a vivid thing in the minds of the audience—it is the central 'personal-

5

ity' of the play. The audience must identify with Denise's driving ambition and Bob's underlying fears.

From the moment when the crash of the bus is heard, action takes over. Denise's reaction to the crash should not seem improbable after the earlier scenes. Bob must show an anger towards her which is all the greater because he does love her. He suddenly comes up against everything in her which he has been dreading; and he can have no idea that the crash of the bus will provide the only kind of shock which can cure her obsession.

Bob and Denise have great opportunities in the dialogue which begins with her words, "Bob! Whatever was all that about?", and ends with the struggle by the front door. So far, she is merely curious. She heard the crash, but did not take it in. Her mind was too firmly gripped by her party. She asks Bob this question, because it is a nuisance for him to have anything to distract him from her preparations.

And Bob has no idea of her coming reaction, when he says "I'm afraid it's really bad." It takes him a little time to believe that from that moment Denise thinks of nothing but her own interests.

She begins, "You told them—," still calm, and incredulous. But by the time she says, "Are you telling me that they're coming to this house?" a brittle hysteria is perceptible in her voice, and it mounts with every speech until the struggle at the door.

It is Bob who has greater variety in his lines in this scene. He is a decent, kindly man. He wants to appeal to her, and make her understand. Anger only comes to the surface when she countermands his order to Amadeo. And when she says, "I'll hate you forever . . .", we feel that his anger is still chiefly aimed at the waste of precious time.

He becomes convinced that the nightmare is real when she says, "Bob, I'm locking the door." Now that he knows she is truly trying to keep the children out, he is angry to the point of white-hot violence. The struggle should be grimly realistic, and the accompanying lines as melodramatic as possible. Denise is thrown to the floor, and gets up slowly. She does not move again until she says, "Bob, are the—ambulances coming?" But there is a great deal of acting for her to do while she stands to the side of the door. Blind rage begins to turn into an unwilling comprehension of what she has tried to do in shutting the children out of her home.

The Doctor and the Man have simple, straight parts. The next line of special importance is Denise's "Doctor Barrow! Come quickly, please! It's this boy." The audience knows that she has changed abruptly. She is scared, and she is stirred.

When Bob and the Doctor reenter after the time lapse, the interest centers on Bob's lines. The Doctor continues to play it straight, but each of Bob's speeches has a fresh inflection and emotion. When Barrow says, "I'm sorry for what it's done to your house," he has no idea what a sore spot he is hitting. Bob's reaction is bitter and violent, surprising the Doctor, who goes on to make another unconsciously loaded comment, "She's quite a girl, Bob." What is Bob to say? He pauses, then gives the conventional reply, flatly spoken. He conveys to the audience the agony he is feeling at the prospect of being alone with Denise again.

Then they are alone. Husband and wife begin this last scene in tired, expressionless tones, with the emotion held back. Denise starts to raise her voice at the second "I hated you." The word 'hated' is repeated, and it shocks us. Denise is sparing herself nothing, for in truth it is herself that she hates at this moment. Later she uses the word again, "I didn't hate him." It may not sound like a turning-point to us, but we see that it was. It was the point of time when something else began to be as significant to her as her living room rug—a dying boy.

The central line for Bob in this scene is, "I knew that I couldn't stay in a house which means more to my wife than human beings." Then he goes back to his flat voice when he says, "The girl's name is Becky." But a question from Denise has a swift effect upon him, "Can I come with you?" He feels his closeness to her returning. He had been near to hating her. Now, when his anger dies down, he sees that she needs pity and love, not hate. Later if their marriage survives and grows stronger (and we are left hoping that it may), they will surely agree that the moment of violence and tragedy was necessary to it. Finally, Denise says, "Bob, I think it's cured." This is not a light-hearted, 'happy-ever-after' ending. A weight has been lifted, leaving the way open for a creative solution to Denise's problem. Bob, still ravaged, is not going to change all in a flash. And Denise is still the tense, hyperactive woman who planned the party—she wants to be DOING something now, in the kitchen. But they are not hiding anything any more. It is out in the open that this is a silly house. Even so, we feel that they may succeed in making it their home.

4. A Note about Music

Several of the plays in this collection were written as musicals. Scores are available, if you would like to use them. The plays to which this applies are indicated in the text. If you wish to order the scores, or to receive a catalog of them, write to:

RELIGIOUS DRAMA PRODUCTIONS,
5910 Camino de la Costa,
La Jolla, California 92037

5. A Note about Books

THE JERUSALEM BIBLE (JB in the text) has been used as the standard text throughout this book. This does not apply to the Verse Plays, in which there are many memories of older versions.

An invaluable companion to the scenes, and indeed to the whole of the three-year cycle of readings, is Gerard Sloyan's A COMMENTARY ON THE NEW LECTIONARY (Paulist Press, 1975).

6. A Note about Use of a Narrator

It may sometimes be helpful to introduce a scene with a short narration, explaining the context. This can be done in a variety of ways: as part or all of the Sermon; as an introduction spoken by one of the actors; or sometimes in the form of a Bible reading (for example the Parable of the Good Samaritan read just before acting WHO IS MY NEIGHBOR? or THE GOOD SAMARITAN).

You will find that a short narrative introduction can be adapted from the notes given before the scenes. You should work out in advance whether you feel an introduction is needed. Do not kill a scene by too much explanation.

1. THE ADVENT SEASON

Christmas Is Coming

Bible Reference: The Advent readings in general. The play is suitable for any Sunday in Advent, but the Third or Fourth are preferable.

Note: The central part of the play is an adaptation of Leo Tolstoy's story, 'Where love is, there God is also.' It can be presented as a musical. (To obtain music, see page 7.) It is a story which brings us face to face with the incarnation in a simple and beautiful way. Martin looked for Jesus to visit him, and was taught that the visitors who came, and to whom he showed love and concern, truly brought Jesus into his home. Because God sent his Son into the world, to live and die and rise again, he is still in the midst of us, and we can see him in the people around us. After a long experience with this play, I know of no story outside the Bible itself which brings Christmas home with greater force.

Scene: For the beginning and end, a family living room, away from the center stage.

Characters: FATHER
JOHN, MARY, SUE, *and* TOM, *his children.*

(*The* FATHER *is sitting, reading a book, when all four children come in, quarrelling, and speaking at the same time.*)

JOHN: I'm the eldest. I'm going to do it.
MARY: You're too dumb. You always mess everything up.
SUE: Boys aren't any good at Christmas stuff. Mary and I can do it.
TOM: I want to do it. It isn't fair!
FATHER: Just a minute! QUIET! That's better. Now, John, what's this all about?
JOHN: It's time to set up for Christmas, Dad. We all want to do it, and—
MARY: We keep fighting. It's silly.

9

FATHER: Very silly. If you can't agree to do it together, perhaps we'd better skip it this year.

TOM: But, Dad, then Santa wouldn't come.

SUE: And we'd miss all the fun.

FATHER: You don't seem to be having much fun now. Do you kids really think Christmas is all about Santa Claus?

JOHN: No, Dad. We know it's Jesus' birthday. Only—

MARY: Sue and Tom aren't old enough to understand that. All they care about is Santa.

FATHER: Then let's use this Christmas to learn some more about what it really means. It's fine to wait for Santa, but what we're really waiting for is the coming of Jesus, isn't it?

TOM: Does he come down the chimney too?

SUE: No, silly! He's in the manger.

FATHER: Let's stop calling each other silly, and do some learning together. Sit down, all of you! I'd like to tell you a story.

Scene: The scene now moves to the center of the stage. Martin's basement workroom is also his living room. To one side is his cobbler's bench, under a window (to be imagined), from which he can see the feet of passers-by in the street above. On the other side of the stage is the stove, with the samovar and the soup pot. This, together with the teacups, can all be just offstage. Martin's bed is at the rear; a table and two chairs front center. An oil lamp or candle is on the table.

Costumes should be old-fashioned and simple: an old military cloak for Stepanich, a black robe for the Pilgrim, with a rough girdle, a burlap apron for Martin, and long dresses for the women.

Characters: MARTIN AVDEYICH *(ahv-dyay-itch): in his 40's, but older looking.*
           A PILGRIM
           STEPANICH *(ste-PAN-itch), an old soldier*
           A YOUNG WOMAN, *with her baby*
           AN OLD WOMAN
           A BOY
           VOICE OF JESUS
           NARRATOR *(the Father of the family)*

(It is daytime in the workroom, but the light is not very bright. MARTIN works at his bench during the opening verses, glancing up sometimes at the feet of people passing in the street.)

NARRATOR: Martin the Cobbler sits by the window;
Watch how his work is nimble and neat!
Over his head the people are passing;
Martin can tell them simply by their feet.
He knew them by their boots.
He never saw their faces.
He knew them by their boots,
Their heels and toes and laces.

These are some boots he fitted with toe caps.
These he had sewed whenever they split.
These needed heels and these needed patches.
These needed padding so that they would fit.
He knew them by their boots, etc.

That is the way with Martin the Cobbler,
Here as he sits and works at his seat.
Most of the day he cannot see people,
Yet all the time he knows them by their feet.
He knew them by their boots, etc.

NARRATOR: (*continues*) In a certain room there lived a shoemaker named Martin Avdeyich. It was a basement room, which possessed but one window. This window looked on to the street, and through it a glimpse could be caught of passing feet. Martin was always busy, because his work lasted well, and his prices were moderate. His wife had died many years before, leaving him with a boy three years old. The boy lived with Martin, and he began to grow up and help Martin, and to be his great joy. But God had not seen fit to give Martin happiness in his child. The boy fell sick and died. Martin mourned for him bitterly, and murmured against God. His life seemed empty to him.

(*There is a knock, and* MARTIN *goes to admit the* PILGRIM, *as the Narrator continues. They sit at the table, and talk in dumb show.*)

One day an old peasant pilgrim came to Martin's shop, and they talked together, Martin told him of his great sorrow, and said that he had no wish left except for death.

PILGRIM: You should not speak like that, Martin. You must learn to live for the God who gave you life, and not for yourself.
MARTIN: But how am I to live for him?
PILGRIM: Tell me first, can you read?

11

MARTIN: Yes, I can.

PILGRIM: Then take this, Martin Avdeyich. Inside this book you will find the answer to your questions.

MARTIN: Thank you, but—(*He looks doubtfully at it, and reaches for his pocket.*) I must—

PILGRIM: No, no. Do not offer me any payment! If you receive what the book has to give, you will owe more than you could pay.

(*The* PILGRIM *goes out.* MARTIN *lights the lamp, picks up the book, still doubtfully, puts on his spectacles, and begins to read.*)

NARRATOR: Now at first Martin only meant to read from his Bible on festival days, but from the beginning it gave him great comfort. Indeed, he became so engrossed that he would read until the oil burned out in his lamp. All day he would work hard and well, and at night he would read.

(MARTIN *sits reading. We hear his voice from a tape recorder, or live.*)

MARTIN'S VOICE: "And unto him that smiteth thee on the one cheek offer also the other; and him that taketh away thy cloak forbid not to take thy coat also. Give to every man that asketh of thee, and of him that taketh away thy goods ask them not again. And as ye would that men should do to you, do ye also to them likewise. (*He turns the page.*) And why call ye me Lord, Lord, and do not the things which I say? Whosoever cometh to me, and heareth my sayings, and doeth them, I will show you to whom he is like: he is like a man which built an house, and digged deep, and laid the foundation on a rock . . . But he that heareth and doeth not, is like a man that without a foundation built a house upon the earth." (*He removes his spectacles, and rubs his eyes.*) Is my house founded upon rock? May the Lord help me to stand firm! Ah well! It is time to go to bed. Yet I must read one chapter more.

(*If a recorder is used, the recorded voice begins again.*)

"And he turned to the woman, and said unto Simon the Pharisee, See'st thou this woman? I entered into thine house, and thou gavest me no water for my feet; but she hath washed my feet with tears, and wiped them with the hairs of her head. Thou gavest me no kiss; but this woman since the time I came in hath not ceased to kiss my feet. My head with oil thou didst not anoint; but this woman hath anointed my feet with ointment." (*He says aloud.*)

12

"Thou gavest me no water for my feet . . . My head with oil thou didst not anoint. . . . "I am just like that Pharisee! I think only of my own needs. If the Lord himself should come and visit me, should I receive him any better?

> If Jesus came to my house,
> Should I be on the watch?
> Should I know his tread, and
> His hand upon the latch?
> Should I be unworthy
> Of so great a guest?
> Should I try to give him
> Warmth and care and rest?
>
> Simon was a Pharisee,
> Rich and full of pride.
> Yet he did not welcome
> Jesus to his side.
> Am I any better
> Than a Pharisee?
> Would he find a welcome
> If he came to me?

(MARTIN's *head nods, and he sleeps. After a pause a voice calls him gently.*)

VOICE: Martin!
MARTIN: Who is there? (*He starts up, looks round, then sits again.*)
VOICE: Martin! It is I, Jesus. Look into the street tomorrow! I am coming to visit you.

(MARTIN *gets up, rubs his eyes, shakes his head, and goes to the bed. During a short music bridge he comes back to the bench and begins to work. He keeps peering up at the window, as pairs of feet pass.*)

NARRATOR: Next day Martin could not get out of his head the words he had heard or else fancied, as he sat asleep. Whenever a pair of boots passed, he peered upwards to see the face, even when he knew the boots. The doorkeeper passed, and a water-carrier. Then an old soldier, a veteran of Tsar Nicholas' Army, shuffled by in old, patched boots, carrying a shovel. He stopped near the window, and began to clear the snow. (*We hear the sound.* MARTIN *peers eagerly up.*)

13

MARTIN: O, I must be getting senile! It's only old Stepanich clearing the snow; and just because he comes I jump to the conclusion that Christ is coming to visit me. He's too old to be doing that work; and he's half frozen. I wonder if he'd like some tea. The samovar must be ready. (*He brews the tea, and opens his door to go up the steps.*) Stepanich! Stepanich! Come in and warm yourself! You must be frozen.

STEPANICH: O, Christ reward you! My bones are almost cracking! (*He enters the room slowly.*)

MARTIN: There! That should help to fight the cold. A stove and a samovar are good friends in weather like this. Here, don't trouble to wipe your boots! I'm always doing it in my job. Come and sit down, and we'll empty this teapot together. (*He kneels in front of* STEPANICH *to wipe the boots. They then drink their tea.* STEPANICH *finishing quickly. He turns his cup upside down, and wipes his mouth with his sleeve.*)

STEPANICH: Thank you, Martin Avdeyich!

MARTIN: Have another cup, Stepanich! (*But his attention is always half on the window.*)

STEPANICH: Thank you kindly. (*A pause.*) Are you expecting somebody?

MARTIN: Expecting somebody? Well, to tell you the truth, Yes. Or—well, I am and I am not. (*We see them continue in dumb show.*)

NARRATOR: And Martin told Stepanich about the words which he had heard the night before, and how the Lord had said that he would visit him that day. Then he filled Stepanich's cup once more with tea.

(*We see this action. Then* MARTIN's *voice resumes.*)

MARTIN: Drink it up! It will do you good. You know, I often call to mind, Stepanich, that when Jesus walked this earth there was never a man, however humble, whom he despised, and how it was chiefly among the common people that he lived. It was from among them, from men like you and me, sinners and working folk, that he chose his disciples. "Whosoever," he said, "shall exalt himself, the same shall be abased; and whosoever shall abase himself, the same shall be exalted. You call me Lord," he said, "yet will I wash your feet. Whosoever," he said, "would be chief among you, let him be the servant of all. "Because," he said, "blessed are the lowly, the peacemakers, the merciful and the charitable."

14

(STEPANICH *has forgotten his tea. He sits still, with tears in his eyes.*)

Oh, but you must drink your tea. I'm talking too much.

STEPANICH: I thank you, Martin Avdeyich. You have taken me in, and fed me, body and soul. *(He rises to go.)*

MARTIN: You must come again. I am only too glad to have you.

(STEPANICH *goes out.* MARTIN *finishes his tea, washes the cups and goes to his work. He works on, humming and watching the window.*)

MARTIN: Who's this? A woman with a baby! And look how thin her clothes are! I must ask her in out of the wind. *(He goes out up the stairs.)* Won't you bring your baby in, my good woman? It's warm in here. Come in and wrap the child up! *(She enters. She is young, but anxious-looking, and her clothes are thin.* MARTIN *points to the bed.)* Sit there and feed him! You'll be near the stove.

WOMAN: I cannot feed him. I have had nothing to eat myself today.

MARTIN: Nothing to eat? Well, I'll find you something. Here! *(He pours soup from a jug on the stove.)* Let me hold the baby! I have had little ones of my own. There! *(He tries smacking his lips at the baby, then wiggles a black finger in front of its face.)*

WOMAN: *(laughing)* You are a friend in great need, sir. When I came to your window I was losing hope.

MARTIN: Have you nothing warmer to wear?

WOMAN: I had a warm shawl, but I had to sell it. I am a soldier's wife, you see, sir; and my husband was sent to a distant station. I have heard nothing of him in eight months.

MARTIN: So he has never seen his baby yet?

WOMAN: No. At first I got a place as a cook, but when the baby came I lost my job. That was three months ago, and I have had no work since. I tried to get other jobs but nobody would have me: they said I was too thin. I have just been to see a tradesman's wife. She promised to take me on, but when I arrived today she told me to come back next week.

MARTIN: Have you a place to live?

WOMAN: Thank God, my landlady allows me shelter even when I cannot pay for it. She's an old widow and likes company.

MARTIN: Here! Hold your baby! *(He stoops to open an old trunk by the bed, rummages in it and produces a jacket.)* Look! It's a poor old thing, but it will at least serve to cover you.

(*She looks at it, then at him, and bursts into tears.*)

15

WOMAN: I thank you in Jesus' name, sir. Surely it was he who sent me to this house.

MARTIN: (*smiling*) He did indeed put me by my window; but it was not for you that I was looking.

(*Again we see his lips moving as he tells his story.*)

NARRATOR: So Martin told her about his dream, and why he was watching so closely when she stopped by his door. Then she thanked him, and went on her way; and Martin returned to his work.

(*We see her get up, thank him, and leave.* MARTIN *works on, glancing constantly upwards.*)

OLD WOMAN: (*from street*) I've got you, you little wretch!

BOY'S VOICE: (*from street*) Let me go! Let me go!

(MARTIN *puts down his work, and hurries out. This scene is best played in front of the main stage.* MARTIN *comes down center, as the* OLD WOMAN *enters, holding the boy by the collar.*)

OLD WOMAN: Don't you try to deny it. You stole my apple!

MARTIN: Now, now, my good woman. Let go of him, please! Pardon him, for the good Lord's sake!

OLD WOMAN: Pardon him! Not until he has felt the policeman's stick.

BOY: I never took it, I tell you! Let me go!

MARTIN: Now, let him go, please! He won't do it again. (*She releases the boy, who turns to run.*) No, you, don't, my lad. You must say you are sorry. I saw you take the apple.

BOY: (*crying*) I'm sorry, Grandmother. I did take it. I'm sorry.

MARTIN: There now. I shall give you one. (*To the* OLD WOMAN) Don't worry! I'll pay for it.

OLD WOMAN: Yes, but you spoil him by doing that! He ought to be beaten so soundly that he wouldn't want to sit down for a week — for two weeks!

MARTIN: That may be our way of giving rewards, but it's not God's way. If he ought to be whipped for taking the apple, what about us and our sins? (*She is silent for a moment.*)

OLD WOMAN: I know, sir, I know. I had seven children of my own at home once. Now I only have my daughter, and my grandchildren. But you should see them run to meet me when I come home from work. Aksintka will go to no one else. "Granny," she calls, "dear Granny, you look tired!" (*She pauses.*) O, God go with him!

16

Everyone knows what boys are like.

BOY: (*as she begins to lift her basket*) No, let me carry it, Grandmother! It will be on my way home.

(*They go off together. Martin watches them, smiling.*)

MARTIN: She forgot all about her money. (*He goes back into the house.*) Now, where are my spectacles? I must put my work away, and light the lamp. (*These actions follow.*) Now for the Book! (*He brings it to the table.*) That's funny! It seemed to open of its own accord. (*He sits and begins to read.*)

VOICE OF STEPANICH: (*after a pause*) Martin?

MARTIN: (*startled*) What? Who is it?

VOICE OF STEPANICH: Martin! Don't you know me?

MARTIN: Who are you?

STEPANICH: (*coming out of the dark corner by the window*) It is I, Martin—Stepanich.

VOICE OF YOUNG WOMAN: Martin! (*coming out of another corner*) It is I, Father.

OLD WOMAN: (*on the other side of the stage*) And I, Martin.

BOY: (*coming out after her*) And I, sir.

MARTIN: (*staring after them*) Yes . . . yes. (*He turns slowly back to the table, puts on his spectacles, and holds his Bible close to the lamp. We see his face brightly lit, and very calm and happy, as he begins to read, slowly.*) "For I was hungry, and ye gave me meat. I was thirsty and ye gave me drink. I was a stranger, and ye took me in. Inasmuch as ye have done it unto one of the least of these my brethren, ye have done it unto me." (*His voice fades away, and the Chorus begins to sing softly in the background. He reads on for a little, then puts his head in his hands. He must not look as though this is a gesture of weariness, but the attitude of a man praying and at peace.*)

STEPANICH: I was hungry, and you gave me meat.

YOUNG WOMAN: I was hungry, and you bade me eat.

OLD WOMAN: I was thirsty, and ready to sink.

BOY: I was thirsty, and you bade me drink.

(*The four come forward, center. The woman with the baby sits, and STEPANICH stands behind her—like Joseph and Mary. The boy kneels in front of her. MARTIN brings each of them tea as the following words are spoken or sung. After one verse the Pilgrim knocks, and MARTIN brings him in, welcomes him and gives him tea.*)

17

NARRATOR OR CHORUS: Who is my neighbor?
He whose cry I hear.
Who is my neighbor?
He whose need is near.
Who is my neighbor?
He whose plight I see.
Who is my neighbor?
He who calls on me.

He is my neighbor,
Who will hear my cry.
He is my neighbor,
Who will not pass me by.
Who is my neighbor,
In my hour of grief?
He is my neighbor,
Who will bring relief.

Go, and do likewise!
Never close your door!
Go, and do likewise!
Seek the sick and poor!
Find out your neighbor!
Serve your God above!
Go, seek your neighbor!
Fill the world with love!

(*As the song ends,* MARTIN *puts out the lamp.*)

(*As the last verse ends, the family scene begins again.*)

FATHER: Does that make things any clearer?

MARY: Yes, Daddy. I'm sorry I got mad with the others.

JOHN: Me too. Can we try now, Dad? Take turns, and help each other?

FATHER: Good idea! Why don't you begin right away? Let Tom have the first turn, because he's the youngest.

(*The children arrange the figures on the center stage as a nativity scene. Martin, the Pilgrim, and the Old Woman kneel with the Boy in front of the baby, holding gifts from the children. Model animals may also be brought in. Meanwhile, a carol is sung.*)

18

2. FIRST SUNDAY IN ADVENT

The End of the World

Bible Reference: General. The Second Coming and the End form the theme of all readings in A, B, and C.

Note: Advent is the season during which Christians think about the coming of Jesus Christ. They prepare to celebrate his first coming, at Christmas, and they study what the Bible says about the Second Coming. And it needs careful study. Uncritical interpretation of the Book of Revelation, and other Bible passages taken (often out of context) from the Prophets and the Gospels, has led some people to make wild and frightening predictions of coming disaster. The 'end of the world' has been predicted a great many times since Jesus' lifetime.

What he most assuredly tells us is to be ready at all times for his coming; but he also warns us not to make calculations and prophecies about the times and the seasons. (Compare Matthew 24:42 with Acts 7:1.)

The scene dramatizes something which has happened to many of us in present-day America. Sincere believers in the imminence of 'the end' often approach other people to warn them about it.

The characters of Stan and Nora can be substantiated by a perusal of a popular book like "The Late Great Planet Earth," in which similar arguments are employed. Henry and Jane represent normal, thoughtful Christians, who have read the Bible, and are trying to see a balanced picture of the words of Jesus.

Also suitable for: Fifth and Sixth Sundays of Easter; 10th, 31st, 32nd, and 33rd Sundays of the Year, and Christ the King.

Fifth Sunday of Easter, Epistle and Gospel C (Revelation 21:1–5) contains John's glorious vision of 'a new heaven and a new earth,' where God 'will wipe away all tears.' No finer picture of the end, or fulfillment, of the world is contained anywhere in the Bible. And in the accompanying Gospel (John 13:34) the evangelist records the perfect advice given to Christians awaiting that end: 'I shall not be with you much longer . . . I give you a new commandment: love one another.'

19

Sixth Sunday of Easter, Epistle C, is a continuation of the description of the end in Revelation 21.

10th Sunday of the Year, OT/A, contains a beautiful link with this scene, in Hosea 6:3: 'Let us set ourselves to know Yahweh; that he will come is as certain as the dawn.'

31st Sunday of the Year, Epistle C, (I Thess. 1:11–2:2) might well have been quoted by Henry and Jane Wilson. 'Please do not get excited too soon or alarmed by any prediction or rumor or any letter claiming to come from us implying that the Day of the Lord has already arrived.' The verse before this has stated clearly Paul's belief in the Second Coming, and the need to be ready. In fact this Epistle sums up the balanced Christian view of the end.

32nd Sunday of the Year, Epistle A, (I Thess. 4:13–18) discusses the end from the point of view of the departed. In this early letter Paul implies a belief in the early Second Coming of Jesus: 'Any of us who are left alive until the Lord's coming will not have any advantage over those who have died.'

33rd Sunday of the Year. All three C readings are concerned with the end. The Malachi verses (4:1–2) give a stark picture of the burning of evildoers, in contrast to those on whom 'the sun of righteousness will shine out with healing in its rays.' Another Epistle from 2 Thess. (3:7–12) finds Paul dealing with the strange problem of members of that Church who were refusing to work because the end was imminent. (The same subject came up in American newspapers during 1976.) And finally, in the Gospel (Luke 21:5–19) appears one of Jesus' warnings against those who say that 'the time is near at hand.'

Scene: The living room of the Wilsons' home, in late afternoon.

Characters: HENRY *and* JANE WILSON, *in their fifties.*
STAN *and* NORA, *evangelists, in their early twenties.*

(HENRY *is sitting reading a newspaper, when the doorbell rings. He opens the door.*)

HENRY: Good evening.
STAN: (*from outside*) Good evening, Sir. My friend and I are evangelists.
NORA: May we talk to you for a few minutes?
HENRY: Evangelists? All right, why don't you come in?
STAN: Thank you very much. (*They come in.*)

20

NORA: We want to ask you whether you are ready for the Second Coming of Jesus Christ.

HENRY: I think I had better call my wife. She is better at this kind of thing than I am. Jane!

JANE: (*off stage*) Yes, dear? Who is it?

HENRY: Two young people. They're here about the Second Coming.

JANE: (*entering*) The Second Coming? That's a surprise. Good evening. I'm Jane Wilson, and this is Henry—you've met him already.

STAN: I'm Stan Evans, Mrs. Wilson.

NORA: And I'm Nora Bell.

JANE: Well, why don't we sit down? I keep my Bible here in the drawer.

NORA: You read your Bible? Then you must know that Christ is soon coming.

JANE: He's coming—there's no doubt about that. But soon? We were discussing that at our Church recently, weren't we, Henry?

HENRY: That's right.

NORA: 'The day of the Lord is near in the valley of decision'—that's what the Bible says.

HENRY: Yes, the Prophet Joel. But he wrote that hundreds of years before Jesus lived. What did he mean by 'near'?

STAN: Look at this, Sir, in Acts, chapter 1. 'This same Jesus, which is taken up from you into heaven, shall so come in like manner as ye have seen him go into heaven.'

JANE: Yes, my dear. But look back three verses, and you find Jesus' own words: 'It is not for you to know the times and the seasons which the Father hath put in his own power.' It seems to me you are trying to know what he told us to leave to him.

STAN: But don't you believe we should be ready?

JANE: Of course I do. 'Watch and pray,' he told us. 'Ye know not what hour your Lord doth come.'

HENRY: But that's no reason to go around frightening folks with quotes from the Bible, slanting it to make it look as though it must be happening soon.

NORA: But, Mr. Wilson, there are so many signs: the return of the Jews to Israel, the ten-horned beast (that must be the Common Market in Europe).

STAN: And the ecumenical movement—the Churches trying to join together, including Rome. They want a super-Church, and it will only help anti-Christ to rule the world.

HENRY: Look, you kids. I'm sure you're sincere, but I'd like to know where you picked up that stuff. Go home and do your homework a bit more thoroughly! Start with Jesus. It's not easy to understand what he was saying about the end of the world, or about his own Second Coming. 'This generation will not pass, till all these things be fulfilled.' That's a puzzle, isn't it? But just after that he says, 'But of that day and hour knoweth no man.'

JANE: And he has warned his disciples earlier in the same chapter: 'Many false prophets shall arise, and shall deceive many . . . If any man shall say unto you, Lo, here is Christ, or, There; believe it not.'

HENRY: We set most store by Jesus' own words. No offence to you. We wish you well.

JANE: You have a lot of courage, going from door to door like this.

NORA: But there's so much more. In Revelation—

HENRY: No, Nora. We've told you where we stand. Now why don't we say a prayer together, and part friends?

STAN: O.K., Mr. Wilson.

HENRY: Then let us bow our heads.

3. SECOND SUNDAY IN ADVENT

John the Baptist

Bible Reference: General. The theme for this Sunday is preparation for the coming of Jesus. In 2 Peter it is called the Day of the Lord or the Day of God (Epistle B), while Paul calls it the Day of Christ (Epistle C). All three Gospel readings describe the preaching of John the Baptist.

As John was the forerunner of Jesus, it is natural for his story to be told during the Advent season. He was surely among the most unselfish great men in history. His whole message was that he was preparing the way for another far greater than himself.

The mistrust which Jesus encountered from the Jewish authorities began in the time of John. He was watched, in case he might be dangerous. But his call to baptism and repentance met with a ready response. Some of Jesus' disciples were previously followers of John, as we learn from John 1:40.

This scene incorporates some of John's actual preaching. The characters are imaginary, except for John and Andrew, but the dialogue is based closely on the Gospel narratives.

Also suitable for: 2nd, 19th, and 26th Sundays of the Year.

2nd Sunday of the Year, Gospel A (John 1:29–34), contains John the Baptist's description of Jesus as 'the Lamb of God.' 'I am the witness,' he says, 'that he is the Chosen One of God.'

19th Sunday of the Year, Epistle B (Ephesians 4:30–5:2), has no reference to John the Baptist; but verse 30 is very much in the spirit of his preaching, with its reference to 'the Holy Spirit of God who has marked you with his seal for you to be set free when the day comes.' John, who taught that he could only baptize with water, while Jesus would baptize with the Holy Spirit and with fire, would have loved to read these words.

26th Sunday of the Year, Gospel A (Mt. 21:28–32), contains one verse about John. It is a scathing criticism of the 'respectable' characters in our scene.

Scene: A desert place, near Bethabara, East of the Jordan.

23

Characters: NICODEMUS, *a Pharisee*
EZRA, *a Sadducee*
A PRIEST
A LEVITE
JOHN THE BAPTIST
A TAX COLLECTOR
A SOLDIER
ANDREW
CROWD

(*The* PHARISEE *and* SADDUCEE *approach each other across the stage.*)

PHARISEE: Greetings, Ezra! What brings you to this wild place?
SADDUCEE: Nicodemus! I might ask you the same thing. But I can guess the answer.
PHARISEE: The so-called Baptist? John?
SADDUCEE: Exactly. I have come to see what is really happening.
PHARISEE: I too. They say he is coming this way soon, with a crowd at his heels.
SADDUCEE: A fine man, I hear. Austere—they say he eats simple desert food, wild honey and locusts—disciplined, knows the Law well.
PHARISEE: And a magnetic speaker. Oh yes. The question is, is he orthodox?
SADDUCEE: You and I might disagree about what that means, Nicodemus. (*Noise of crowd offstage.*) Well, here they come! We shall soon know.

(*Enter* JOHN, *with a crowd following him.*)

SOLDIER: Stop and talk to us, Master!
LEVITE: Master, I want to ask you a question.
ANDREW: Please, Master, give me an answer!
JOHN: All right, my friends! Stop here, and ask your questions. I see we have distinguished visitors from the City. Good evening, gentlemen!
SADDUCEE: You are John-ben-Zacharias? I am Ezra, a Sadducee, from Jerusalem.
PHARISEE: And I am Nicodemus, a Pharisee of that City.
JOHN: I have no soft, smooth words to say to you. Go back and tell the leaders in Jerusalem that I see in them a generation of vipers,

24

bloodsuckers and traitors to God's word. Repent, and be washed clean by baptism, if you truly wish to humble yourselves before God!

PHARISEE: You dare to say that to us, the children of Abraham?

JOHN: Oh, Abraham! If God wanted to do so, he could take these stones and turn them into children of Abraham.

PRIEST: That is blasphemy!

JOHN: I dare to say to you what the Prophet Isaiah said: 'Prepare the way of the Lord, the coming Messiah!'

SOLDIER: But, Master, if I seek baptism, what will it mean? I'm a soldier. How can I follow you, and do my job?

JOHN: A soldier? Then you are trained to observe discipline, and preserve peace. Don't use your power to oppress the people you are meant to protect! Do your job without cruelty or favoritism!

TAX COLLECTOR: And me, Master? I'm a tax collector.

JOHN: It's the same thing with you, friend. Be fair and honest, avoid extortion, and follow God's Law. Listen, all of you! This is a call to simple justice, and love. If you have spare clothes, and plenty to eat, share what you have with the cold and hungry!

LEVITE: May I ask what your authority is for saying all this?

JOHN: Indeed you may, Sir. I have no authority, except that God has sent me to make the way clear and straight for the Savior who is coming.

PRIEST: The Messiah? You really believe that?

JOHN: If you have read the Scriptures, how can you not believe it? What I say or do is not important. I am only here to point the way for him who is to come soon—a leader so great that I am not good enough to kneel and untie his shoelaces.

ANDREW: And what does it mean, being baptized?

JOHN: Washing away your sins, after true repentance. I can see you are a man of faith, my friend. I only baptize you with water, but he who is coming after me will baptize you with God's Holy Spirit. It will be like fire, filling your life!

ANDREW: This leader—how shall we know him when he comes?

JOHN: Oh, you will know him, if you look for him with pure eyes. But first a lot of dead wood has to be cleared away from among our people. I tell you, the axe is ready to strike, and to cut down those who refuse to recognize the Messiah.

PHARISEE: May I ask why you preach out here, in the wilderness?

SADDUCEE: And wear that camel's hair shirt?

JOHN: Out here nobody can accuse me of hypocrisy. I am no popular preacher, seeking gold, and eating fine food. I stand for simple, stark repentance, to make men and women ready for the coming of the Christ, the Messiah.

PRIEST: And if he does not come?

JOHN: God forgive you for your unbelief, Sir! He will come, I promise you—and soon!

Also suitable for this Sunday: Camels for the Ark (Epistle C): see First Sunday after Christmas.

4. THIRD SUNDAY IN ADVENT

Granny Is Coming for Christmas

Bible Reference: General. The readings continue to look towards the coming of Jesus. Epistle B (I Thess. 5:16–24) adds the injunction: 'You must all think of what is best for each other.'

Note: This is a scene which explores the whole spirit of the Advent season. Rightly understood, it is a time of preparation and of joy. In an average American city you certainly see plenty of preparation for Christmas. It is the busiest time of the year in stores, and there is a real spirit of generosity and good will. But the reason for the preparation is often difficult to see. At the middle point of Advent, it may be a good thing to look inside a typical home, and to ask how the family inside it are getting ready.

Scene: A family living room, at breakfast time. The scenery and characters are the same in both parts.

Characters: FATHER
MOTHER
KATHY (16)
JERRY (14)

Part One: Who'd Want to be Granny?

KATHY: (*entering*) Mom! Isn't breakfast ready yet? I have to leave.
MOTHER: Why can't you get your own breakfast for a change? Is Jerry up yet?
KATHY: How would I know?
FATHER: (entering). Don't you talk to your Mother like that, Kathy. Where's the paper?
MOTHER: I don't suppose anyone brought it in yet. It's Jerry's job.
JERRY: Hurry up, Mom! I need my breakfast.
MOTHER: You need—You have a nerve, coming in late, looking as though you haven't even washed your face.
FATHER: Go fetch the newspaper—fast!
JERRY: Oh, don't bug me!

MOTHER: Look, all of you, Granny's arriving today at 3:30 at the Airport. Jerry, I told you to have your things out of your room, so that I can get it ready. And Kathy, don't forget you're to pick her up.

KATHY: Today? Oh, Mom, I can't. I forgot all about it. Dan wants me —

FATHER: Oh, for crying out loud! You forgot—that's all you kids ever do—forget. Here's Granny coming for Christmas, your Mother needs help, and all I hear is I forgot, I can't, I don't wanna. What is this?

JERRY: Do I have to move out of my room? It's such a drag. Why doesn't Kathy move out?"

MOTHER: (*sits down crying*) I can't stand it! You all shout at each other, and complain. I wish Granny weren't coming at all. I wish there were no such thing as Christmas! What a curse you make of Christmas with all your bickering!

Part Two: It's Christmas When Granny Comes

KATHY: Need any help, Mom?

MOTHER: No, dear, it's all ready. Give Jerry a hand with his things, will you? I have to get his room ready for Granny.

KATHY: I know. 3:30 at the Airport. I can't wait to see her!

FATHER: Time you sat down and had your own breakfast, honey. Morning, Kathy! (*He kisses both of them.*)

MOTHER: It's all on the table. Start in, Jerry!

JERRY: Coming, Mom! (*entering*) Here's the paper. Dad. The Rovers won in overtime.

FATHER: They did? That's good. Thanks, Jerry.

MOTHER: Is your room ready?

JERRY: Almost. Will Granny be here when I get back from school?

FATHER: If the flight's on time. I'll be home early today.

MOTHER: Maybe we can all walk down to the beach before dark, if she isn't too tired.

KATHY: It really feels like Christmas when Granny comes. We must get the decorations up.

FATHER: Don't forget you're coming to get the Christmas tree with me tomorrow, John.

JOHN: Can we take Granny with us?

FATHER: If she wants to come, yes.

MOTHER: Time for you two to leave. I'll finish your room, Jerry.

Have a good day! And Kathy, drive carefully this afternoon.
Christmas traffic at the airport is bad.

KATHY: I will, Mom. 'Bye, Dad!

JERRY: 'Bye Mom, Dad. See you! (*The children go out.*)

FATHER: It's time for me to leave, too. You know something? I'm
proud to have Granny come to our home.

Also suitable for this Sunday: Bible as Drama, page 116 (Epistle A);
Job (verse play or musical.

5. FOURTH SUNDAY IN ADVENT

Joseph and Mary

Bible Reference: Gospels A and B (Mt. 1:18–24 and Lk. 1:26–38).

Note: The story of the angel Gabriel's annunciation to Mary of the birth of Jesus is very well known, and is the subject of many great paintings. Saint Matthew's account of the dream of Joseph is less familiar. It was this dream, described in Gospel A, that convinced Joseph that he should take Mary to his home as his wife. In a simple dialogue, this scene describes Joseph's visit to Mary after his dream. An understanding of the thoughts and actions of Mary and Joseph is part of our own thoughtful preparation for Christmas, for Jesus was born into a loving home.

Also suitable for: January 1st (Solemnity of Mary, Mother of God). In the Epistle for that day (Gal. 4:4–7) Paul writes that 'when the appointed time came, God sent his Son, born of a woman.' The short scene between Joseph and Mary would fit in well with this reading.

Scene: The home of Mary in Nazareth.

Characters: JOSEPH
MARY

(MARY *is sitting and sewing, when there is a knock at the door, and* JOSEPH *enters.*)

MARY: Joseph!
JOSEPH: Mary, my dearest! Oh, it's so good to see you! (*He embraces her.*)
MARY: And you, Joseph! I have been so bewildered and troubled.
JOSEPH: I want you to stop worrying, Mary. You're coming home with me.
MARY: You mean you're going through with the marriage?
JOSEPH: Yes, dear. You know how deeply I care for you. And now God has sent me a clear command.
MARY: You also?

30

JOSEPH: Yes. A dream. I know that you had a vision of the angel Gabriel. I have always believed in you, Mary—you know that. But until last night I didn't know what to do.

MARY: Tell me what happened! It makes me so happy to hear it.

JOSEPH: I went to sleep worrying about us, and what people would say about you when they knew about the baby. While I was asleep, I heard a voice, coming out of a bright light. I knew that it was the angel of the Lord.

MARY: He came to you, too! Oh, thank God!

JOSEPH: The voice said, 'Joseph, son of David, do not be afraid to take Mary into your home. She has conceived her baby through the power of the Holy Spirit. She will bear a son, whose name will be Jesus, the Savior.'

MARY: It was the same vision. God has spoken to both of us.

JOSEPH: He reminded me of the Prophet Isaiah's words: that a maiden will conceive and bear a son, called Emmanuel, 'God with us.' Then I woke up, and hurried here to tell you.

MARY: Oh, Joseph! I cannot tell why this has happened to us. I only know that I must do my best to serve him. I could not do it alone, but with your help I can.

JOSEPH: You shall not be alone, Mary. I am proud that God has chosen me to give you and your son a home. Now, get ready! I want to carry out his command without delay.

6. CHRISTMAS

(or First Sunday after Christmas)

The Innkeeper

Bible Reference: Luke 2:1–4, the Gospel for Christmas Mass at Midnight.

Note: This Scene is imaginary. We do not know what kind of man the Innkeeper at Bethlehem was. But the spirit of the Scene is faithful to the Bible story. It may help to make the situation of Joseph and Mary more vivid and understandable.

Scene: The main room of the Inn at Bethlehem. Christmas Eve.

Characters: INNKEEPER
A MAN *and* A WOMAN, *guests*
MAID
JOSEPH *and* MARY

(*The two* GUESTS *are sitting at a table, eating. The* MAID *serves them, while the* INNKEEPER *stands close by, talking to them.*)

INNKEEPER: I hope you're enjoying your meal.
MAN: It tastes great, after that journey.
WOMAN: We feel so lucky to have got the last room.
INNKEEPER: We've had a dozen people ask for rooms since you came. (*The bell rings.*) That'll be some more. Susannah!
MAID: (*entering, after having carried out some dishes*) Yes, Master?
INNKEEPER: Answer the door! Remember, we're full. No room.
MAID: Yes, Master. (*She opens the door.*)
JOSEPH: (*outside*) Good evening. May I speak to the Innkeeper?
MAID: I'm sorry, Sir. He's busy. And we don't have any room.
JOSEPH: I understand that. We've tried several places. But could I just have a word—
INNKEEPER: What's the trouble, Susannah? There's a draught com-

ing through that door. (*near the door*) I'm sorry, Sir. We just don't have any space.

JOSEPH: May I come in a minute? We have an emergency.

INNKEEPER: An emergency? All right, then, come in. But—

(JOSEPH *and* MARY *enter.*)

JOSEPH: Come inside, Mary dear! It will be warmer in here.

MAID: Come and sit down nearer the fire!

JOSEPH: She's very near her time. The rough journey has been too much for her.

INNKEEPER: She's going to have a baby? Where have you come from?

JOSEPH: Nazareth.

INNKEEPER: Nazareth? In Galilee? You must be mad!

JOSEPH: When the Romans give an order, you obey it, pregnant or not.

INNKEEPER: I don't know what to do. We've already doubled up in every room.

WOMAN: We'd like to help. But I don't see how.

MAN: Keep out of this, Anna! It's not our business.

WOMAN: It has to be somebody's business.

JOSEPH: I know you have no rooms. But what we need really is any kind of shelter. She'll die out there in the cold.

INNKEEPER: This is what happens in our trade. Feast or famine! A month ago every room was empty.

MAID: They could go in the stables, Sir.

INNKEEPER: Let a baby be born in the stables?

MAID: That's where the animals keep their young ones warm. (*to* MARY) I'll help you, if my Master will let me.

JOSEPH: We'll accept that gladly, and pay you.

MARY: Please, Sir!

INNKEEPER: I don't know what to say.

JOSEPH: Then say yes! And God will bless you!

INNKEEPER: All right, then. Susannah, show them where to go, and send some food from the kitchen. But don't linger down there! We have too much to do as it is.

MARY: We shall never forget your kindness, Sir.

INNKEEPER: Kindness? I don't know. We'll do what we can for you, but—a manger in a stable! What a way to be born!

33

7. CHRISTMAS

(or First Sunday after Christmas)

The Animal That Didn't Speak

Bible Reference: Luke 2:1–14

Note: This short scene is self-explanatory. It has general reference to the Christmas story in Saint Luke's Gospel.

Scene: The stable in which Jesus was born. The time, midnight, the moment of his birth.

Characters: THE HORSE
THE OX
THE CAMEL
THE DONKEY
NARRATOR

NARRATOR: There is a legend that at midnight, as Christmas morning begins, the animals are able to speak just for a minute. On the first Christmas morning, four of them were watching what was happening at one manger in their stable. A baby was coming to life, and there were strange rumors that the child was some kind of King—although it seemed most unlikely.

HORSE: You heard what they were saying? A King?
OX: That kid? It's a little hard to believe.
CAMEL: You never know. Stranger things have happened.
HORSE: One thing I do know. If he grows up to be a King, he will need a fine horse, a stallion like me, for instance, so that he can ride in processions and be seen by his subjects.
CAMEL: Processions! That won't do him much good. He will need to make long journeys to far-off lands. That is where I can help him. Communications are the key to a King's strength.
OX: I am sure you can both be useful in a minor degree. But a King's power depends on the lands that he owns, and it is my strength which pulls the plow. If this baby is really a King, he will need me most.

DONKEY: Excuse me—

HORSE: Probably the rumors are worthless.

CAMEL: His father and mother look like very common people.

OX: Galileeans, I'd say, from their accent.

NARRATOR: That was all that they had time to say. The poor Donkey never got in a word, and the others took no notice of him. But, in spite of that, it was the Donkey who carried the baby away to Egypt, and bore the Son of God into Jerusalem.

(*The* NARRATOR *could read G.K. Chesterton's poem,* THE DONKEY, *at the end of this Scene. It can be found in the Oxford Book of English Verse, Number 931.*)

8. FIRST SUNDAY AFTER CHRISTMAS: THE HOLY FAMILY

Camels for the Ark

Bible Reference: Luke 2:22–40 (Gospel B)

Note: The Song of Simeon, or 'Nunc Dimittis,' is part of this passage. 'Now, Master, you can dismiss your servant in peace.' In the play chosen for this Sunday, two elderly men find peace and fulfillment.

Henry Vogel is a victim of a very common ailment, the emptiness of retirement. It often strikes unexpectedly, bringing with it an ache of disillusionment. To be free of the office, free of the daily grind, sounded so wonderful. But free for what? Henry needs Anastas Bata, perhaps even more than Anastas needs him. Through their friendship, both men recover a sense of purpose.

Anastas' return to creative work recalls the haunting verses of Psalm 90, another Bible passage which depicts old age. 'Teach us to count how few days we have . . . Let us wake in the morning filled with your love . . . May the sweetness of the Lord be on us.'

The production of this play, Anastas' room should be the center. Fit the other scenes, which are short and simple, around it. Use music bridges to show the passage of time. Props are very simple.

Also suitable for: Second Sunday in Advent, First Sunday in Lent, and 26th Sunday of the Year.

Second Sunday in Advent. Epistle C (Phil. 1:4–6, 8–11) contains a wonderful description of friendship. 'My prayer for you is that your love for each other may increase more and more and never stop improving your knowledge and deepening your perception, so that you can always recognize what is best.' The shoddy wooden camels which Henry was about to send to his grandchild forced Anastas to try to produce his best—and so to be himself again.

First Sunday in Lent. The link here is that OT/B and Epistle B

(Genesis 9:8–15 and 1 Peter 3:18–22) are concerned with Noah and the Ark.

27th Sunday of the Year. Epistle A (Phil. 4:6–9) is another passage from this letter of Paul, close to the spirit of this play. 'If there is anything you need, pray for it.' Henry called on Anastas prayerfully. As a result, he and Anastas found themselves doing what Paul urges in verse 8: 'Fill your minds with everything that is noble . . . good, worthy of praise.' And this led them towards 'the peace of God, which is so much greater than we can understand.'

Scene: See individual scene headings.

Characters: ANASTAS BATA, *in his late 60's, of Czech origin*
GERRY TODD, *10, son of Anastas' neighbors*
HENRY VOGEL, *early 60's*
LORNA VOGEL, *his wife*
THE REVEREND STEPHEN CARTWRIGHT
DOCTOR BROOK

Scene One

(The scene is ANASTAS' living room. He lies on a couch. Simple furniture for the rest of the room. One chair with carved arms. ANASTAS is reading a newspaper. Sound of whistling offstage, and a bouncing ball. The silence, and a pause.)

GERRY: *(from off left)* Mr. Bata? I'm sorry. It was my ball. Would you mind throwing it back?
ANASTAS: You'll have to come through and get it yourself, Gerry. The door's open. Come along through!
GERRY: O.K. I'm coming.*(Pause. Knock on door. He enters.)*
ANASTAS: Come on in, Gerry.
GERRY: Thanks, Mr. Bata.
ANASTAS: You go along and fetch it. Through the kitchen.

(GERRY *goes off, and returns a few seconds later.)*

GERRY: I've got it, Mr. Bata. Thanks. Gee! Are you sick?
ANASTAS: It's just my leg, Gerry. It's sore. Won't last long. You run along now.
GERRY: Sure. *(He starts towards door.)*
ANASTAS: Oh, Gerry. Take this bread out for the birds, will you? Leave it by the birdbath?

37

GERRY: Yes, Mr. Bata. (*Again he goes out and quickly returns.*) I put it there, Mr. Bata. And thanks for letting me come through the house.

ANASTAS: That's all right, Gerry. Those balls sure do bounce high, eh?

GERRY: You said it! Say, Mr. Bata—can I tell my Mom you're sick? Gee, you need someone to—kinda clean up the place, and—

ANASTAS: (*sharply*) No! I'm sorry, Gerry; but I'll be all right.

GERRY: O.K., Mr. Bata. Thanks. I'll be seeing you. (*He goes out.*)

ANASTAS: That's no trouble, Gerry. You come any time. And don't worry about me. I'll be all right. (*Pause.* GERRY *has now gone out.*) I'll be all right.

(*If the stage is large enough,* ANASTAS *should sit still while the next scene is acted out in front of him. If the stage is small,* ANASTAS *moves off.*)

Scene Two

(LORNA *is in her front garden. She is working with a trowel. After a pause, enter* CARTWRIGHT.)

CARTWRIGHT: Mrs. Vogel?

LORNA: Yes. Mr. Cartwright, isn't it?

CARTWRIGHT: That's right. You have a good memory. We just met once for a minute at the Church.

LORNA: Yes. Henry and I have been here nearly a month, but we've only got across to the Church once so far, I'm afraid. You know what it's like moving house.

CARTWRIGHT: Sure do. Do you like the house?

LORNA: Oh, the house is pretty good.

CARTWRIGHT: You don't sound very enthusiastic.

LORNA: It's just what we want, really. But I'm worried about my husband. Henry's always been so active. Now he's got nothing to make him get up in the morning. He should be back any minute now.

CARTWRIGHT: Just retired, has he?

LORNA: Yes, from a shipping office.

CARTWRIGHT: Retirement's always a problem, until you get adjusted. You expect so much, I suppose, and then come down to reality with a thud. (*laughing*) But who am I to talk? I've never tried it.

LORNA: Henry's out with the dog now—and buying some coffee. And that's the big event of the day.

CARTWRIGHT: I think I see him coming.

LORNA: Oh, yes. I'm glad. He'd have been sorry to miss you.

CARTWRIGHT: I hoped to see him, too. I have something for him to do, if he'd take it on.

LORNA: You have? That's fine, Mr. Cartwright.

HENRY: *(entering)* Hello there! Duke! *(Whistles to dog.)* Oh, well! He's off on his own.

LORNA: Henry, you remember Mr. Cartwright.

HENRY: Sure. Nice to see you. Won't you come inside?

CARTWRIGHT: If you don't mind, I won't come in today. I'll pay you a visit soon, if I may. You must come up and meet my wife and the kids.

HENRY: We'd like that.

CARTWRIGHT: But I want to ask you something, Mr. Vogel, if you won't think I'm springing it on you too suddenly.

HENRY: What is it?

CARTWRIGHT: Well, several of us Ministers in the area have got together to try to tackle a problem that we keep meeting: I mean the problem of lonely people. There are too many of them and we're aiming to try to break some of it down.

LORNA: Sounds like a great idea.

CARTWRIGHT: So I wanted to ask you to pay a call on someone, if you aren't too much tied up.

HENRY: Tied up? No, no! Mr. Cartwright, I'm sure I could find the time. Three months ago I could hardly wait to get out of the office door in the evening. Now—well, the days are pretty empty. I used to look forward to just that—not having eight hours of desk work; but I really don't see how it's going to work out.

CARTWRIGHT: Sounds like an attack of retirement blues.

HENRY: Retirement blues—that's good! Well, what do you have in mind?

CARTWRIGHT: I'd like you to go and visit an old man named Anastas Bata. He's Czechoslovakian by origin—has lived over here most of his life, but he's still very much of a foreigner in some ways, they say. He lives by himself, in one of those little houses up Arden Place.

HENRY: Oh, yes. I know that neighborhood. I sometimes walk the dog out that way.

CARTWRIGHT: Our Committee heard about Bata through Doctor Brook. The old man's very independent; doesn't want a woman

39

fussing around his home. And now he's laid up with an infected leg, and we're trying to find a man to drop in on him—see if he needs anything. Then if you'll get back to me, we'll try to help.

HENRY: I'll look in on him, of course; but I'm not sure I'm any good at that kind of thing. I mean—

CARTWRIGHT: We don't need a trained social worker, Mr. Vogel. What Anastas Bata probably needs is a friend—a link with the outside world.

LORNA: You can try, Henry, can't you?

HENRY: Sure, I'll try. Is that the address?

CARTWRIGHT: (handing him paper) That's it. I must be on my way; but thanks, Henry. I certainly appreciate what you're doing. And it was good to see you, Mrs. Vogel.

LORNA: We'll see you again soon, Mr. Cartwright. Now that we're settled in the house, we'll aim to be down at the Church each Sunday. Good-bye!

(CARTWRIGHT and VOGEL say good-bye. CARTWRIGHT goes out.)

HENRY: (reading) Anastas Bata, 74, Arden Place. Well, it's something to try anyway. Do you suppose he'll need anything from me?

Scene Three

(Back in ANASTAS' living room. He is on the couch.)

GERRY: (Knocking on door.) Mr. Bata?

ANASTAS: Come in, Gerry! (Enter GERRY carrying covered pitcher.)

GERRY: It's some soup, Mr. Bata. My Mom sent it.

ANASTAS: Thanks, Gerry. And you tell your mama thanks. You put it over there, will you? That's right. (GERRY goes to kitchen.)

BROOK: (walking in) Door seems to be open, so I'm coming on in. How are you doing, Stas?

ANASTAS: Oh, hello, Doctor! You know Gerry Todd? His Mother just sent me some soup.

BROOK: Yes, I know Gerry. We had his tonsils out last year. Hi there, young rascal!

GERRY: Hi! I'll be getting along, Mr. Bata. Hope your leg's better soon.

ANASTAS: Thanks, Gerry. And don't forget to thank your Mon. (GERRY goes out.)

BROOK: Nice to find you've got good neighbors. Now let's have a look at that leg. (*He rolls up* ANASTAS' *pants, and squeezes his leg.*) Hurts you pretty bad, eh?

ANASTAS: Ja.

BROOK: Well, it's beginning to mend; but you are a stubborn old cuss not to call me sooner, Stas. I know it's a problem, living alone. Anyway, we caught it in time, and the drugs are working. You're taking them as I told you?

ANASTAS: Yes, Doctor.

BROOK: Somethin's got to be done about your meals, and looking after this place; otherwise we may have to put you in the Hospital.

ANASTAS: I don't want to go there.

BROOK: We'll do our best. Any relatives?

ANASTAS: Just my daughter. In Pittsburgh. She—can't come. She's got her own children.

BROOK: I see. Well, we'll have to think. But meanwhile, you take your medication, and the problem may solve itself. (*knock on door*) Hey, you're busy today.

ANASTAS: I don't know who it could be. Come in.

HENRY: (*entering*) Mr. Bata?

ANASTAS: Ja, I am Bata.

BROOK: I'm Doctor Brook. Come on in.

HENRY: Doctor Brook, I'm Henry Vogel. Mr. Bata, you don't know me, but Mr. Cartwright, from St. Peter's Church, gave me your address.

ANASTAS: My address?

HENRY: Yes. He'd heard you were sick. If there's anything we can do. . . .

BROOK: Good of you to come, Mr. Vogel. Anastas here could probably do with a little company while this leg is keeping him out of action for a little while.

HENRY: What's the trouble?

BROOK: Nothing that won't take care of itself right soon. Well, I must be going. I'll call again soon, Stas. Good to have met you, Mr. Vogel.

HENRY: And you, Doctor. So long. (BROOK *goes out.*)

ANASTAS: Please, you sit, Mr. Vogel. I would get up, but my leg—

HENRY: There's no need. (*he sits*) Comfortable place you have here.

ANASTAS: Yes. Everything close: bed, chair, the radio.

HENRY: And kitchen and yard through there? It's compact, isn't it?

ANASTAS: You please have some coffee?

HENRY: Sure. I'd like it. Let me fix some.

41

ANASTAS: Yes, thank you. (HENRY *goes for coffee pot on dresser, pours two cups of coffee. But they continue talking.*)

HENRY: Does your leg trouble you much?

ANASTAS: Ja. Two weeks of trouble; but the Doctor fix it good now.

HENRY: You've lived here since you gave up work?

ANASTAS: Before I give up work, I live here with my Maria. But . . . nineteen years, since my Maria died.

HENRY: Cream and sugar? You've lived here a long time then?

ANASTAS: A little cream, no sugar, please. Thank you kindly.

HENRY: You've lived here a long time?

ANASTAS: Fifty-two years in United States. When I was sixteen years old my father say to me, "Anastas, here in Bratislava life is hard. America is the land of opportunity." So we come.

HENRY: And it was true? You found your opportunity?

ANASTAS: I work with my father. He teach me woodwork and carving. I found good work, building houses, and I earn good wages. All my life I work hard. Then my Maria died; and Anna, my daughter, she's married and lives in Pittsburgh.

HENRY: How long ago did you stop working?

ANASTAS: Nine years now I do not work. It is not good, ha?

HENRY: I'm beginning to see that. I gave up work and retired less than three months ago. Anyway, Mr. Bata—Anastas—is that the name?

ANASTAS: Yes, Anastas. Stas, if you like.

HENRY: Stas it is. Mine's Henry—just plain Henry. Well, I'd appreciate it, Stas, if you'd let me drop by sometimes and talk with you for a few minutes. There's not much around this town for a retired man to do.

ANASTAS: I'll be glad if you come, Mr. Vogel.

HENRY: Now, if you're Stas, I'm Henry, Okay?

ANASTAS: Okay, okay.

HENRY: (*rising*) I'll be round again soon. (*Drops paper bag on the floor.*) Oh! Clumsy! I hope they aren't damaged.

ANASTAS: What you got in there?

HENRY: (*unwrapping package*) Camels. Sounds funny, I know. But that's what they are. Camels for the Ark. Noah's Ark. I bought an Ark for one of my grand-children—oh, must be seven years ago. Each birthday I give her a fresh pair of animals. She'll be fourteen next week; and this year it's camels.

ANASTAS: (*looking at camels.*) Tt, tt! Such camels, Henry. It is quick, bad carving, not right for Noah's Ark.

HENRY: It's hard to find things carefully done these days. These were the best I came across; but they look machine-made, I know. Did you carve this kind of thing?

ANASTAS: I carved the arms of that chair where you sit.

HENRY: You—did this?' I'm no expert, but—this is wonderful work.

ANASTAS: I carve it for Maria forty years ago. A pair of doves.

HENRY: What a craftsman you are! Well, Stas, I mustn't overstay my welcome. It's been a real pleasure to be with you.

ANASTAS: It is good that you come. Always you will be welcome, Henry.

HENRY: Don't get up. I can—

ANASTAS: No, no. I get up. It is bad to sit too long. See? I'm on my feet.

HENRY: That's fine; but don't forget what the Doctor said about common sense and rest. I'll call again very soon, Stas.

ANASTAS: Ja, soon. Come soon, Henry.

Scene Four

(*Table, telephone and chair, in the Vogels' house. Telephone rings.* LORNA *comes to answer it.*)

LORNA: Hello! Oh, Mr. Cartwright! Yes, this is Lorna Vogel. Friday? Yes, we'd like that very much. Henry isn't here just now. He went off to see his new friend, Mr. Bata. Yes, I know. Yes. He has some scheme in mind, I don't quite know what. Well, Friday, then. 6:30? Thanks a lot, Mr. Cartwright. We'll look forward to it. Yes. Good-bye!

Scene Five

(*Music bridge then back to* ANASTAS' *room.* HENRY *is sitting by the couch on which* ANASTAS *lies.*)

HENRY: It hit me last night after I saw you, as I was packing up those two sorry little camels for Celia last night. My wife thought I was crazy. But I suddenly realized that I could ask you to carve something twenty times as good for Celia.

ANASTAS: I carve? Since I leave working I never handle my tools, not one time, Henry. No, no! My hands are dead.

HENRY: That's not true; and I'll take a bet on one thing—you didn't throw your tools away or sell them.

43

ANASTAS: No, I did not do that.
HENRY: Then where are they?
ANASTAS: Wait, Henry. I tell you—
HENRY: Stas, where are your tools?
ANASTAS: In the little shed behind my house. But they must be rusty.
HENRY: I don't believe it. Listen, Anastas—your hands are no more dead than mine. We could fit up a small bench with a lathe. Look, I made a sketch over my coffee this morning.
ANASTAS: But, Henry, I—
HENRY: No, listen to me. Last night I knew you were meant to carve those camels, so I won't take "No" for an answer. Now I'm going to look in the shed. That is, if you don't object.
ANASTAS: It is not that I object, but—
HENRY: That's all right, then. I'll go and take a look.

(*He goes out.* ANASTAS *sits silent.*)

ANASTAS: The Ark of Noah. If my hands were not so dead!

Scene Six

(*Music bridge then back to the Vogel's home.* LORNA *is sitting at the table. Enter* HENRY, *whistling.*)

LORNA: You sound cheerful.
HENRY: I am. I'm just off to see Stas, to show him Celia's letter.
LORNA: It means a lot to you, doesn't it, Stas doing that work?
HENRY: It surely does. I can't quite explain how, but it's done something to me. (*He kisses her.*) Well, I must be off, honey. See you at lunch.
LORNA: (*laughing*) I'll believe it when I see you. The two of you seem to forget about time. And to think that it wasn't so very long ago I wondered how you were ever going to fill up your days, Henry!
HENRY: Well, I think He really had something up his sleeve this time. I must be off.

Scene Seven

(*Music bridge, then back to* ANASTAS' *room. He is working at a small bench, carving.* HENRY *enters, after knocking on door.*)

ANASTAS: Who is it?

HENRY: (*hurrying to him*) Hi, Stas! How's it going?

ANASTAS: You look and see.

HENRY: I certainly will. What in the—what have you got there? It's—

ANASTAS: He is the panther. Always I like the panther. He is strong, yes; but he is graceful.

HENRY: Stas, this is like the arms of that chair. It's the work of a genius!

ANASTAS: It is like the chair, yes; because I make that chair when I was alive—I make it for my Maria, out of my love. But my love, she dies; and for years I let my hands lie dead also. Now I think I am alive again, because someone knocked at my door.

HENRY: I have something to read to you, Stas. Listen to this. (*he sits*) It's from Celia.

ANASTAS: Ach, Celia. The little lady with the Ark. You read me what she says, please.

HENRY: She says, "The camels are so beautiful that they make the other animals in my Ark feel rather ashamed."

ANASTAS: She is a sweet girl.

HENRY: Wait! There's more. "Please tell Stas that I know he loved my camels very much; and already I love them, too. That makes us very close."

ANASTAS: (*after a pause*) Thank you, Henry. That letter is good.

HENRY: You know, Stas, I've got something to say to you. It's a kind of confession, I guess.

ANASTAS: How? A confession?

HENRY: Yes. You see, that first day I came here, I thought I came out of charity—I suppose you'd call it that. You know, Mr. Cartwright suggested it, and I thought you needed a friend.

ANASTAS: Ja, a friend. Everybody need friends. Ja?

HENRY: If I thought at all then, I had some silly notion that I came to do you a kindness. Instead, I found out that it was I who needed you. That's the plain truth, Stas.

ANASTAS: We need each other, Henry. We need to be two friends, not to be separate. Two, like the camels, eh?

(*Sound of* GERRY'*s ball bouncing in the yard.*)

HENRY: Hey, whatever is that?

ANASTAS: That is another friend. I think sometimes God brings that ball over my fence, Henry, so that my friend comes to fetch it back.

GERRY: (*knocking at door*) Mr. Bata? I'm sorry about my ball. Do you mind if I come through?

ANASTAS: Come in, come in, Gerry. (*Enter* GERRY) And don't forget to take that bread there for the birds. By the kitchen door.

Also suitable for this Sunday: Honor Your Father (OT); see 3rd Sunday of Lent; also see *Bible as Drama,* page 31 (Gospel A) Joseph and his Brethren (verse play and musical).

9. EPIPHANY

The Road to Bethlehem

Bible Reference: General. The OT, Epistle, and Gospel all proclaim the universality of faith in Jesus.

Note: The festival of Epiphany celebrates the coming of the Three Wise Men from the East to the cradle of Jesus. In a wider context, it symbolizes the fact that he was born to save all people without regard for geography, race, color, creed, or background. 'The nations come to your light, and kings to your dawning brightness,' Isaiah wrote in the OT reading (Isaiah 60:1–6). 'Pagans now share the same inheritance,' Paul says in the Epistle (Eph. 3:2–6).

The events described in this scene may be imaginary: but it fits in beautifully with the story of the star which guided the Wise Men to Bethlehem, to end the search which they had undertaken.

Also suitable for: Pentecost, 16th Sunday of the Year.

Pentecost: The first reading (Acts 2:1–11) describes how people of many tongues and countries encountered the power of the gospel on this first day when the Church went out to witness. The story of the Wise Men is an appropriate reminder that the infant Son of God drew men from far away to seek and to worship him. God is for all people at all times. The Apostles had to struggle to reach this clear conclusion (see Acts 15, the account of the Council of Jerusalem); but there were no restrictions at Pentecost, or at the manger in Bethlehem.

16th Sunday of the Year: Epistle B (Eph. 2:13–18) reaffirms this universality of faith in Jesus. 'You that used to be so far apart from us have been brought very close, by the blood of Christ.' He has 'broken down the barrier which used to keep them (Jews and Gentiles) apart.'

Scene: On the road from Jerusalem to Bethlehem. A campsite, near a well.

Characters: The Three Wise Men, whose names are traditionally given as CASPAR, MELCHIOR, *and* BALTHAZAR

(The WISE MEN *are standing near the well.)*

CASPAR: One more campsite! I've lost count of the nights we have spent in the open along the way.

MELCHIOR: Hundreds. I know that.

BALTHAZAR: And we've lost the Star again.

MELCHIOR: It's a gusty night. Those clouds come and go.

CASPAR: The servants should have supper ready in a minute. I'm hungry! This is a biting wind.

BALTHAZAR: A real January night. And it has been a long day. I was glad to get away from that King Herod.

MELCHIOR: I don't trust him. A shifty, cruel man, I'd say.

CASPAR: And a great deal too anxious to pry into our plans.

MELCHIOR: He doesn't have to worry. It isn't likely the Star is leading us to a place like this. More likely on towards Greece, or North to Cilicia.

BALTHAZAR: But these Jews are strange people. I have read what some of their prophets have written. Great men of vision! And they were looking for the same thing as ourselves.

CASPAR: A King to be born?

BALTHAZAR: Yes. A Messiah, they call him—an anointed one, that means, to be the successor of the Kings they once had. Not foreign tyrants like Herod, but their own Jewish leaders—David, Solomon, Hezekiah.

MELCHIOR: It would take a remarkable leader to do anything for the Jews now. Herod and the Romans have them tied down and helpless.

CASPAR: And they squabble among themselves. But I met some fine thinkers in Jerusalem, nevertheless. Men of great quality.

BALTHAZAR: *(walking to the well)* Look at this old well—these solid stone blocks!

CASPAR: Deep, too, by the looks of it.

MELCHIOR: It's too dark to see the water. Wait! Oh, God! Do you see?

BALTHAZAR: See what, Melchior?

MELCHIOR: The Star! It's a sign! Don't you see it?

CASPAR: That's right! Look up there! The clouds have parted, and there it is!

MELCHIOR: The Star came down! Of course it had to be this

way—a reflection in water! We've found the place!

BALTHAZAR: But what place is it? Where did they say this road led?

CASPAR: To the Coast, ultimately. But they mentioned the name of a town: Beth—I can't remember.

BALTHAZAR: Bethlehem. Of course! I remember now. That was the home of their King David.

MELCHIOR: Do you really think this is where we shall find another King?

CASPAR: It's too late to do anything tonight. God has sent us the sign. Now let us eat and rest, and in the morning we will find the King.

BALTHAZAR: A Jewish child! A strange ending to our search.

MELCHIOR: Our whole search has been strange. But the finger of God is pointing the way, and it is for us to follow. Come and eat, my friends!

10. EPIPHANY

Three Wise Men

Bible Reference: Mt. 2:1–12

Note: Look around at the faces of the people in the congregation at your Church. What a wealth of talent and skills the Church ought to be generating! If only all of the wise men and women who come to worship would do as the Magi did—offer on their knees the treasures which they possess and control. At the Epiphany season we should reassess what we have to give, and compare it with what we are actually giving, in terms of talent and dedication as well as material things. That is what Larry asks his two friends to do in this scene.

Scene: The comfortable home of Larry, a business executive. Evening.

Characters: LARRY, DAVE, GREG

(LARRY *is opening the front door as the Scene opens.* GREG *is standing in the center of the room.*)

LARRY: Come in, Dave! Greg is here, so we can start.
GREG: Evening, Dave.
DAVE: Greg! How are you doing?
LARRY: Help yourself to some coffee.
GREG: Thanks. It's chilly out there.
LARRY: Sit down, both of you. And thanks for coming. We're all busy, so I don't want to waste time.
DAVE: I'm intrigued, Larry. This is the card I received. (*He reads*): 'Will you join Greg Simons and me for an Epiphany evening— prayer and planning—January 6th at 8 p.m.? It's important.'
GREG: That's what you sent me, too.
LARRY: Let's start by reading what happened at Epiphany. I brought three Bibles, so that we could read the verses in turn. It's in Matthew, chapter 2. (*They either read the verses aloud or look at them in silence for a few seconds.*)
LARRY: Ever since Christmas I've been thinking about that story,

and wondering what I could do to make it real, here, now, in our Church.

GREG: Sounds interesting. What do you have in mind?

LARRY: It may sound a little wild, but I'll tell you. One night when I read that passage I thought about the three of us.

DAVE: Wise Men? Kings? I'm flattered, but I don't think it fits me.

LARRY: It could, Dave. What's your official title, and your company's full name?

DAVE: President, Rocky Mountain Atomic Development Corporation.

LARRY: Right. I see you as the Wise Man bringing gold as his gift. You deal in precious, deadly dangerous elements, vital to God's world. You see what I mean?

DAVE: The gift of gold?

GREG: And you are the myrrh, Larry? Simmons Incorporated, makers of Sweetskin Soap? But how about me?

LARRY: Oil into frankincense? You may call it a little far-fetched. You oilmen are always causing pollution. But you also give us something we must have, in order to live and move. Maybe if we learn to use our oil and gas the way God means us to, we won't call it dirty names we shouldn't have cause to. And our cities would smell sweet again.

DAVE: So what are you proposing, Larry?

LARRY: Nothing very definite; but I have the germ of a plan. I want to see us three, and others like us who believe in God, and who welcomed the birth of Christ two weeks ago, go down on our knees and offer our gifts to him. I want to see us discuss together how our companies can be more Christian, more dedicated to what God wants.

GREG: Some people would laugh at that, and say your competitors would be the ones who would thank you.

LARRY: Yes. And I think they'd be wrong. I'm for free enterprise all right; but as we are now, here in the city and all over the world, I think we're acting like a bunch of selfish, savage kids.

DAVE: I go along with that.

LARRY: So I thought, begin with three wise men—we're not fools, or we wouldn't be where we are—in one average American Church. Maybe we can pull in others, from other churches. Maybe—just maybe—we can have an impact on our own community.

DAVE: You know, this is the first time I've thought about the Wise Men—I mean THOUGHT. I've heard it a hundred times, but you don't relate it to here and now. You're right, Larry. I often sit at my desk and pray. I'd feel a lot less lonely if I knew you were doing the same.

GREG: Sometimes we're too shy or embarrassed to say what we believe.

LARRY: And, you see, we'd actually run our Companies much better if we at the top put God and the Sermon on the Mount first. It would be better for the employees, better for the shareholders, better for the community. Because honesty combined with dedication is infectious—and it works in the long run.

DAVE: You're right, Larry. I'm with you.

GREG: But how many are willing to take a chance? Well, it would have to start with one—or twelve. How do we begin?

LARRY: Tonight, I thought we'd sit quietly, with a pad and a pencil. And at the end of half an hour let's share what we've thought and prayed about. God will surely want to help us. Isn't that what his Holy Spirit is for—if you listen? Now, who's embarrassed?

GREG: Well, everybody, for all I know. But, what does that really matter? Better shy about the good than bold about the bad. And, who knows, as including God in our calculations becomes a habit, we could very well lose that shyness and become bolder. . . .

LARRY: And stronger.

DAVE: And richer, where it really counts.

LARRY: And wiser, too. Wiser. Shall we read about the Three Wise Men bearing gifts to the Infant Jesus on that fateful night 2,000 years ago?

Also suitable for Epiphany: God's Tumbler (general): see 32nd Sunday of the Year.

52

11. BAPTISM OF THE LORD

Baptism

Bible Reference: General.

Note: The subject of Baptism is treated in many readings throughout the year. On this Sunday, when the Gospels deal with the Baptism of Jesus, it is timely to launch a discussion of the whole subject of Baptism.

In this scene, three young mothers express different, and by no means uncommon, views. Does the New Testament contain instances of infant Baptism? Regardless, it was undoubtedly a very early custom in the Church. On the other hand, some Christian Churches teach that to be baptized, a boy or girl must be old enough to choose independently for himself or herself. Then there is the very widely held view, though it is usually a rather loose, uninformed view, that there is no hurry, and a choice of religion will be something which a child can think about later. The prevalence of this point of view comes partly from a wrong emphasis in Church teaching in the past. A clear understanding of the meaning of Baptism, and a loving welcome into the Church, would be the best way to bring Hilary and her husband closer to Jesus Christ.

Also suitable for: Lent 1, Second Sunday of Easter, 13th, 15th, 17th, and 27th Sundays of the Year.

First Sunday in Lent: Epistle B (I Peter 3:18–22) contains a rather strange comparison of Noah's Flood with Christian Baptism. 'That water is a type of the baptism which saves you now.'

2nd Sunday of Easter: Epistle A (I Peter 1:3–9) does not mention the word Baptism, but it is a glorious passage about 'new birth.' Because of this new birth 'we have a sure hope and the promise of an inheritance that can never be spoiled or soiled and never fade away.'

13th Sunday of the Year: Epistle A (Rom. 6:3–4, 8–11) embodies one of Paul's clearest statements about Baptism. He has been stung by criticisms that he has been preaching that 'we should remain in sin so as to let grace have greater scope.' In Baptism we died with

Christ, so that 'we shall also imitate him in his resurrection.' He talks of 'new life,' where Peter talked of 'new birth.' It is a passionate passage, in which Paul's writing rises to great heights.

15th Sunday of the Year: Epistle B (Eph. 1:3–14) comes from a late letter of Paul. It sets Baptism in the context of the Church, the body of Christ. 'Such is the richness of the grace which he has showered on us . . . we were claimed as God's own . . . and you too have been stamped with the seal of the Holy Spirit . . . which brings freedom for those whom God has taken for his own.' After reading a statement like this, we can imagine what Baptism meant to the men and women of courage who offered themselves in the first years of the Church.

17th Sunday of the Year: Epistle C (Col. 2:12–14) restates what Paul said in Romans (see 13th Sunday of the Year). 'You were buried with him when you were baptized; and by baptism, too, you have been raised up with him . . . he has brought you to life with him, he has forgiven us all our sins.'

Twenty-seventh Sunday of the Year: Gospel B (Mark 10:2–16) incorporates the rebuke which Jesus gave to disciples who tried to hustle children away from him. 'Let the little children come to me.' Joan and Elizabeth interpret this in different ways in the Scene. Anyone who worships regularly side by side with children knows the trustfulness and simplicity (in the true sense) which they bring to their faith. It is this which Jesus here demands.

These are some of the readings which deal with the many facets of Baptism. It would be challenging indeed to act this scene side by side with the dramatization of Paul's Baptism from THE BIBLE AS DRAMA ('In the house of Judas,' page 239).

Scene: Joan's home. This Scene contains a discussion between three mothers, who have different views about the Baptism of their children.

Characters: JOAN, ELIZABETH, *and* HILARY, *all about 30 years old*

(*They all enter together.*)

JOAN: Come in and sit down. There's some coffee all ready.
ELIZABETH: Thanks, Joanie. I'd love some.
HILARY: So would I. Oh, it's good to sit down. I can hardly wait for the weekend, to get out of the city and camp in the mountains.
JOAN: Here you are. Cream and sugar on the table.

54

HILARY: Looks so good!

JOAN: Do you take Paul with you camping, or leave him with your mother?

HILARY: Oh, we take him. He loves it. And even though he's only four, he can be quite useful sometimes.

ELIZABETH: Well, our weekend is going to be busy. Sarah is being baptized.

HILARY: Oh, Liz! How exciting! Do you have a big party planned?

ELIZABETH: Not big, no. The real party is the service—all of our congregation welcoming her into the Church. But I know we three don't agree about Baptism.

JOAN: Our two Churches don't agree, you mean. It's just as important for us as for you; but we don't feel it can have any meaning until the person being baptized can think and speak for himself.

HILARY: In a way that's what George and I think—he more than I. I don't really know what I think. He says Paul will make up his mind for himself when he's old enough. He says you shouldn't force it on him.

ELIZABETH: No offence to George, but I've never thought much of that argument. You don't leave him to make up his own mind whether he will brush his teeth, or be an American citizen.

HILARY: But that's different. I mean he MUST wash, to keep healthy.

ELIZABETH: Exactly.

HILARY: Oh, I see what you mean. You think—

ELIZABETH: It's hard to put it right. I'm not a theologian. But I do believe in the Bible. And it says what you've just said, Hilary: 'Let us draw near with a true heart . . . having our bodies washed with pure water.' That's one of my favorite verses, from Hebrews. And there's a lot more.

JOAN: I agree with that, Liz. What I can't understand is your Church baptizing babies. They can't repent. And that's what John the Baptist called it: baptism of repentance.

ELIZABETH: They can't brush their teeth either, Joanie. But you don't wait. You do it for them, until they can understand.

JOAN: But do you really believe a child is condemned to Hell if he dies unbaptized?

ELIZABETH: You're asking some tough questions! No, I don't. I think it's up to the love of God. We can't put limits on his love. But according to Saint Matthew, Jesus' last words to his friends were: 'Go ye therefore, and teach all nations, baptising them in the name of the Father, and of the Son, and of the Holy Ghost.' So I don't see how you can believe in him without wanting your child to be baptized.

JOAN: But the point is, when? At our Church the children are very much a part of everything, and join in worship and Bible study. But Baptism—I still can't see how it means anything to a baby.

ELIZABETH: One book I read had two things to say about that, which I've never forgotten. It said Baptism of a baby is like carefully sowing a seed in your garden, in good soil, and then keeping it watered, and weeding the flower-bed. You don't make the seed grow, but you give it the best possible chance.

HILARY: I like that, Liz.

JOAN: And the other thing this writer said was that the New Testament makes it probable that children were baptized then—not certain, but probable. Pass me your Bible, will you? Here—Acts, chapter 16, the keeper of the prison at Philippi, after the earthquake. It says, 'he was baptized, he and all his family, straightway.' And in First Corinthians Paul says he baptized the household of Stephanas. The book said that the natural interpretation was that it included children.

JOAN: I never thought of that.

HILARY: In some ways I envy you two. You know so much about all this, and I'm so vague. And you're always talking about the friends you make at Church.

JOAN: The most important thing to me is the children. If they can go there regularly, and feel that they are wanted and loved, and taught the foundations of a good life, that's everything to me.

HILARY: I'm going to have to get George to think about it again. He's so independent, but—

ELIZABETH: I hope I didn't sound as if I was lecturing you, Hilary. I didn't mean to.

HILARY: No, it's been a good discussion. I don't think about these things enough. George says you are just as close to God in the mountains as in Church—or closer—but I don't know. Anyway, I have to run now. Thanks for the coffee, Joanie.

ELIZABETH: I must be on my way too. Enjoy your trip!

HILARY: And you, Liz—have a lovely Baptism! I wish I could be there.

Also suitable for this Sunday: Bible as Drama, Page 239 (Gospels A/B/C); In the House of Judas.

12. SECOND SUNDAY OF THE YEAR

Cana of Galilee

Bible Reference: John 2:1–12 (Gospel C)

Note: John describes in this Gospel reading the first miracle of Jesus' ministry. There are many overtones to this story of the wedding at Cana. It is one of many passages which point forward to the Last Supper and the institution of the Eucharist. In this respect it is complementary to the story of the feeding of the five thousand (John 6:1–15).

If Jesus is invited into the home, as this family invited him, he will always come. He will transform the home, and meet every need shown to him. In a truly Christian home, or association of any kind, the presence of God will continually make the wine taste better, the friendship grow sweeter, the love grow richer.

Also suitable for: 6th Sunday of the Year, Corpus Christi, 32nd Sunday of the Year.

6th Sunday of the Year: OT/C (Jeremiah 17:5–8). Like Psalm 1, this short passage describes the man who trusts in God and not in man. The difference is that one who 'relies on things of the flesh' is like 'dry scrub in the wastelands,' while the God-centered man 'has no worries in a year of drought.'

Corpus Christi: general. All of the readings are concerned with God's gifts of food, actual and spiritual: the manna of OT/A (Deut 8:16); the 'blessing cup' of Epistle A (I Cor. 10:16); the five loaves and two fish of Gospel C (Lk. 9:16).

32nd Sunday of the Year: OT/C (I Kings 17:10–16). Here Elijah does the same thing for a home in need, as Jesus at Cana. The widow was as open and generous with the little she had as the boy with the five loaves and two fish. In return, she experienced the riches of God's gifts: 'the jar of meal was not spent nor the jug of oil emptied.'

Scene: The kitchen of the home in Cana where the wedding is taking place.

Characters: JACOB *and* MIRIAM, *the father and mother of the bride*
MATTHEW *and* BARTHOLOMEW, *servants*
MARY
JESUS
EZRA, *the Master of Ceremonies at the wedding*

(The two SERVANTS *are working at a table piled with food.* MIRIAM *hurries in.)*

MIRIAM: We need more cakes and fruit, Matthew.

MATTHEW: As quick as we can, Ma'am. We don't seem to be able to keep up with them.

BARTHOLOMEW: What a mob! And eat—I never saw such appetites!

MIRIAM: I suppose I ought to be thankful that everyone came, but—

JACOB: *(bursting in)* Miriam! In Heaven's name hurry up and bring in some more wine!

MIRIAM: More wine? I can't believe it! Two casks! They can't have drunk all of that.

JACOB: They have. And we have to get hold of some more.

MIRIAM: That's your job, Jacob. I'm having enough trouble keeping them fed. Whoever would have thought that Jonas would have come, and Joanna with all her children, and that flock of cousins from Magdala?

JACOB: Well, they came, and they have to eat and drink!

MARY: *(entering)* Is there anything I can do to help, Miriam?

MIRIAM: Oh, Mary! We're at our wits' end. We're running out of wine!

MARY: Don't worry, Miriam! It's one of the loveliest weddings I have ever seen.

JACOB: But we've got to do something! I'll go back and see that what we have left is served. *(He goes out.)*

MIRIAM: There's a small flagon left in the storeroom. I'll fetch that.

MATTHEW: One flagon, Ma'am? That won't be much help. Not with this lot. (MIRIAM *goes out.)*

MARY: Wait, both of you! I have an idea. *(She goes out.)*

BART: Come on, Matt! Let's get this stuff loaded up. At least they can eat! (MARY *comes back with* JESUS.)

MARY: Can't you help them, Jesus? Jacob and Miriam have been so hospitable.

MATTHEW: Let's go, Bart! Have you got it?

BARTHOLOMEW: All set. *(They go out.)*

JESUS: You really believe in me, Mother, don't you? You think I'm ready to show signs in God's name.

MARY: I think your gift of love is strong enough to meet the needs of people who turn to you. (MATTHEW *and* BARTHOLOMEW *return.)*

JESUS: Thank you, Mother dear. You understand a great deal. *(To the* SERVANTS) Will you please fill these jugs with water?

BARTHOLOMEW: Look, Sir, if you'll excuse us—we're very busy.

JESUS: Please do what I ask. I want to help your Mistress.

MATTHEW: O.K., then. If you say so. Come on, Bart! Out by the pump.

JESUS: I will come with you. *(They go out.* MIRIAM *returns.)*

MIRIAM: This is the last we have. If only there were a store open!

MARY: Wait just a moment, Miriam. I think everything will be all right.

MIRIAM: I don't see how—*(The* SERVANTS *and* JESUS *return.)*
Whatever is that, Matthew?

MATTHEW: The young gentleman told us to bring it in, Ma'am. To serve to the guests, he said.

JACOB: *(entering)* That's it! We're out of wine!

MIRIAM: Wait, Jacob! I want to taste this. It's—why, it tastes different from anything I've ever tasted before.

JACOB: *(tasting)* It's wine all right—good wine. Get in there with it quick, Matt! How did you manage to get it so quickly? And what is it doing in those water jugs?

MIRIAM: I don't know. You'd have to ask Mary that—or Jesus.

JACOB: I don't understand. What have you got to do with this, Jesus? You're a carpenter, aren't you?

EZRA: *(entering)* Jacob! Miriam! What are you doing out here in the kitchen? Come back to the guests, all of you—Mary, and Jesus!

JACOB: We're coming, Ezra.

EZRA: I thought the party was breaking up; but now your servants have given us a real surprise, and we're starting a new round of toasts. Where did you get that wine?

JACOB: You mean, what's in the jugs?

EZRA: That's right. I can't place it, but there's something very unusual about it.

JACOB: There's something very unusual about this whole thing. Never mind! We'll figure that out later.

EZRA: It's a funny thing, Jacob. Most people serve their best wine early, and make do with inferior stuff later in the evening. Why did you and Miriam keep this wonderful wine to the last?

JACOB: Why did we, Miriam?

MIRIAM: We'll ask the questions later. This is Rebekah's wedding, and I'm so thankful that we found what we needed. You know that, don't you, Jesus? And you, Mary?

MARY: Yes, Miriam. We know.

MIRIAM: Come on, dear! Let us all go back to the guests!

Also suitable for this Sunday: John the Baptist (Gospel A); see 2nd Sunday of Advent.

13. FOURTH SUNDAY OF THE YEAR

The Rosebush

Bible Reference: Epistle C (I Cor. 12:31–13:13)

It is hard to single out a play to go alongside this great passage about love. But there are many verses which describe Franz and Gretchen Schultz and their type of love: 'Love is always patient and kind . . . it does not take offense . . . it is always ready to excuse, to trust, to hope . . . love does not come to an end.' Franz Schultz refuses to give up, knowing that the hostility shown by Corky is an inevitable result of the way in which his early life was spent. Every character in the play shows love for Corky, in a different way.

Also suitable for: Third Sunday in Lent, 16th, 25th, and 30th Sundays of the Year.

Third Sunday in Lent: Gospel C (Lk 13:1–9) contains the parable of the barren fig tree. When Corky cut down the rosebush, Franz might well have said that he in return should be discarded—'Cut it down: why should it be taking up the ground?' Instead, he said in spirit, 'Give me time to dig around it and manure it: it may bear fruit next year.'

16th Sunday of the Year: Gospel A (Matt. 13:24–43) contains the parable of the wheat and the weeds. It is appropriate to this play, with its portrayal of patience and understanding as vital ingredients of love.

25th Sunday of the Year: Gospel B (Mk. 9:30–37). 'Anyone who welcomes one of these little children in my name, welcomes me.' This is the same basic truth as that contained in 'Martin the Cobbler' (see page 10).

30th Sunday of the Year: OT/A (Exodus 22:20-26) contains some of the moral and religious laws relating to widows, orphans and strangers.

Scene: The home of Franz and Gretchen Schultz in a small American town.

The main stage represents the living room, with simple furniture. The bedroom scenes could be heard offstage, or acted to the side.

Characters: FRANZ SCHULZ (*with heavy German accent*), *a gar-
dener; about 50*
GRETCHEN SCHULZ (*also with accent*), *his wife*
SLIM, *their 10-year-old adopted son*
CORKY, *a boy, aged 12*
MR. MANSOLA, *Probation Officer*

Scene One

(*Main stage. The living room of the* SCHULZ *home. Two armchairs
near center with a small table between. Entrance from the street is
L.: and the R. side of the stage leads to the kitchen and stairway.
When the curtain rises, enter* SLIM L., *followed by* MR. MANSOLA
and CORKY.)

SLIM: Wait here, and I'll get Pa—Mr. Schulz. He's in the yard.
MANSOLA: Thanks. You're Slim, aren't you?
SLIM: Yes, Sir.
MANSOLA: I heard about you, in Mr. Schulz' letter.
SLIM: I'll be back in a minute.

(*He goes out L. Short silence.*)

CORKY: Why do I have to come to a place like this, Mr. Mansola?
MANSOLA: Now, Corky, we've been through all that. Mr. and Mrs.
Schulz want to give you a home.
CORKY: I don't want to come here. Take me back to New York. I
hate this place! It's dead!

(*Enter* FRANZ L., *with* SLIM.)

FRANZ: You Mr. Mansola?
MANSOLA: That's right, Mr. Schulz; and this is Corky.
FRANZ: Welcome, Corky! You too, Mr. Mansola. How was your
trip?
MANSOLA: Pretty good. Made good time.
FRANZ: This is Corky's suitcase? We'll take it to his room.
CORKY: I can carry it myself.
FRANZ: O.K., Corky, you carry it. And you show him the room,
Slim. You met Slim, Corky?
CORKY: Yeah.
SLIM: Come on, Corky! (*They go out R.*)
FRANZ: Sit down, Mr. Mansola. Can I offer you anything?

62

MANSOLA: No thanks, Mr. Schulz. While they're upstairs, I think I ought to tell you something.

FRANZ: Corky didn't want to come here. Is that it?

MANSOLA: That's right. Mind you, a kid like Corky doesn't know what he wants. He's had no care, no home—not what you and I mean by home.

FRANZ: We thought about that. That's what we want to give him, Gretchen and I.

MANSOLA: He mistrusts all of us; and it's only fair to tell you, Corky thinks a gardener in a country place is a poor exchange for the gang leaders he admired back in the city. You've got a job ahead of you.

FRANZ: We know that. Maybe we'll fail—but if we don't, it's something worth trying, is it not?

MANSOLA: I just wish there were more people who thought your way, Mr. Schulz. Some of the problems we meet would break your heart; but at least you're giving Corky a fine chance. Well, I'd better be leaving now. I'm sorry to miss Mrs. Schulz; but you'll be in touch with me, I know, if you need help over Corky.

FRANZ: That's right. Mrs. Schulz, she'll be sorry she missed you too. We can only do our best, she and I; but we'll sure do that; and so will Slim. He's a good boy, Slim, and he's been wanting Corky to come.

MANSOLA: Say goodbye to them for me, Mr. Schulz. May as well leave them to get acquainted now.

FRANZ: I'll do that. And I'll come to the car with you. You a gardener, Mr. Mansola?

MANSOLA: (*laughing*) I would be, if I had the chance. My job keeps me too much in the city. I can see you're a real expert.

FRANZ: Let me show you my new rosebush. I'm breeding a new rose out there; and pretty soon we'll all be able to enjoy it.

MANSOLA: A new type, eh? That's really something, Mr. Schulz.

(*They go out L. After a short pause,* SLIM *enters R., followed by* CORKY.)

SLIM: Shall I show you the rest of the house, Corky, and the garden?

CORKY: Guess you might as well. Where's she?

SLIM: Ma? She's at the market. She'll be back soon. Guess you came sooner than we thought.

CORKY: Is she like him? Foreign?

SLIM: Yes. I suppose so. I'm—used to it, so I don't notice. Do you think you'll like it here, Corky?

CORKY: Why should I like it? Mr. Mansola says I have to come here; but I don't have to like it, do I? And nobody can make me stay.

(*Lights fade. Short music bridge.*)

Scene Two

(*Front stage:* CORKY *and* SLIM *are lying in two beds, R.C. a little light from R., as from a window.*)

SLIM: D'you like the bed, Corky?

CORKY: It sure is soft.

SLIM: When I first came here, I couldn't sleep in this bed. I'd never slept on anything soft like this.

CORKY: You didn't have a real bed?

SLIM: Uh-huh. My Auntie had too many of us. I slept on the floor, or sometimes with the others on the bed. Where did you live, Corky, before—

CORKY: Before I got arrested? With my mother—that is, sometimes I lived there.

SLIM: Where'd she live?

CORKY: New York. We moved around a lot. And sometimes she wouldn't want me there.

SLIM: So what'd you do then?

CORKY: I'd sleep in the Park.

SLIM: You slept in the Park? On one of the benches?

CORKY: Sure. Sometimes I did. Or on the grass.

SLIM: Gee! I never did that. How come you got arrested, Corky?

(*Sound of heavy steps on stairs, off L.*)

CORKY: Is that him coming upstairs?

SLIM: Yes.

CORKY: I hate him, with his dirty boots, and that crazy foreign voice!

SLIM: You shouldn't say that. Pa's real good.

CORKY: Pa! He's not your Pa.

SLIM: I tell you he's good, Corky. When we're out of school I go in the truck almost every day, and help him.

(*Knocking L.* FRANZ *comes just inside the room.*)

FRANZ: How are the two roommates? You looking after him, Slim?
CORKY: I don't need a kid to look after me.
FRANZ: Sure you don't, Corky. We're all going to help to look after each other, eh?
CORKY: I didn't ask to come here. I want to go back to New York.
FRANZ: First you try to like it here, Corky. We want you to stay, don't we, Slim?
SLIM: We sure do.
FRANZ: So if you need anything, just come and ask. Now go to sleep. We got plenty work tomorrow. Good-night now!
SLIM: Good-night, Pa!

(*Lights fade. Music bridge.*)

Scene Three

(*Main stage. The living room. The boys are sitting at a table R. of the arm-chairs. GRETCHEN comes from kitchen R.*)

GRETCHEN: More milk, Slim?
SLIM: Yes, please, Ma.
GRETCHEN: You, Corky?
CORKY: No.
FRANZ: (*entering from L.*) My rosebush. It's beginning to bloom.
GRETCHEN: The new bush out front?
FRANZ: That's right. I'm very proud of my roses, Corky.
SLIM: Some of them nobody ever grew before. A new type. They'll be famous one day, maybe.
FRANZ: Maybe—maybe not. But they'll sure be beautiful. Corky, you want to come with Slim and me in the truck today? See where we work?
CORKY: You want a slave, Mr. Schulz? No, thanks!
GRETCHEN: Don't say that, Corky. That's not right. Here's your coffee, Franz.
FRANZ: (*sitting at table*) Thanks.
CORKY: You get money for keeping us, don't you? Anyway, why do I have to come and live here, and do dirty work? Just to get you the scratch, huh?
FRANZ: Wait and see, Corky, before you say things like that. You don't have to come with us, not 'till you want to.
CORKY: Then it'll be a long time. I'm not going to grow up messing around in other people's yards. I'm going to be a lawyer one day—

so's I can get kids like me off and look after myself, and not be kicked around.

FRANZ: Sure, that's right. If you study hard at school, we help you to do that, Corky. But don't despise the people who grow the flowers and the food. A lawyer doesn't grow things, Corky. He's useful, but he doesn't grow the food we need.

CORKY: He's too smart to work—just uses his brain and gets a lot of money. I'm not going to get you money for having me. (GRETCHEN *has sat at the table, and is watching* CORKY.)

FRANZ: I don't want the money, Corky. Part of the money we get for you, and for Slim, I put in the bank. When you grow up, it's there for you. Then one day maybe you become a great lawyer—and you can help us, too. I just want to be proud of you—and you can make us proud of you, I know.

CORKY: Proud of me? Don't feed me that garbage! I tell you I don't want to be here. I don't want to be here!

(*Lights fade. Music bridge.*)

Scene Four

(*Front stage. The bedroom as before.*)

SLIM: Corky?

CORKY: Yeah?

SLIM: Can't you go to sleep?

CORKY: No.

SLIM: Corky, you never told me—in the city, how did you get arrested?

CORKY: Simple. The leader of our gang left me behind when the cops came along.

SLIM: Who was he?

CORKY: Arturo. He talked big, so we thought he was a great guy. But he just cared for his own self, like everybody else.

SLIM: Were you in a street fight?

CORKY: We used to beat up the guys on the other streets, see? Now, this night, we bumped into some of the Front Street kids, and there was a fight. I can't remember much, 'cause somebody hit me with a bottle.

SLIM: And this Arturo—he left you?

CORKY: Yeah. Sure he left me. He heard the cops coming, so he left me and ran.

SLIM: (*after a pause*) Corky?
Yeah? Corky?
CORKY: Yeah?
SLIM: You still want to run away?
CORKY: Sure I'm going to run away. But there's something I have to do first. See if they'll still want me. Ha!
SLIM: What?
CORKY: Never you mind. You go to sleep.
SLIM: Don't run away. They want you to stay, and—
CORKY: Oh, sure, sure! They love me like I was their own son. Yeah, yeah.
SLIM: (*after a pause*) Corky, I want you to stay.
CORKY: Oh, go to sleep!

(*The dim light from the window grows less, and there is a short music bridge.* CORKY *climbs out of bed.* SLIM *sits up soon afterwards.*)

SLIM: Corky? What's the matter?
CORKY: (*at the window R.*) Ssshh. Keep quiet! They'll hear you.
SLIM: You're running away. Oh, no, Corky, don't run away! Please!
CORKY: I'm not, I tell you. Now you be quiet!
SLIM: You've got your knife.
CORKY: So what? You shut your mouth, and be quiet, or I'll use it on you.
SLIM: But—
CORKY: Look, what I'm doing is just between Mr. Dirty-Gardener Schulz and me, see? If you know what's good for you, just put your head under those sheets and stay out of this.

(*He goes L. out to stairs. Lights fade to darkness. Music bridge, and light from window comes bright, to show early morning. Both boys are in bed.* CORKY *puts his head up, then gets out of bed and goes to window R.*)

CORKY: Slim! Slim, wake up!
SLIM: M-m-m? What is it?
CORKY: Want to come here, and see the show?
SLIM: What do you mean?
CORKY: Come on over here. Old Schulz'll see it in a minute.
SLIM: See what? (*goes to window*) Oh, Corky. What've you done?
CORKY: Neat, isn't it?
SLIM: You've ripped it up! His favorite rosebush! Why did you have to do that, Corky?

67

CORKY: Why? To show the great Schulz what I think of him and his lousy plants, that's why. Here he comes!

SLIM: Oh, Corky. I wish you hadn't done it. It's the new bush—

CORKY: Ssh! Here he comes. Look—he's seen it. Isn't that better than the movies?

SLIM: Oh, Corky! Poor old Pa! (*He starts to cry softly.*)

CORKY: Don't be so soft! Now he'll come after me. You see. Well, he'll have to beat me, that's all. But it'll be worth it, to see his face. Maybe I can bite him. I bit one of the guys that came to our room once. Maybe I'll hit him back. Worth it to see him get all red and mad and throw me out. Love me like his own son, eh? Ha!

SLIM: He's not moving, Corky. (*pause*)

CORKY: You wait. He'll move soon enough. (*longer pause*) What's he doing? What are those things he's holding?

SLIM: Those are his hedge clippers. He sometimes does his own garden before going off for the day's work.

CORKY: Why's he going round there? Why doesn't he come after me? Is he scared of me, or something?

SLIM: Maybe he isn't angry, Corky.

CORKY: Not angry? Don't be so stupid! That was his favorite rosebush, wasn't it? He really cared about it.

SLIM: P'raps he doesn't know you did it.

CORKY: No, he's just playing it cute. That's it. He thinks I'll get scared, and go crawling to him. Well, he can go on thinking. Come on, you big clod! Come and hit me! Shout at me! I cut it down, see? Yeah . . . 'Cause I don't like you or your flowers or the way you smell, or anything about you. And before I run away back to New York I want you to know it, see? So that it hurts.

SLIM: Oh, Corky, look! He's coming to clip this hedge.

CORKY: (*Returning to bed.* SLIM *follows.*) He thinks I'll be sorry if he waits. He's a cagey number, but he doesn't know me. If he thinks I'll be sorry, and go crawling up to him, he don't know me.

(*Lights fade. Music Bridge.*)

Scene Five

(*Main stage.* CORKY *is sitting on the floor L.C. near TV. He switches it off, goes to armchair C. and flings himself down. Enter* GRETCHEN *from kitchen R., carrying tablecloth. She lays it on table R.C.*)

GRETCHEN: You not want to watch any more TV, Corky?

CORKY: No. It's boring.

GRETCHEN: You want to help me with the dishes?

CORKY: No. (*pause*) Why aren't they home yet?

GRETCHEN: They'll come soon. It's light a long time still, so they work late even Saturday. You hungry, Corky? There's my new gingerbread in the kitchen.

CORKY: No.

GRETCHEN: Carry this tray back to the kitchen, will you? In a minute we'll be all ready for them.

CORKY: O.K. (*Goes out R. with tray.* GRETCHEN *finishes the table.* CORKY *returns to C.*)

GRETCHEN: They'll be mighty hungry after all that work. One day you go too, Corky; and you'll be as hungry as Slim. (*Sound of truck off L. in driveway.*)

CORKY: That's them.

GRETCHEN: Franz! Slim! Supper's ready.

SLIM: (*entering L.*) Hi, Ma! Something sure smells good. And I'm starved. Hi, Corky!

FRANZ: (*entering L.*) Hello there! You both have a good day?

GRETCHEN: Sure. I baked gingerbread, and Corky watched TV.

FRANZ: There's rain coming pretty soon. That's why we work so late this evening.

GRETCHEN: Thanks to Heaven! We sure need the rain.

FRANZ: That's right. Make the roses grow. Slim and I, we go wash. Then we'll have our supper. You're right, Slim. Something smells mighty good.

> (*As he goes R. lights fade. Music Bridge. When lights come up again,* FRANZ *is alone, sitting in armchair.* GRETCHEN *enters from kitchen.*)

FRANZ: Are they both in bed, Gretchen?

GRETCHEN: Yes, Franz. Poor little Slim! He's so tired he could hardly take off his clothes.

FRANZ: That's a good way to be at the end of the day. Slim worked very hard today.

GRETCHEN: Franz.

FRANZ: Yes, Gretchen?

GRETCHEN: When you going to speak to him about it?

FRANZ: About the rosebush? Oh, at the proper time. Not just yet, I reckon, Gretchen.

GRETCHEN: He was sure jumpy all day—like he was waiting for the execution.

FRANZ: One day he'll let us love him and come near him. And then he'll learn to love, too, like Slim. Remember how Slim didn't know how to take us, when he came first? That's the same with Corky.

GRETCHEN: Yes, Franz. Only Corky's older. That makes it harder.

FRANZ: This rosebush—he has to work it out his own way.

GRETCHEN: His way? I don't see how poor Corky knows what his way is.

FRANZ: It's like Mr. Mansola said—the Probation Officer. Everything in Corky's life has been hard. He don't know about love. I know he don't like coming here, and I can see why. So he cuts down my rosebush—to show me he don't like that I'm a gardener—and to show me he don't want us.

GRETCHEN: Won't he ever see things different?

FRANZ: I hope, I hope, Gretchen. But it takes time. He thinks I'll punish him, because that's what he understands—and so that's what he wants.

GRETCHEN: Poor Corky! But, Franz, do you think he's going to understand if you don't punish him?

FRANZ: Nobody can be sure, Gretchen. I just know that's what I think is right—that's what I think the good Lord wants us to try to do for Corky. When my plants don't grow straight, I don't punish them. I help them. They need to be tied up and given nourishment—so that's what I do, because I care about them. Boys have to grow, Gretchen, just like plants. Only thing is, it's harder to tie them up and help them to stand straight.

GRETCHEN: I'll go fix some coffee.

(*She goes out to kitchen.* FRANZ *picks up newspaper and reads. After a pause,* CORKY *enters R. hesitantly. He comes forward and stands by* FRANZ's *chair.*)

FRANZ: Why, hello there, Corky. Can't you sleep, huh? Come over and sit down. You like some hot chocolate, maybe?

CORKY: O.K.

FRANZ: Gretchen! Corky's come down. He'd like some hot chocolate, please. Make him sleep better.

GRETCHEN: (*at kitchen door*) That's right. I fix it, Corky, in a minute.

FRANZ: Now, Corky—

CORKY: I want to talk to you, Mr. Schulz.

FRANZ: Sure, Corky. Tell me what you're thinking.

CORKY: You know I cut it down?

FRANZ: Yes, I know.

CORKY: Then why didn't you hit me? Why didn't you throw me out yet? When will you do it?

FRANZ: I don't think I have the right to do that, Corky.

CORKY: But you—didn't want it cut down, did you? You didn't like losing it.

FRANZ: No, no, I didn't. I can tell you, it hurt me bad when I saw it lying there—my bush that I raise, different from any other.

CORKY: But you didn't get mad. How come you didn't get mad and yell at me?

FRANZ: I was mad, Corky, when I saw it. I sure was mad. I say to myself, Corky did this: why would he do a thing like that to me? Then I say to myself, if I'm mad at him, he'll probably run away. If I beat him—and that's what I felt like doing, Corky, soon as I saw how it had been cut and broken with that knife—if I beat him, we don't see him again. And who'd be any better off then? You see, Corky, we want you to stay. We think this is the right place for you to be.

CORKY: You still want me? After I did that?

FRANZ: May sound strange, Corky; but we want you more because of that. You see, this is the way we figure it. You know why we wanted Slim to come here, Mrs. Schulz and I? And why we want you to come too?

CORKY: Yeah, I know. To get the money.

FRANZ: That's not it, Corky. We had a son—a good boy, strong and big. That's his picture there, on the table. We loved him very much. He was a smart boy, and he wanted to be a lawyer, like you, or maybe a doctor. Well, he went away to war. He was wounded bad, and he died. (*pause*) He died all alone on a hill, no buddies around, and we felt bad, Corky. But we didn't want to feel bitter. If you spend your life with things growing all round you, you get so you want to see everything grow—not die. We lost our son, and we asked God to look after him; and I reckon God does that for us. But we still had to help things to grow right—that's what we figured. So we got Slim, 'cause he had no garden to grow in. And now we have you, Corky; and we want to help you to grow strong and tall and straight.

CORKY: But—you still want me to stay, when I cut down your best bush? I wanted to make you mad before I ran away.

FRANZ: We want you, son. We want you. (GRETCHEN *has come in*

71

from kitchen, and stands by him.) Don't we, Gretchen?

GRETCHEN: That's right.

FRANZ: And you don't have to be a gardener. If you want to go to school and learn to be a lawyer, then that's what we want, Corky—whatever's the best way for you to grow.

GRETCHEN: Here's your coffee, Franz. And Corky—be careful! That hot chocolate is hot. And eat the cookies.

CORKY: Thanks, Mrs. Schulz.

GRETCHEN: You're very welcome, my son. This is your home, if that's what you want it to be.

(*She goes out to fetch her cup, and returns quietly to C. during the next speeches.*)

CORKY: Mr. Schulz? That rosebush. It's dead, isn't it? You can't plant it again and make it grow?

FRANZ: No. You can't plant it again. Not that one.

CORKY: Well, can you plant another one in the same place—where I cut that one down?

FRANZ: If that's what you think you'd like to see, Corky, we can do it. It's not difficult. We just need to be patient, that's all.

CORKY: Could I help you to do it?

FRANZ: That's what I'd like, Corky. Then it'll belong to all of us, won't it? We can watch it grow.

CORKY: Yeah. I'd like that. I'd—like to see it grow again.

(GRETCHEN *is standing between their chairs.* CORKY *suddenly gets up and buries his head in her arms.*)

14. FIFTH SUNDAY OF THE YEAR

Who Is My Neighbor?

Bible Reference: OT/A (Isaiah 58:7–10)

Note: The courage and standards required of a Good Samaritan are clearly set forth in this passage of Isaiah. The true 'fasting' in Yahweh's eyes is to 'share your bread with the hungry . . . to clothe the man you see to be naked,' to do away with 'the yoke, the clenched fist, the wicked word.'

Just as important as what Uncle Dan did in this play is what the other neighbors failed to do. It is a familiar story. I based the play on an actual incident, which happened to a parish priest in a large city. He and his high school group were discussing the sociological background of crime, when they heard a violent assault on a boy outside the window.

It is dangerous and difficult to be a Good Samaritan in present day American life. But the one course which a Christian cannot take is to close his eyes and refuse to be involved.

The play can be presented in one of two ways. First, as a radio-type program, with voices coming from several locations. This will probably require several microphones. You should choose different areas to represent Uncle Dan's room, the Silvers' apartment, Dave and Judy's apartment, the bar, and the street scenes. In one Church I have used locations behind the organ, in the pulpit, behind the reading-desk, and behind the choir pews on either side. If you do it this way, the whole play is heard, none of it seen.

But I have marked some scenes as taking place on a visible stage, and this will usually be preferable. Uncle Dan's appeal in the last scene gains force if he is seen looking up at the various places from which the voices have been heard.

The play is suitable for any season in the Church year.

Scene: An American city street, on a hot, sultry summer evening.

Characters: UNCLE DAN
PETE, *a College Student*
NANCY, *15*
MR. SILVERS
MRS. SILVERS *her parents*
JUDY
DAVE *a young couple*
RUSTY
BO-BO *hoodlums, about 18*
BUD, *hoodlum, 16*
SAM, *a bartender*
GIUSEPPE, *18*
AMBULANCE DRIVER
SECOND AMBULANCE

Scene One

(*On stage and visible.* UNCLE DAN *and* PETE *are walking down a street. Sound of baby crying. A boy goes by on a skateboard.* NAN-CY's *voice is heard.*)

NANCY: Hi, Uncle Dan!
DAN: Hi there, Nancy!
PETE: That kid'll wear a rut in the sidewalk.
DAN: If he hasn't already, he never will. Anyway, where does a kid skate in this neighborhood? Everybody lives above the street.
PETE: Does everyone around here call you Uncle Dan?
DAN: Oh, quite a few of the kids do, Pete. If you stick around long enough, and walk with an artificial leg, you get to be known as a character. Come in and have some coffee.
PETE: Thanks.
DAN: And tell me some more about college, and that psychology course you're taking.
PETE: (*as they go offstage*) O.K. If you promise to listen.

Scene Two

(*The* SILVERS' *apartment* [*heard from offstage*].)

SILVERS: There's that baby next door yelling again.
NANCY: Get with it, Dad! Babies have to cry. Anyway, maybe he's as bored as I am. I wish there was something to do.

74

SILVERS: Oh, be quiet, Nancy! You're always complaining. Haven't you any studying to do?

NANCY: I've done it. And it's too hot to study.

MRS. SILVERS: Then turn on the tv.

NANCY: I don't want to watch tv, Mom. I want to go out and do something.

SILVERS: Well, you can't. Not at this time of night.

NANCY: Aw, come off it, Dad—

SILVERS: I'm going to bed and read a magazine. Anything to get away from that belly-aching of yours.

Scene Three

(DAVE's *apartment* [*heard from offstage*].)

JUDY: Dave, put down that paper and talk to me! (*He slaps the newspaper down angrily.*) Now—are we going to be able to make the payments, or aren't we? How about the money?

DAVE: Judy, I told you—I don't know. It depends on my commissions.

JUDY: And if we can't?

DAVE: Then we lose some of our things—they have to go back.

JUDY: Dave! How can you sit there and say that? Do I have to starve in an empty room because my husband doesn't make enough money?

DAVE: I earn as good money as a lot of people, but where it goes I don't know. You've got to be more careful, that's all.

JUDY: Careful! Look at me—my clothes—this room! How dare you say that to me?

DAVE: I'm sorry, Judy. Don't get all worked up! Here, let me fan you.

JUDY: (*after a pause*) That feels good.

DAVE: Don't worry, honey! We'll come through all this. Honest!

JUDY: I didn't mean to complain, Dave. It's just I'm so worried with the baby coming—and it's awful hot, isn't it?

DAVE: Yeah. It's sultry, like a storm coming up, or something.

Scene Four

(UNCLE DAN's *room* [*heard from offstage*].)

PETE: Uncle Dan! Coffee's ready.

DAN: Make mine black, will you, Pete? (*A pause. Sound of cups put down.*) That's fine. Now—to get on with our debate. What you're saying is—the kids on the street who steal or commit crimes aren't responsible—that we just haven't made enough social progress to solve their problems.

PETE: That's right. But we are making progress. As we understand what makes people anti-social or violent or frustrated, we can educate them out of it—not shut them up behind bars.

DAN: Does crime go down in proportion to the number of college degrees we hand out?

PETE: It's not that simple. But give it time. It takes time to make progress.

Scene Five

(*A Bar [heard from offstage].*)

RUSTY: Stick a dime in that jukebox, Bud.

BUD: Okay, Rusty. (*He does so.*)

RUSTY: I'm having one more drink. Then we're getting out of here.

BO-BO: Let's go now, Rusty, and look for some girls.

RUSTY: We'll do what I say, Bo-Bo. And this time, smart guy, you pay.

SAM: Look, fellas, you don't want any more liquor. I told you, I shouldn't be serving you under age.

RUSTY: Hey, a smarty pants bartender! Who said anything about age?

BUD: Yeah. Who said anything about age?

SAM: You're not more'n 16. Anyone can see that.

RUSTY: That's our business. And if you don't want any trouble, you just give us those drinks, now!

BO-BO: (*dropping money on counter*) There's your money, and he said NOW!

SAM: Okay, okay. But—it's against the law. If the cops find out—

RUSTY: We can handle the cops!

SAM: Well, if that's the kind of damfool ideas they bring you up on, you're in for some trouble. (*slaps down drinks*) There you are!

BO-BO: Let's drink up and get out of here. I'm hot!

RUSTY: Give Bud a chance. He's not old enough to take his liquor fast.

BUD: Aw, lay off! I can take it. Down the hatch!

RUSTY: Good boy, Bud! Goodnight, Grandpappy! Tell the cops we're sorry we missed them.

SAM: I'll do that. And don't hurry back!

Scene Six

(UNCLE DAN's *room* [*heard from offstage*].)

DAN: You keep talking about progress, Pete, but it seems to me we haven't made very much in thousands of years.

PETE: How can you say that? Look around! Better hospitals, better schools—

DAN: And printing presses and radios and movies and TV. Take those kids down on the street. They get ten times the book learning that a kid 2,000 years ago had, but how much different are they when it comes to a crisis?

PETE: You don't believe education will eventually change things?

(The clock strikes three quarters.)

DAN: 9:45. When do you have to get back?

PETE: I've got a good hour yet.

DAN: Good! You asked me, will education change things? I'll tell you something, Pete. There's just one thing that keeps us from being like wild animals, and that one thing is love—being loved and needed and having someone care about us. And in reverse— loving people, caring about them. It's a two-way street.

PETE: I know. That makes sense. Better sense than some of the text books.

DAN: Flattery, my son, will get you another cup of coffee.

PETE: I'll fetch it—and some for you.

Scene Seven

(The SILVERS' *apartment* [*heard from offstage*].)

NANCY: *(singing)* Ya-ya-ya, I'm in love, I'm in love—

MRS. SILVERS: Nancy, quiet! Your father's sleeping.

NANCY: What a terrible night! How can it be so hot? Maybe if I get the window clear up, I can get some more air. (*She pushes it up.*) No more air to be had, I guess.

(Sound of whistling below.)

Hey, Mom, there's Giuseppe leaving the delicatessen.

MRS. SILVERS: Where? Oh, I see him. He's a good-looking boy. Nice, too. Always happy and whistling.

NANCY: Kinda square. But I guess he's okay.

MRS. SILVERS: Who are those three boys?

77

NANCY: Where?
MRS. SILVERS: Coming the other way.
NANCY: I never saw them before. Hey, they're real creeps!
MRS. SILVERS: Nancy—look what they're doing.
NANCY: They're moving in on Giuseppe!

Scene Eight

(*The street* [*heard from offstage*].)

BUD: (*in a thick voice*) Who you pushin'?
GIUSEPPE: (*Italian accent*) I don't push nobody—
RUSTY: He said you were pushin'.
GIUSEPPE: I don't mean to push. I'm sorry.
BO-BO: He's a jerk. That's what he is.
BUD: Hey, Rusty, he pushed me.
RUSTY: Let's get him!

   (*Sound of a fight.*)

GIUSEPPE: Let me go! Oh, God! Let me go!
BO-BO: Kick his teeth in, the dirty, pushin' Wop!

Scene Nine

(*The* SILVERS' *apartment* [*heard from offstage*].)

NANCY: (*screams*) Oh, no! Look!
MR. SILVERS: What's goin' on? What's the matter, Nancy?
NANCY: They're beating up Giuseppe!
MRS. SILVERS: Can't you do something, George?
MR. SILVERS: No, no. Now—it's not our business. No use getting
   involved.
NANCY: Oh, it's awful! (*crying*)

Scene Ten

(DAVE'*s apartment* [*heard offstage*].)

JUDY: Dave, they're kicking a boy down on the sidewalk. We've got
   to stop them!
DAVE: Take it easy, honey. We can't do anything.
JUDY: You mean you won't! Well, I can. I'm going to call the police!

DAVE: No, Judy. If you do that you have to give our name and we'll be involved. Let the kids work it out!

JUDY: Work it out?! Dave, they'll kill him!

DAVE: And I tell you it's not our business. It's dangerous to interfere.

Scene Eleven

(*The street [on stage, visible].*)

GIUSEPPE: (*Staggering on stage, followed by the three hoodlums.*) Madre mia! Someone help me, please!

PETE: Uncle Dan, what's going on?

DAN: (*to window*) Good God, it's Giuseppe! Come on, let's go! Take that whistle—on the desk—get outside, down the street a ways so they'll think it's the police! And blow it for all you're worth!

PETE: What about you? You might get hurt!

DAN: I've got to stop them before they kill him. Get going, Pete!

DAN: (*running in*) Get away from him, you young punks! Get away!

RUSTY: Aw, shut your mouth, Peg-Leg, and keep out of this!

DAN: Why, you young—

(*He wades into them, and catches* BUD *by the arm. They surround him.*)

BUD: Aaah! Lemme go, Mister! You're hurting my arm!

(*Loud whistle from distance, again approaching.*)

BO-BO: Hey Rusty, the cops! Let's get out of here!

RUSTY: This way—down the alley!

BUD: Rusty, don't leave me! Aaah, Rusty! He's breaking my arm!

DAN: I'll break more than your arm if you try to get away.

PETE: (*running up*) Uncle Dan—you all right?

DAN: Sure. I know enough Judo to deal with a drunken schoolboy. I just couldn't manage to hold the other two at the same time. Easy, Giuseppe, boy. It's all over. We'll take care of you.

BUD: (*crying*) I tell you he pushed me. He jumped me! I was just walking along peaceful and—

DAN: Shut up! We'll deal with you when the police get here. What we need first is an ambulance. Have any of you called the police? I'm talking to all you people who live up there. Did any of you call the police? Or an ambulance? In God's name, what's wrong with you? There's a boy down here dying, maybe.

79

DAVE: O.K. Uncle Dan. I'll call the police.
DAN: Tell them an ambulance—hurry! Pete, hold our prize catch.
PETE: Come here, you!
BUD: I tell you, he—
PETE: Be quiet! You make me sick!
DAN: Now, now Giuseppe, easy does it! Your friends are here.
GIUSEPPE: Thanks, Uncle Dan.
DAN: You're a good boy, Giuseppe. You've got courage, you have.
We'll have help any minute now.
PETE: (*in a whisper*) God, he looks awful! Isn't there something we can do?
DAN: Just try to keep him still. If they haven't injured his spine or his kidneys, he'll be all right. God knows they tried!
PETE: It's all so stupid! I can't believe—
DAN: Progress, eh? I guess it came along too slow to help Giuseppe.

(*Ambulance siren approaching.*)

Over here! (*Ambulance men bring stretcher.*)
This fine boy—beaten to a pulp!
1ST MAN: Come on, Joe, let's get him to the hospital!
DAN: His name is Giuseppe Mancini. Lives down the street.
2ND MAN: Thanks, friend (*They put him on the stretcher and hurry away.*)
DAN: God help him, poor kid! You people up there—what are you staring at? The show's over, unless you want to wait for the cops to take away this hoodlum. But I warn you—you'd better not be looking when the police get here—you might be wanted as witnesses! You might be involved, and that would never do, would it? (*Police siren*) Yes, you up there! A boy gets half-killed under your eyes, and you didn't move even a finger—a finger on a telephone dial—to help! Because you might get hurt. Someone might ask you some questions. What kind of neighbors are you, anyway? And what are you going to do the next time? Only the next time it may be you!

Also suitable for this Sunday: The Perfect House (OT/A); see Fifth Sunday of Easter: The Good Samaritan (OT/A); see 15th Sunday of the Year.

15. SIXTH SUNDAY OF THE YEAR

Go, Show Yourself

Bible Reference: Leviticus 13:1–2, 44–46, and Mark 1:40–45 (OT and Gospel B)

Note: Leprosy. Even now the word has overtones of irrational fear. In the time of Jesus it was the worst sickness which could befall a man or woman. Lepers had to live apart, dependent on uncertain charity, and their hope of returning to normal life was slender.

The reactions of the leper's family, and of their neighbors, after this cure described by Mark, are not recorded. It is these reactions which the play explores, in a modern context—or rather a timeless context.

If the reactions of the characters in the play seem to be exaggerated, you should look back at accounts of the Black Death in England, in the 14th century, or the London plague of 1665, or nearer to home, the polio epidemic of 1916, when "outlying communities began treating New York City refugees as if they were lepers or vagrants, turning them back with guns." (Richard Carter: *Breakthrough, p. 10.*)

The play is written as a radio play, and may be given with microphones and unseen actors. This would emphasize the timelessness.

It can also be acted visibly, in part or in whole within a flexible staging area, so that the scenes can be presented in quick succession.

A good compromise would be to act onstage all the scenes in the Simonsons' home. This only requires two areas: the living room, and Mary's room to one side. The initial scene could be presented in the same area later used as Mary's room. But the scene at the Matthews' home and the roadside conversation scene would be heard radio-style.

Also suitable for: 22nd and 28th Sundays of the Year.

22nd Sunday of the Year: Gospel B (Mk. 7:1–8, 14–15, 21–23) deals with the question of 'clean and unclean.' Jesus is clear that it is the things that come out of a man that make him unclean. He is concerned with the heart, not with the 'observances' which loomed so large in the minds of 'the Pharisees, and the Jews in general.'

28th Sunday of the Year: Gospel C (Lk 17:11–19) contains the story of the healing of ten lepers. There is a great poignancy in the words, 'they stood some way off.' The lepers knew, and Jesus knew, that they could not approach him without breaking rigidly established customs. He healed without touching—by saying the words, 'Go and show yourselves to the priests.' Notice that this reading, and the play, bring out in different ways how hard it is to be grateful. Only one of ten lepers came back to thank Jesus; and almost all of John Simonson's circle of family and neighbors found it difficult to feel thankful for his return.

Scene: See individual scene headings.

Characters: JOHN SIMONSON, *18; tall, thin, handsome*
A PRIEST
JOHN SIMONSON, SR. *Parents of John*
MARTHA SIMONSON
JOE SIMONSON, *13; John's brother*
MARY SIMONSON, *19; John's sister*
DOCTOR KING
ANDY MATTHEWS *Neighbors of the Simonsons*
SUE MATTHEWS
PETE MATTHEWS, *19; their son*
BOB MATTHEWS, *13; their son*

MUSIC: Introduction, Fading

NARRATOR: 'Go, show yourself to the Priest.' The words were spoken to a leper, outside a Jewish village, nearly two thousand years ago. Prove to the Priest that your skin is clean and unbroken, and he will give you the certificate of healing. You can go home . . .

Scene One: The Priest's House

(Sound: Running footsteps growing nearer. Loud breathing. Loud knock on door.)

PRIEST: Who is it?
JOHN: Let me in, Father. I must see you, quickly.
PRIEST: All right, all right. Don't be impatient. I'm coming.

(Sound: Chain on door. Door creaks open slowly.)

82

PRIEST: Well?
JOHN: Father, I'm John Simonson, from the leper compound.
PRIEST: A leper? You—
JOHN: No, no. I've come to show you. I'm cured. He touched me—
PRIEST: Come in, my son.

(*Sound: Door closed.*)

PRIEST: There! That's better. Now what's all this?
JOHN: Look! You see my arm? This wrist was half eaten away. And
it's the same all over my body.

(*Sound: Tearing clothes.*)

JOHN: If you don't believe me, look for yourself. And it's not just my
skin. If you knew what it feels like, to have life in you, and
strength, and hope—

(*Music bridge.*)

NARRATOR: John Simonson had been a leper for five years. When
he was thirteen years old, his mother saw a white patch on his
neck. She fainted, and when neighbors came to the house they
rushed the boy away to the compound outside the village, before
she even saw him again. There he lived, with the others, for five
years. Some families forgot their leper relatives, perhaps because
they could not bear the memories and the reality. But John's father
and mother did not forget. They did what they could for their son.
They left him food, and clothes, and letters; and in these letters
they told him how much they loved him, and longed to have him
back.
   It could all have happened in Galilee or in Rome, in India or in
the Philippines, in Omaha or in New York.
   John Simonson is running home. He has proof of his cure, not
only in his skin, but in the pocket of the makeshift clothes which
he put on at the Priest's house, when for the last time he tore away
the matted rags of the outcast. John is running home. What will he
find there, the grown man who went away a boy?

Scene Two: The Simonsons' Home

JOE: Mom!
MOTHER: I'm in the kitchen. What is it?

(*Sound: Steps.*)

83

JOE: I can't get that old engine to work. Can I go down to the hobby shop?

MOTHER: How much money do you have?

JOE: Two dollars. If it's more, I'll have to wait and get it done later.

MOTHER: Why not ask your father first? He might be able to fix it.

JOE: O.K., Mom. Gee! I'm sure glad you found it. How come that stuff had been in the attic so long?

MOTHER: Oh, it all got put away years ago, and forgotten. I'm glad we can bring it out and use it. Now run along, Joe, and play with the rest of it. I'm sure Daddy will have some ideas about the engine.

> (*Music bridge. Steps, coming to a halt, and door-bell. Rattling door.*)

JOHN: Mother! Dad! Let me in!

> (*Sound: Steps, door opens.*)

MOTHER: Who is it? Oh, God! No!

JOHN: Mother, I'm—

MOTHER: Don't touch me! Don't come inside! Oh, John, John, go back! Please, go back!

JOHN: Mother, don't! You don't understand! Look at me! I'm cured! I've been to the priest, and got my clearance. I'm cured!

MOTHER: I don't believe it. It's not possible. Oh, John!

> (*Sound: Whistling and approaching steps. Stops abruptly.*)

JOE: Who is it, Mom?

MOTHER: Joe, go back to your room—

JOHN: Joe?

JOE: Yeah. Who—Mom, it's—what's he doing here? Get him out!

MOTHER: It's all right, Joe.

JOE: But we'll all get it. We'll be lepers.

JOHN: Cut it out, Joe. Look, Mom, I know it's hard for you to believe it, but here's the form—my clearance. Funny; I didn't think about this on my way here. I could only think about getting home, and seeing you, and the house; not about what it would be like for you.

MOTHER: John, I'm sorry. It was just too much, coming suddenly. Sit down, John. Joe, leave us for a little while, dear.

> (*Sound: Steps receding, door closes.*)

JOHN: Oh, Mom! (*breaking down, sobs*) You don't know what it's like. You don't know—

MOTHER: I understand, Johnnie. I do. It's just that it was such a shock, seeing you there. One moment, I was cleaning house, and then—you were at the door.

JOHN: Where's Dad?

MOTHER: He should be back from the office quite soon. Johnnie, it is true? There are no marks?

JOHN: No, Mother. It's gone. All of it. The smell, and the taint, and the feeling inside me that I was rotting away all through.

MOTHER: Oh, my boy! My dearest boy! I can't believe it. You look so fresh, and strong.

JOHN: (laughing) Fresh—that's it. New life inside, new flesh outside. As for strength—I was strong before. We had to be, out there, to control the ones who went mad.

MOTHER: Don't, John!

JOHN: No, I won't talk about it. I just want to forget. Oh, these cushions—and the rug! The flowers, and pictures, and—

MOTHER: Johnnie, your clothes. Are they—

JOHN: Infected? Don't worry! The Priest keeps spare clothes there, and I threw mine away. Not that I think it mattered. When Jesus cured me, I don't think any infection had a chance.

MOTHER: That was how it happened?

JOHN: Yes, that was how it happened. I'll tell you about that, and about the compound, one day. Can I go and look at my room now, Mother? I've thought about it so much, all these years.

MOTHER: Of course, John. It's—well, naturally, Joe uses it now.

JOHN: Joe? My room? (laughs) How stupid can you be? Five years, and I never thought about that. All the same, I think I'll just go in and look. You don't mind, do you? I'd like to be alone in there, just for a minute.

MOTHER: That's all right, John.

(Sound: Steps receding, sobs. Music bridge. Sound: Door opens. Steps approaching.)

JOE: Oh, Mom! You're crying. Where is he?

MOTHER: Oh, Joe. He's gone to—his room.

JOE: Which room? (pause) You mean, my room? He can't go in there! I won't dare touch anything. And it's not his, it's mine!

MOTHER: Joe, Joe! Be quiet! We have to get used to this, Joe. Johnnie's come back to us, Joe. He's cured, truly cured. God has given him back to us, and we have to get used to it.

JOE: I just don't understand. They said at school nobody gets cured of leprosy. What if it isn't real?

85

(Sound: Car on driveway. Horn. Car stops.)

MOTHER: There's your father. You wait in here, Joe. I want to speak to him first.

(Sound: Car door slammed. Steps on driveway.)

FATHER: Hi, Sally! What's new?

MOTHER: Oh, John! *(sobs)*

FATHER: Here, here, here! What's up, honey? What's come over you?

MOTHER: John, before you come into the house, I've got news for you. Johnnie's home.

FATHER: Johnnie? What Johnnie? You mean the Robertsons are back from Europe?

MOTHER: No, no. Our Johnnie. Our son.

FATHER: Johnnie? You must be crazy?

MOTHER: Hush, John! He may hear you.

FATHER: Johnnie's a leper. If he's come near here, the only thing to do is to call the police.

MOTHER: Oh, John don't! You've got to understand. You—

(Sound: Steps on driveway.)

JOHN: Hello, Dad!

FATHER: Johnnie! Johnnie, you have to go away—

JOHN: No, Dad. I can understand how you feel; but I'm cured. Mom knows, don't you, Mom?

MOTHER: He has the certificate, John, signed by the Priest.

JOHN: Look, Dad. You needn't come any closer until you see for yourself. My arm was dead white, except where it was eaten away into a raw mess. Look at it now! And my face, and my legs. It started here, remember? On my back. I know I look like a scarecrow now; I just saw myself in the glass. But give me a chance to take a shower, and shave, and put on some decent clothes. I tell you, Dad, it's all over.

FATHER: But—things like this don't happen, son.

JOHN: They happened today. *(laughing)* I'm beginning to think they happened almost too fast—but they happened, all right.

MOTHER: We'll get used to it soon. It isn't that we don't want you back, Johnnie. You know it isn't that . . .

(Music bridge.)

86

Scene Three: The Matthews' Home

(Sound: Hammering. Then woman's steps on wood floor.)

SUE: Andy! Andy! Quick! Come down!
ANDY: Just a minute! *(hammering)* I'm coming!

(Sound: Heavy steps on ladder and wooden floor.)

ANDY: Now, what's it all about, Sue?
SUE: *(hysterical)* Oh, Andy! We've got to do something. That leper boy has been seen going back into the Simonsons' house.
ANDY: Which boy? Not—
SUE: Yes. Johnnie. The hopeless case. He must have broken out of the compound. Andy, find Pete and stop him from going there to pick up Mary.
ANDY: Now, just a minute, Sue. Let me find out about it first.
SUE: Do we all have to become lepers just because they won't keep away from us?
ANDY: Sue!

(Sound: Face slapped.)

ANDY: Now, calm down, Sue. Let me try to call Pete, and stop him going to their house. I think Bob may be riding his bicycle with Joe Simonson, too. We'll see.

(Music bridge.)

Scene Four: The Simonsons' Home

(Sound: Drink being poured. Icecubes.)

FATHER: Boy! I need this drink. Do you feel better, darling?
MOTHER: I hardly feel anything. I'm torn—just torn up inside.

(Sound: Steps. Door opens.)

FATHER: How do you do, Doctor King?
DOCTOR: Hello. Let me reassure you, he's cured.
MOTHER: *(breaking down)* Oh, God!
FATHER: Take it easy, darling.
DOCTOR: You're bound to be under a severe strain, Mrs. Simonson. I'll give you something to help you sleep.
MOTHER: It's not that I'm not thankful. I—

DOCTOR: I know. The adjustment is too much, coming all at once.

FATHER: You do believe it will last, Doctor? It's not something that will lift us up and then let us down?

DOCTOR: In my opinion, no. It may sound strange to say this, but if he had been healed by drugs I should be more suspicious than I am now. Johnnie put it best himself, while I was talking to him. He said, "I haven't just been cured of a disease. I've been made whole." His body is whole and healthy.

FATHER: And you believe in faith healing?

DOCTOR: My dear Mr. Simonson, I believe in healing. Most healing is brought about by the patient, by his common sense and confidence working together with nature. Some healing is contributed by the doctor—by his confidence, which is another way of saying, by faith. And the rest is drugs—they do help, but they aren't much use without faith.

FATHER: You feel so helpless, in face of a thing like this. I mean, he's back—that's the central, wonderful fact. But you can't just change everything in a moment—rooms, routine, everything.

DOCTOR: It's the same with any family which experiences a sudden change. The cure has to cover every member.

(*Sound: Running steps outside. Front door flung open.*)

MARY: Hi, everyone! Oh, Doctor King! What's wrong? Somebody sick?

DOCTOR: Nothing like that, Mary. In fact, just the opposite. There's good news for you all.

MARY: What sort of good news? The way you all look, it doesn't seem so good. Mother—

MOTHER: Mary, dear, we've had a shock; but it *is* very wonderful news.

MARY: Well, nobody seems to want to tell me what it is.

FATHER: It's about Johnnie.

MARY: Johnnie? You mean—my brother who's a leper?

DOCTOR: Let me tell you, Mary, as your family Doctor. I've examined Johnnie, after your mother and father told me that he had been cured. It's true.

MARY: (*hysterical*) I don't believe it! Where is he? He's not coming here? He's—no, no. (*screams and sobs*)

FATHER: Mary! Be quiet.

MARY: Where is he?

DOCTOR: He's in his room, Mary; asleep.

MARY: His room! He has no room! He doesn't belong here! Get him away!

(*Sound: Sobs and running steps. Door slams.*)

Scene Five: The Matthews' Home

(*Music bridge.*)

BOB MATTHEWS: What's wrong with you, Joe? Aren't you going to help me mend this wheel?
JOE: Oh, I dunno, Bob. I think I'd better go home.
BOB: There's plenty of time. Gee, Joe! I don't know what's got into you.
JOE: Leave me alone! I'm all right.

(*Sound: Footsteps along path, approaching.*)

ANDY: (*shouting from a distance.*) Bob! Bob, where are you?
BOB: Down here, Dad. With Joe.
ANDY: Did your brother John come home?
JOE: Yeah.
ANDY: And you were with him?
JOE: Yes, Mr. Matthews, but—
ANDY: Well, you get out of here! Get back home, and don't come near my place again! Tell your father I'll call the police. I'll do anything to have him out. Is that clear?
JOE: You haven't got any right to talk like that—
ANDY: Get out! You and your whole family. Don't spread the plague here.

(*Music bridge.*)

Scene Six: The Simonsons' Home

DOCTOR: There, Mary! Do you feel better?
MARY: I guess so, Doctor. I'm—sorry.
DOCTOR: Just relax. You've always had a horror of leprosy, haven't you?
MARY: Yes, I can't help it. Do you remember Joanna Thomas?
DOCTOR: Yes, I remember. She died, didn't she?
MARY: Yes, she died. She was one of the lucky ones. She died in three years. We shared a desk in Fifth Grade. And then one day—

89

DOCTOR: All right; don't think about it.

MARY: I can't help it. I try to forget, but she haunts me, till I hate her—and myself. We all used to envy her skin, and she had the most wonderful hair, dark and smooth. I saw her from the edge of the compound, a few weeks before she died.

DOCTOR: All right, Mary dear. Tell me.

MARY: Her face was dirty white, pudgy and shapeless. Her hair was falling out, and she looked like a half-empty sack. Where her hands had been—

DOCTOR: All right, Mary. Don't worry.

MARY: She called out to me, and I turned and ran. I ran away. And I remembered Johnnie too. I tried to shut it all out; and now—Is it really true that Johnnie won't pass it on to us, breathing the same air, touching things?

DOCTOR: It's true. Look, nobody could possibly blame you for how you felt about leprosy, after what happened to Joanna and Johnnie. But do you know the only thing to do about something that makes you as much afraid as this?

MARY: What can I do?

DOCTOR: Face up to it. You're engaged to Pete Matthews, aren't you?

MARY: Practically engaged. We were going to announce it next week, but now—

DOCTOR: I know. You're frightened about John, and what the Matthews family will say.

MARY: I just want to forget Johnnie.

DOCTOR: But you can't, Mary. When you realize what has happened, you are going to be so, so happy. And remember, John needs you very badly. Before you go to sleep tonight, make up your mind that you will try to give him what he needs. Will you promise me that?

MARY: I'll try. I promise.

DOCTOR: And I give you my word that John is as healthy and strong as your Pete. Next thing you know, he'll be getting married himself . . .

(*Fading. Music bridge.*)

MOTHER: It's going to be all right, John. Once we get used to the idea of having him back, it's going to be all right.

FATHER: I keep thinking of what it means. He has no clothes, nothing. They gave him that high school diploma last year; but was it genuine? Or just charity? Is he going to be—like an ordinary person?

MOTHER: Don't, John! We'll face that when it comes. Just now he needs love, so desperately. If we can give him that—

(*Sound: Front door flung open. Running Steps. Sobs.*)

MOTHER: Why, Joe!

JOE: Oh, Mom!

MOTHER: What is it, my darling?

FATHER: Try to tell us, son.

JOE: I went out to play with Bob, then Mr. Matthews came from their house.

(*Sound: Sobs.*)

FATHER: Whatever it is, Joe, it's nothing for you to worry about. Just tell us. We'll look after it.

JOE: He was all mad. He shouted at me to come home, and tell you to send Johnnie away or he'd call the police.

FATHER: Why, the . . .

MOTHER: Oh, no!

JOE: He said he was coming over to make sure.

FATHER: He'd better not, that's all! He'd better not!

JOE: Oh, Mom, I'm so mixed up. Is he going to have my room?

FATHER: We'll work it all out later, Joe.

JOE: And what am I going to say to my friends?

FATHER: I know, Joe. It's hard for us all, coming suddenly. But think about Johnnie first. He's the one who needs the breaks.

JOE: I'll try, Dad. Goodnight.

(*Sound: Car on driveway. Door slammed. Steps. Door bell.*)

FATHER: I'll go.

(*Sound: Steps. Door opened.*)

PETE MATTHEWS: Good evening, Mr. Simonson.

FATHER: Hello, Pete.

PETE: I'm a bit early. Came straight from work. May I wait for Mary? We have a date.

FATHER: Come in, Pete.

MOTHER: Mary is in her room. I think she's resting now. I'll go see.

PETE: For Heaven's sake, what's the mystery?

FATHER: Well, Pete, it's like this . . .

(Sound: Steps on driveway. Loud knock on door and bell.)

FATHER: Excuse me a moment. Oh, hello, Andy.

ANDY: Is my son in there?

PETE: Hi, Dad! Here I am.

ANDY: Get out of this house, Pete. Run straight home and strip off those clothes. I'll burn them, and you scrub yourself in the shower.

(Sound: Door opens.)

DOCTOR: Just a minute, Mr. Matthews. Will you please calm down?

ANDY: I've no time to argue, Doctor King. Is that leper out of this house yet?

PETE: Leper!

DOCTOR: There is no leper in this house, Mr. Matthews. There hasn't been at any time. John Simonson is cured.

ANDY: Cured! You don't know what you're talking about. Is he back in the compound, or not?

JOHN: Here I am, Mr. Matthews.

(Sound: A long silence.)

JOHN: Perhaps you'd like to see for yourself.

ANDY: How dare you come here? Pete, get out of this house quick.

PETE: Dad, shut your mouth! Do you want me to be more ashamed of you than I am? Johnnie, remember me? Shake hands. It's— wonderful that you're back.

JOHN: Thanks, Pete, thanks. Now, Mr. Matthews, if you're so keen to see me go back to the compound, come and get me.

ANDY: You're mad! Don't come near me!

(Sound: Steps walking. Other steps running. Heavy breathing.)

JOHN: Don't worry. I'm just closing the door. We don't want all the world to hear this.

(Sound: Front door closed.)

ANDY: If it's money you want, I'll pay you—

JOHN: Money? That's great, isn't it? How much? Ten thousand dollars, twenty thousand? To go quietly back to the compound and lose myself. Or perhaps you don't mind my being out, so long as I keep away from you—so long as I don't try to breathe your air, or perhaps kiss your daughter. Actually, that's rather funny. She's the only girl I ever have kissed. Gina, her name was—is that right? It was in fourth grade, and we didn't get much of a kick out of it. That was before—

ANDY: Someone get him out of here. He's crazy!

JOHN: No, Mr. Matthews, I'm not mad. I could be, easily; but thank God I've kept this side of madness all the years in that place—until today. And today I've been made whole, my body and my mind and my spirit. It's going to take some getting used to, but I'm probably the sanest person in this room. And I'm not a leper, Mr. Matthews. I was; but I'm not now. You're going to touch me and see.

(*Sound: Slow steps, then a quick scuffle.*)

ANDY: Stand back! If you won't go back quietly, this is the only way to force you.

MOTHER: Johnnie! The gun! Keep back!

ANDY: Pete, go to that phone and call the police! Nobody else is to move.

DOCTOR: You might have spared us that, Mr. Matthews. If you're going to shoot anyone, it will have to be me. Now, give me that gun, please!

ANDY: Get out of my way, Doctor! Don't be a fool! Do you want us all infected?

JOHN: Leave this to me, Doc.

(*Sound: Quick steps and a struggle and fall.*)

ANDY: Don't touch me! A-a-a-h!

JOHN: We learned a good deal about self-defence out there, Mr. Matthews. Guns don't settle the problem. Do I look like a leper? Do I feel like a leper?

FATHER: Johnnie, let him go!

JOHN: I'm sorry, Dad. I don't want to hurt him. It would be a betrayal of my own healing, a denial of the power of love. Get up, sir. I assure you it won't do you any harm to have touched me.

ANDY: I'm—sorry, Johnnie. I still don't understand; but I'm sorry. I behaved like a brute.

DOCTOR: You behaved like a frightened man, Mr. Matthews. Look, Johnnie, I have a suggestion. You and I are the same build, and you have to get some clothes from somewhere. Why not drive over with me to my place and look for something?

JOHN: Sounds like a good idea. That is, if you've got the time.

DOCTOR: If we go quick, I've got time before my next call.

FATHER: Thanks, Doctor.

DOCTOR: Pete, take your father home. He's had a shock, like all of us. And Mary will be all set for a date tomorrow. Come on, Johnnie!

(*Music bridge.*)

Scene Seven: A Car by the Roadside

(*Sound: Car driven slowly.*)

DOCTOR: Remember this place. Let's stop under the trees.

(*Sound: Car slows and stops.*)

DOCTOR: There!

JOHN: Thanks, Doctor King. You seemed to be the only person who wasn't turned inside out by my arrival.

DOCTOR: Oh, don't get me wrong. I was taken aback, all right. I've seen it happen before—not often, but occasionally, when faith gets the better of logic. Will you go back to school now, Johnnie?

JOHN: (*laughing*) Give me a chance! I'll have to think about it. It'll be College of some kind. You know they sent us correspondence courses, and I did pretty well—graduated last summer. I'd like to have a stab at being a Doctor myself, but I don't know about Dad's finances.

DOCTOR: Ever done any fishing?

JOHN: Why do you ask? I did a bit, up the river. But remember I was only thirteen when I caught leprosy.

DOCTOR: Listen! I've got a cabin up near Freshwater Lake, about seventy miles inland. I keep it stocked. I'm going to take you up there, tonight. This is Wednesday; I'll be back there myself on Friday evening, and we'll catch some fish.

JOHN: You mean, not go home now? Go straight there?

DOCTOR: It's up to you, Johnnie: but that's my advice; that is, if you're not afraid of being alone. I'll call round and tell your parents that I'm taking you there. What they need is time, and so do you.

JOHN: I need it?

DOCTOR: I think so. Up there you'll have time to think, and find out how to behave like a healthy man. Climb some of the mountains—read the papers and magazines. It'll get you more ready for the next steps, like going downtown, and meeting girls again. Even more important it'll give your folks a chance to get used to a miracle.

JOHN: I believe you're right.

94

DOCTOR: Come on! Let's go and look for those clothes for you.

(*Music bridge.*)

Scene Eight: The Simonsons' Home

(*Sound: Door opened, then quietly shut. Steps.*)

FATHER: Hello, dear. Mary still quiet?

MOTHER: Fast asleep. Doctor King said she wouldn't stir till morning.

FATHER: Joe went to sleep on the camp bed, fully dressed. I left him. Didn't want to wake him!

MOTHER: No, let him sleep. We're all exhausted. What are you writing?

FATHER: Calculations. How we can adjust our income to send one more boy to college.

MOTHER: We didn't believe it, did we? I used to write twice a week without fail, and every time I said, "We want you back so badly." It was true, John, wasn't it? We did want him back; but we gave up believing it.

FATHER: We were only human, darling. We had to treat him as dead, emotionally, even when we sent the things and letters. I suppose it was like putting flowers on somebody's grave.

(*Sound: Car on driveway.*)

MOTHER: There they are.

(*Sound: Car stops. Door slammed. Steps outside. Steps inside. Door opened.*)

FATHER: Hello, Doctor! Where's Johnnie?

DOCTOR: Can I come in a minute?

MOTHER: Nothing's happened, has it?

DOCTOR: No, no. He's fine. He's at my house, trying on some clothes. We had a talk, and worked out a plan.

FATHER: A plan?

DOCTOR: I'm taking him away to my cabin, perhaps till Monday, perhaps a little longer.

MOTHER: But—

DOCTOR: I'm sure it's right, Mrs. Simonson. Families have a problem, even when one of them comes back from a long stay in hospital. With a returning P.O.W., after a War, it's even harder. But a leper—

95

FATHER: Are you sure he won't feel—unwanted?

DOCTOR: No. Johnnie's got a pretty good head on his shoulders. He knows that ordinary people can't live with a miracle. You and he have to lower the temperature, to allow the routine of daily life to work at all.

MOTHER: You mean—we can't accept a miracle until we forget that it happened?

DOCTOR: That's about it, Mrs. Simonson. Our need for security drives us to hate the abnormal. We like to read about it, but we can't stand it in our own lives.

FATHER: Then—isn't it wasted, if people forget so soon?

DOCTOR: Healing is never wasted. Johnnie's life will be the fruit of what happened, the miracle. But you don't convert crowds by healing a leper. They don't want to remember: so they forget. Johnnie may become a short paragraph in the history books, along with the earthquakes, the murders, the plane crashes. What happened to him doesn't matter in the end: but what he can be now, that's different.

FATHER: Yes. Yes, I see.

MOTHER: Oh, John! I hope we're worth all this—you and I, and Mary and Joe—and Johnnie himself. I hope we're worth it.

(*Music. Conclusion.*)

Also suitable for this Sunday: Cana of Galilee (OT/C); see 2nd Sunday of the Year; also see *Bible as Drama,* page 263 (Epistle B); Corinth: Second Episode.

16. THIRD SUNDAY OF LENT

Honor Your Father

Bible Reference: Exodus 20:1–17 (OT/B)

Note: This reading includes the Ten Commandments. Next, after respect for God, comes respect for parents. As Paul says (Eph. 6:2) 'The first commandment that has a promise attached to it is: Honor your father and mother, and the promise is: and you will prosper and have a long life in the land.'

In our society family ties have been weakened. It is wonderful that older people can be well cared for together in retirement or convalescent homes; but it can plainly be seen that some people use this as a too simple answer to the problems involved in caring for them at home.

Also suitable for: 1st Sunday after Christmas; Trinity; 20th, 21st, and 22nd Sundays of the Year.

1st Sunday after Christmas: OT/A and Epistle A (Sirach 3:3–7, 14–17 and Col. 3:12–21). This epistle is a commentary on the Fifth Commandment; and in verse 4 we read that 'he who honors his mother is like someone amassing a fortune.' Later there is the injunction: 'Even if his mind should fail, show him sympathy.' The play shows the different reactions of old Mr. Forsberg's children to these verses.

Trinity: Epistle A (2 Cor. 13:11–13) and Epistle B (Romans 8:14–17). The first passage is about 'the spirit of sons.' It also contains the words, which need to be pondered in the context of every family: 'If we are children we are heirs as well.'

The second reading sums up the perfect family spirit: 'Help one another. Be united; live in peace.'

Twentieth Sunday of the Year: Gospel C (Lk. 12:49–53). 'A household of five will be divided . . . son against father.' Jesus is saying that the standards and beliefs which he demands will often not be accepted by the family members.

21st Sunday of the Year: Epistle B (Eph. 5:21–32). The following verses, 6:1–4 (quoted above), are needed to complete the reading as

97

it touches on this scene. Family life with 'no speck or wrinkle' is a rare dream. But the key to happiness in a family lies in the word 'honor.'

22nd Sunday of the Year: OT/C (Sirach 3:17–18, 20, 28–29). The opening verses are a fair description of two of the Forsberg family, Stan and Marge, as well as Stan's wife Ethel: 'Be gentle in carrying out your business, and you will be better loved than a lavish giver.'

Scene: A very humble home, somewhere in a remote country area, the home of Jacob Forsberg, eighty years old. It is the day of his wife's funeral, and four of his five children are returning from it to the house. His sister, Dora, has been looking after him during the funeral.

Characters: STAN FORSBERG, *and his wife* ETHEL *(early fifties)*
GLORIA FORSBERG HOLT, *and her husband* DESMOND, *a Doctor (about 50)*
PETER FORSBERG *and his wife* HARRIET *(late forties)*
MARGE FORSBERG *(late forties)*
AUNT DORA *(80)*

(All except DORA *enter.)*

MARGE: Quietly! He may be asleep. *(She crosses and goes to the bedroom.)*
GLORIA: Let's sit down. I'm exhausted!
DESMOND: Over here, dear. *(She sits on the only couch.)*
PETER: Leave room for Harriet, Gloria.
GLORIA: What do you mean, leave room? I'm not that large, Peter!
HARRIET: I'll be all right here. *(She sits on a chair.)*
PETER: We don't have enough chairs for everyone.
STAN: I'll fetch two more.
ETHEL: No, Stan, I'll get them. *(She goes out one way, as* MARGE *comes in with* DORA *from the bedroom.)*
MARGE: Father's fast asleep.
GLORIA: Good! That gives us a chance to talk.
MARGE: Aunt Dora, I don't think you've met Harriet, Peter's wife.
DORA: Pleased to meet you, Harriet. I'm Mr. Forsberg's sister.
ETHEL: *(entering with two folding wooden chairs)* Sit here, Aunt Dora!
DORA: Thank you, Ethel dear.
GLORIA: Is there a drink in the house?

STAN: You know Father never kept liquor in our home, Gloria.

PETER: Well, let's get our discussion over, and we can go back to the motel.

GLORIA: Who's going to begin?

PETER: First there's the will. Did Mother leave one?

STAN: She made a will last year, when she knew she was sick. Just five lines. She left everything to Father.

MARGE: Mr. Jensen, the Attorney in White Falls, said it was a good idea. Not that she had much to leave.

GLORIA: There's her wedding china. She always said I ought to have that?

PETER: Always? That could hardly include the last thirty years. You've hardly seen her.

GLORIA: You know what I mean. When we were all at home.

MARGE: A lot of things were different when we were all at home, Gloria.

STAN: It makes no difference. Everything belongs to Father.

GLORIA: What use is it to Father? I mean, he can't—

PETER: Can't what? Why don't you come out and say it?

DORA: You two still quarrelling, like when you were kids? You should be ashamed! Nobody's going to move that china while I have anything to do with looking after your Father. Memories are all he has now—memories, and Marge's care—with Stan and Ethel to help.

HARRIET: But—how much does he understand? I mean, isn't he—

MARGE: Feeble-minded? You're a doctor, Desmond. What would you say?

DESMOND: Oh, it's not my line at all. You'd need an expert opinion. Of course, no doctor would ever use that term.

STAN: It doesn't take a doctor to see that Father forgets things, and needs help with his food, and a lot more. But what difference does it make?

PETER: Well, Stan—I mean, none, I suppose, unless—

GLORIA: Peter's worried Father may need to go into a 'home' of some kind, and then he'd have to help pay for it.

HARRIET: Gloria, you've no right—

GLORIA: Oh, come off it, Harriet! It's true, and you know it.

PETER: I haven't noticed the noble Doctor Holt and his wife offering to lift a finger to help.

DESMOND: You watch what you're saying, Peter! Of course Gloria and I will do anything we can.

MARGE: You mean that, Desmond?

DESMOND: (*alarmed*) Certainly! I—don't think I quite understand you.

MARGE: I think it's time we got right down to what we're going to do. A home is no place for Father. He'd give up, and die. And don't try to tell me that would be merciful, Gloria!

GLORIA: I never—

MARGE: You hinted at it in your last letter.

STAN: Well, he's not going to a home, so we can forget it.

PETER: Then that clears the air.

ETHEL: Does it, Peter?

PETER: Yes. I mean, you've agreed that what he needs is Marge, and—

ETHEL: What he needs is for his children to care for him, and repay all that he and your Mother did for all of them.

DORA: 'Honor your father and your mother, so that you may have a long life in the land that your God has given you.'

GLORIA: That's fine for you to say, Aunt Dora. But Desmond and I aren't in any position to help.

ETHEL: And Marge is?

GLORIA: Of course she is! She's always lived at home, and has no ties—

STAN: Why don't you tell them, Marge?

PETER: Tell us what, for God's sake?

MARGE: I'm thinking of getting married. (*A horrified pause*)

GLORIA: Married? You?

MARGE: Yes, Gloria, me. It's not impossible, you know. You've managed it twice.

PETER: But—What would happen to—

DORA: To your Father? That's the point, Peter. It's for the four of you to work out together, isn't it? At least you came here for the funeral. I hear Norman didn't even answer Stan's telegram. So you can write him off.

GLORIA: It isn't for the four of us! It's nothing to do with me! I got myself out of this place thirty years ago—

STAN: So, if Marge gets married, you'll do nothing. It's not what Desmond said a moment ago.

DESMOND: Naturally we would do what we can. I could put you in touch with the right doctors, and help to make any arrangements. But, as Gloria says, our commitments—

STAN: It's not doctors we need. We've agreed Father is not going to be shunted off into a home.

PETER: I'm still staggered! I can't believe it! Marge, are you sure—

MARGE: No, I'm not sure. A decent man, a widower, has asked me to marry him. While Mother was alive, I never gave it much thought. Now I think it's up to you to help me make up my mind.

PETER: Tell her about some of the pitfalls of matrimony, Gloria!

ETHEL: It's not a joke, Peter.

PETER: No, it isn't. I apologize. My nerves are all on edge. If we could only help—

STAN: There's no 'if,' Peter. Between the four of us, we have a solemn duty to love and care for the Father who worked himself unsparingly to give us all we have. Aunt Dora said it in Bible language. I'm saying to you, you're not going to run away from your responsibilities.

GLORIA: I need that drink. Isn't there anything—

DORA: Brandy—but you aren't sick enough for that.

DESMOND: Are you suggesting that your Father might live— stay—with each of us in turn, Stan?

STAN: I'm not ruling it out. The only place where there has been too little room is here—right here, where Marge has put up with it for a generation. You have plenty of room. So does Peter. We can fit Father in, by shifting the kids to the living room. (*A long silence.*)

GLORIA: If no one else will say it, I will. This is one world—yours, Stan, and Marge's. Where we live is another world. You can't mix them. Isn't that right, Peter?

PETER: I never even thought of it. I mean, we knew Mother couldn't travel, so we never suggested—

DORA: But your Father could travel, Peter, if he had to.

MARGE: Be honest, you two! You've let Stan and me do everything all your lives, and now you can't believe we won't stand between you and any kind of burden. Not that it is a burden. Dora reminded us of what the Bible says, 'Honor your father and your mother.' Well, it comes back to you, like in the parable, a hundred-fold. I've seen you every few years, Gloria; and I wouldn't have changed places with you. Oh, I've envied you and Peter some-times. I'm no saint. But in the end I'd take the life I've lived over all of your money, and your moves, and your marriages. I love Father—yes, and honor him. I'm happy and proud to have held Mother's hand as she died, and seen her eyes open wide to let in the light of heaven. And I'll tell you something else. I wouldn't let Father go and visit either of you, and feel your discomfort and your shame, and hear you trying to get out of explaining to your flashy friends who it was tucked away in a back room. He's not so feeble-minded that he can't tell the difference between love and its opposite. If I get married—and I think I shall—I shall go on caring for Father. And it will be possible, because of Stan and Ethel, who are worth a dozen of you two, and because of Aunt Dora, and because my Steve is a decent and generous fellow. But this house needs a lot of changes: an extra room, a toilet and a bath, a new heating system. I'll send you the bills, divided in half. That's the least you can do. It's also all you can do. I'm not a fool, Gloria. You DID cut yourselves off when you went away. It's not really your fault. And if we've said some hard things today, perhaps that's good. From now on we can be more honest. (*a pause*) That's the longest speech I ever remember making. (GLORIA *gets up, after another pause, and kisses* MARGE.)

GLORIA: I wish I could—

MARGE: That's all right, Gloria. There's plenty you can do, if we work together.

ETHEL: Why don't you all go out and have dinner? You too, Aunt Dora. Stan and I will stay with Father.

PETER: No. I'd like to stay, if you don't mind. Father didn't know me, earlier. If I sit with him a while, and talk about the old days—

DORA: That's good, Peter. It's decided. You stay. I stay. I don't like hotel food. Off you go, all of you!

Also suitable for this Sunday: The Rosebush (Gospel C); see 4th Sunday of the Year; also see *Bible as Drama,* page 47 (OT/C): Moses: The Burning Bush; page 243 (Epistle B): Peter and the Baptism of Cornelius.

17. FOURTH SUNDAY OF EASTER

Takeover

Bible Reference: John 10:1–18, 27–30 (Gospels A, B, and C)

Note: Scenes like this can and do happen. This is the age of the takeover. A rich company, or a rich man wanting to own a company, looks out for new enterprises to control. A tempting proposal is made to the shareholders of a smaller company, offering them immediate profits. Sometimes this is a good thing, fairly done, as part of the operation of the free marketplace. Sometimes it is unscrupulous and deceptive. The result may easily be the substitution of 'hirelings' for 'shepherds.' This scene includes a discussion of the difference between the two.

Also suitable for: Third Sunday of Easter, 16th Sunday of the Year.

Third Sunday of Easter: Gospel C (John 21:1–19). 'Feed my lambs . . . look after my sheep,' Jesus says to Peter. It is as true in the Church as in any other institution that personal relationships produce concern and understanding, while distance and size breed a different kind of attitude, often in the name of efficiency. This Gospel, and the scene to go with it, could form a searching introduction to a discussion of the whole problem of 'size.'

16th Sunday of the Year: OT/B (Jeremiah 23:1–6). 'Doom for the shepherds who allow the flock of my pasture to be destroyed and scattered!' Later in the reading the Prophet uses three key words: honesty, integrity, confidence. Jeremiah shows his withering contempt for the Kings of Judah who have failed to stand up to their responsibilities and lead their people.

Scene: The boardroom of George Watson's Fabrics Incorporated.

Characters: GEORGE WATSON, *President, in his 50's*
BRIAN WATSON, *30, his son and partner*
TED HOLLISTER, *Company Secretary*
MARK ANNIGONI, *a Director*
GRAHAM MUNCH, *a Director*

(GEORGE *is standing at one end of the table. The others are sitting.*)

GEORGE: You all know why I have called this meeting. In practice, you and I will decide whether Magnaweave's takeover succeeds. To make the position absolutely clear, I'd like Ted to tell us again the terms of the offer.

TED: They are offering to pay the shareholders $18.50 per share.

MARK: $18.50! I hadn't realized that it was that big.

GEORGE: It's not that big, Mark. But it's a clever offer. Big enough to be a temptation. But they are only making it because they know I have brought the company within reach of going much higher. That's the damnable thing about these men who look for takeover opportunities. They wait for other people to do the work. They want a company that has proved its worth, but not yet reaped the benefit. We have proved that we are making a good product efficiently. We've come through a hard time with credit. We have a fine labor force.

BRIAN: They think everything is for sale.

MARK: They might be right. Their offer takes some fighting.

BRIAN: Not if we stand up to them.

MARK: What about the distribution of shares, George? I don't know the details.

GEORGE: I hold 28%, my wife 6%, Brian 10%. That's 44%. Not a controlling interest, but close to it. The rest is owned by a good many people, some of them with no personal interest in the company. Many of them will want to accept Magnaweave's offer. The key lies with you, Graham, and your 11%.

TED: Then we can stop them, George!

GEORGE: We can stop them, if Graham agrees with my position. He's under no obligation to do so.

MARK: You haven't said anything yet, Graham. How about it?

GRAHAM: I haven't said anything, because I wanted to listen. I knew the terms, of course. It will be no surprise to you to know that Magnaweave have approached me—and given me some tempting bait. I haven't been on this Board for long, but I respect the Company. I'm a businessman. I've come here to see whether there is a strong enough reason to turn down a lot of money.

BRIAN: Isn't loyalty a strong enough reason?

GEORGE: No, Brian! This is not an emotional issue. I want to convince Graham, if I can, and I'm going to try hard to do so.

MARK: It won't be easy to do it by logic or figures, George.

GEORGE: That may or may not be true. Fact one is that Graham could get out of this with a handsome profit. Fact two is that you have your reputation to think about, Graham. You're respected in this community. Fact three is that this move by Magnaweave, even looked at in cold business terms, is liable to be bad for the company, and for the city. What the Bible says about the shepherd and the hireling holds true in business—or at least that's my experience. I pride myself I'm a shepherd. I know this place, and I know the people. When I talk, they listen. I base my faith in this company on that. I built this business up from nothing, by a combination of hard work, skill, and faith. Anne and I mortgaged our home, and risked everything to make it succeed. If I'm bought out now, I can put my feet up and live comfortably. But I don't want to see it happen, because I have no use for the men who are trying to take over. They won't run a good operation, because they don't care enough. They're hirelings, and when the wolf comes near, they'll turn and run—just you see!

(*There is a long silence.* GEORGE *sits.*)

GRAHAM: Thanks, George. I wasn't really in any doubt, but I appreciate what you have said. Ben Street, who was sent by Magnaweave to sweet-talk me, was too cocky by half. He thought I was a pushover. I'm going to take great pleasure in telling him he can tear up his proposal. My money is safer in your hands than with some Magnaweave whizz-kid on the make, who knows nothing about this city or the company.

GEORGE: That's great, Graham. Thank you all. For the time being, at least, we can say 'no takeover.'

Also suitable for this Sunday: Baptism (Acts/A): see Baptism of the Lord, Honor Your Father (Epistle B): see Third Sunday of Lent; also see *Bible as Drama,* pages 223–283, The Young Church.

18. FIFTH SUNDAY OF EASTER

The Perfect House

Bible Reference: I Peter 2:4–9 (Epistle A).

Note: This play could be linked to the readings of almost every Sunday in the year. Here it is paired with the words: 'Set yourselves close to him so that you too . . . may be living stones making a spiritual house.'

Denise Gibson was making an idol of her house, as Dene Peck made an idol of his tennis racket in 'The Champion,' and Elise Morgan of her desk and her cat in 'The Empire' (see 14th and 23rd Sundays of the Year). Bob Gibson, who loved her, and saw what she was doing, was not strong enough to stop her. The play describes how their house began to turn into a home.

Also suitable for: 5th, 8th, 9th, 18th, 20th, 23rd, 26th, and 28th Sundays of the Year.

5th Sunday of the Year: OT/A (Isaiah 58:7–10). 'To share your bread with the hungry, and shelter the homeless poor,' reminds us that Denise was spending a great deal of money on the caterers that evening, but found it hard to accept the idea that injured children equalled her guests in priority.

8th Sunday of the Year: OT/B (Hosea 2:16, 17, 21–22). The Prophet writes about his attempts to win back his wife from unfaithfulness. Bob Gibson is trying to win Denise back from her fixation about her house, to 'betroth her with integrity and justice, with tenderness and love.'

9th Sunday of the Year: Gospel A (Mt 7:21–27). The contrast between the house built on rock and that built on sand is too clear to need comment.

18th Sunday of the Year: Epistle B (Eph. 4:17, 20–24). Here Paul describes Denise Gibson's condition from another point of view: 'You must put aside your old self, which gets corrupted by following illusory desires.' Do you think that Denise has a good chance of experiencing the 'spiritual revolution' which Paul mentions in the next verse? Or would the effect of the accident wear off, and leave her back where she was?

20th Sunday of the Year: OT/B (Proverbs 9:1–6). Read the whole chapter which contrasts Wisdom and Folly as hostesses. Folly's house is 'a throne commanding the city' — which is what Denise was trying to build for herself.

23rd Sunday of the Year: Epistle B (James 2:1–5). The contrast between the man 'beautifully dressed, and with a gold ring on' and the 'poor man . . . in shabby clothes' is less violent than the contrast between Denise's fashionable guests and the dying children. The point is the same.

26th Sunday of the Year: OT/C (Amos 6:1, 4–7). No more vivid picture of self-satisfied materialism exists in the Bible. 'Woe to those ensconced so snugly . . . Lying on ivory beds, and sprawling on their divans . . . they bawl to the sound of the harp . . . they drink wine by the bowlful.' But, in the final verse, 'the sprawlers' revelry is over.'

28th Sunday of the Year: Gospel B (Mk 10:17–30). Before the day of the accident, Denise would have had little understanding of this reading, and of the words 'you will have treasure in heaven.' The daughter of the dead driver, Becky, might now become part of her treasure.

Scene: The living room of the Gibsons' new house, in a comfortable California suburb. The lights are lowered once during the action, or a music bridge is played, to denote the passage of time.

If you think it helpful, the following introduction may be given by a Narrator:

'Denise Gibson has built herself a home. You will hear more about it as the play proceeds. It is some home! We are in the living room, which is like a small cathedral. Over here are doors to the patio and the pool. Over here is the front door. This way you pass through to the other rooms in the house. Even the architect thought that Denise was over-reaching herself. And Bob, her husband? He was on a business trip abroad when the house was planned. Oh, yes, Bob has his misgivings, about the house, and about the party Denise has planned to show it off. You must imagine most of the luxuries she has put together—the drapes, the rugs, the furnishings, the chandeliers. The middle of the room has been left clear for the party. The guests will be here in less than two hours, and I see Amadeo, Denise's Filipino houseman, coming to take a look around. Things had better be in good shape, if Denise Gibson is to be satisfied.'

Characters: BOB GIBSON, *early 50's; businessman*
DENISE GIBSON, *late 40's; his wife*
AMADEO, *their servant*
LESTER SUMMERFELD, *architect of the house*
A MAN
DOCTOR BARROW
YOUNG CHILDREN, *(non-speaking parts)*

(AMADEO *enters, and looks around the room, preoccupied. He has a duster in his hand, and is near the patio entrance when* DENISE GIBSON *comes from the house R.*)

DENISE: Amadeo!
AMADEO: Yes Mrs. Gibson?
DENISE: Are the folding chairs all set out?
AMADEO: Yes, Mrs. Gibson; beyond the pool, just like you said.
DENISE: And the piece of matting that they forgot this morning?
AMADEO: They delivered it a few minutes ago, Mrs. Gibson. It's all in the right place now.
DENISE: Good! I'll come and take a look. And, Amadeo, I'd like to try out that microphone again. You go and say something into it, and I'll be at the far end of the pool. I'll follow you in just a minute.
AMADEO: O.K. Mrs. Gibson.

(DENISE *stands R.C., and writes a note on a pad. After a pause,* BOB GIBSON *enters from patio.*)

BOB: What's on your mind, honey? Where's Amadeo going in such a hurry?
DENISE: To test the mike just once more. I'm not sure that sound engineer knew his job.
BOB: Relax, Denise! I'm certain it's all right.
DENISE: You're too trusting, Bob. When you're paying through the nose for a singer like Lee Holden, it better be perfect! I'll be back in a minute. *(front door bell)* Now who could that be? It's too early for the Band. You see, will you? I'll go and join Amadeo.

(*She goes out to patio.* BOB *opens door. Enter* LESTER SUMMERFELD.)

BOB: Hi, Lester! Come on in!
LESTER: As your architect, Bob, I was just too curious to stay

away. I know you're too busy for a visitor, but I was on my way home, and couldn't resist.

DENISE: (*from off L.*) Who was it, Bob?

LESTER: (*L., looking out towards patio.*) It's me, Denise—Lester. I had to come by to see how my handiwork looks under its first test.

DENISE: (*still offstage*) If you've come for the party you're an hour and a half early.

LESTER: Don't worry! I still have to go home and pick up Sally. Gee, Bob! Denise has really gone overboard. Wow!

BOB: It's her big day, Lester.

LESTER: And yours?

BOB: This sort of thing means more to her—the house, and the party, and so on. But if it fulfills what she wants, that's fine by me.

LESTER: Well, you know what I thought all along, as an architect who's been building fair-sized houses out here for twenty years— this place is just too big for the two of you to live in as a home. I still don't agree with all the things Denise told me to put in, but I have to hand it to her—she certainly knows her stuff and sticks to her ideas.

BOB: That's right. She does.

LESTER: And now that I see the kind of thing she was planning, I can understand her point of view.

BOB: I see your point too, Lester. Takes some living up to, a place like this. But I'm an outdoor nut, anyway, and I think I'll get used to it.

DENISE: (*entering from patio*) Hi, Lester! Good of you to stop by before the crowd comes.

LESTER: Denise, you're a marvel. You win hands down. How many are coming this evening?

DENISE: Two hundred and sixty, without the gate crashers. And this is one time when I really want the gate crashers to see my house.

LESTER: Two hundred and—! You think big all right, Denise.

DENISE: I could stop the clock forever at this moment, Lester. All the years we've been trailing around the world after Bob's job, I've dreamed of this. My own house, and guests filling it. And I really mean a house, and I really mean filling. Well, you've given us all of that. Thanks, Lester!

LESTER: Don't thank me. You're my most profitable clients. It's odd, you know. I haven't often cared so much about a job, and I certainly never before battled with a client to reduce the scale of his plans. I'll be frank with you, though, I just hope you enjoy the house as much on the normal days—you know, the golfing-and-dishes days.

DENISE: Don't worry! We will, won't we, Bob?

BOB: Sure, honey, sure!

LESTER: That reminds me, Bob. We haven't had that game yet. How do you like the course?

BOB: It's fine. I'm still a little rusty, after being away so long; but once this party's out of the way I should be out there every day. Give me a week or two, and I'll take you up on the challenge.

LESTER: Well, I must hurry back, or Sally will wonder how we're going to get here in time. Good luck, Denise! The balloons are really going up now. Speaking of luck, you had your rain just at the right moment. It seems to be all over now.

BOB: Yes. The radio forecast is fine for the evening.

DENISE: It had to be. California sun is one of the things I paid for in advance. It comes with the house.

LESTER: Everything's wonderfully fresh after the showers. Roads are still slippery, though. I came by the side road, where the new construction is. It's a bad corner.

BOB: Most of the guests will come the other way, luckily, from town.

LESTER: So long, then! I'll be back soon.

DENISE: Goodbye, Lester. And thanks!

BOB: 'Bye. (LESTER *goes out by front door.*)

DENISE: I must hurry, Bob, and put myself together.

BOB: You look fine! Well, I'm all set, so I'll see if Amadeo needs anything. It all looks great, Denise.

DENISE: Thanks, Bob. It has to be great. We're going to show them that the Gibsons have come to town.

(*She goes off R., and* AMADEO *enters from patio with some ash trays. He is humming.*)

BOB: You sound happy, Amadeo.

AMADEO: Well, it sure makes a lot of fuss, this party. But now I think we got everything straight. The flowers O.K., the platform O.K., the mike O.K.—

BOB: You've done fine; and all your helpers from the caterers' should be here any moment. (*Crosses to look out patio.*) Parking's the biggest problem. I wish it hadn't rained, from that point of view. There goes the school bus. Time's getting on.

110

AMADEO: Yes, sir. Quarter of four, nearly. Soon as we have the band, and the bar-tenders, we can—

(From a distance comes the noise of the bus crashing: a squeal of brakes, a collision, then some distant screams, children's voices, a few, not exaggerated.)

BOB: What in . . .

AMADEO: The bus! It was the school bus! All those kids!

DENISE: *(running in from R.)* What was that?

BOB: *(already by front door)* School bus, I'm afraid. I'll—

DENISE: Bob! You can't go now. The Band will be coming. (BOB *takes no notice, but runs out.)* Oh! Why can't he leave it to somebody else? There's quite enough to do here as it is. Amadeo!

AMADEO: Yes, Mrs. Gibson?

DENISE: I just thought, while I was in my room. This would be the moment to get that rubber broom, and sweep once more round the Patio. It's nearly dried up from the rain, but there may be a few patches.

AMADEO: Sure, Mrs. Gibson; but hadn't we better wait—

DENISE: We can't wait. There isn't time to worry about other people's problems today. There's too much to get ready here.

(She goes off again R. AMADEO stands irresolute.)

AMADEO: Yes, Mrs. Gibson. (BOB *enters front door, running.)*

BOB: It was the school bus. Small car skidded at the corner, and they collided and overturned. 'Fraid there are quite a few bad injuries.

AMADEO: Oh, my God!

BOB: I've told them that this is the nearest house and telephone. First kids'll be up in a minute. Amadeo, we'll need mattresses, those patio cushions, and all the boiling water you can manage— fast!

AMADEO: Yes, sir. *(He runs towards patio.)*

BOB: And sheets. *(He runs to the telephone, which is on a small table near the front door R.)* Get me the police! Hello, police? Look, there's been a bad accident near the foot of Flower Hill, on Garnet Road—the 38-hundreds. Yes, Garnet. School Bus— overturned. Yes. My name's Gibson. Bob Gibson. 3846 Garnet. 3846. I'm bringing as many as I can up here. Yes. All right then and hurry, please!

DENISE: *(Running in on his last words.)* Bob! Whatever was all that about?

BOB: I'm afraid it's really bad, honey. School bus overturned. I told them to bring the kids that could be moved up here.

DENISE: You told them—

BOB: Listen, Denise, hurry! You know what to get ready.

DENISE: Are you telling me that they're coming to this house?

BOB: Of course they're coming to this house, and to any other house where they can be helped. Now—

DENISE: They can't come in here now. The guests are about to arrive. Why, use your head, Bob!

BOB: Don't be crazy, Denise! These are people—dying, some of them. Amadeo! For God's sake, Denise, let's go!

DENISE: They'll spoil everything. Not now, Bob!

(*Enter* AMADEO *from patio, with patio mattress and sheets.*)

BOB: That's right, Amadeo. Put them down there. (*He puts them down center, on the rug.*) Kettles all on? We may need to tear up these sheets for bandages—

DENISE: Stop this madness, both of you! Do you have no consideration?

BOB: Get going, Amadeo!

AMADEO: Sure, Mr. Gibson. (*He runs out to patio.*)

DENISE: I'll hate you forever if anyone comes in and messes up my house today. I'll hate you, do you hear?

BOB: Oh, for God's sake, stop wasting time! There's a spare mattress on each of the beds. Spread them out, Denise! Do you hear?

DENISE: Bob, I'm locking the door! (*She goes towards the door.* BOB *looks up from his kneeling position center, by the patio mattress. He runs to the door, and they wrestle for the handle.*)

BOB: You must be out of your mind. Get out of my way, or I'll—

DENISE: Take your hands off me! This is my house. I—

(BOB *throws her aside, and she falls center. He flings open the door. A car is heard outside. It stops, and we hear the door slammed.*)

BOB: Here they are! Now, get to work, Denise, or get out!

DENISE: (*As he runs out.*) I'm finished with you! I tell you, I'm finished.

(*She gets up, and stands R. with hands clenched.* BOB *enters, carrying a child. By his side a boy stumbles, crying.*)

BOB: That's all right son. We'll see that you're looked after. Amadeo!

AMADEO: Yes, Mr. Gibson?

BOB: We'll put the first of them in the bedrooms beyond the patio. There are more just coming by the other entrance.

(*He goes out to the patio with the boy.* DENISE *still stands R.* BOB *hurries back, as a man enters the front door carrying a small girl.*)

MAN: This girl's bleeding badly. We did our best—

BOB: Here. On the mattress. (*They lay her down C.*) Amadeo! Bandages and hot water! She's unconscious. I wish I knew more about this.

MAN: I'll get back. There are more to come. (*Exit by front door.*)

DENISE: Bob, are the—ambulances coming?

BOB: Shouldn't be long now. Poor kid! (*Sound of another car outside.*) Here come the next lot. Out on the patio next!

DENISE: Bob—I'll bandage this girl up. You get the spare room mattresses.

BOB: Fine! (*Man enters carrying another child.*) Bring him out here, will you? (*We hear him from the patio.*) That's right. The Doctor must be here in a minute. (*As he returns R.*) About how many were injured, do you know?

MAN: Fifteen, I'm afraid; and two killed, the driver and one child.

BOB: Fifteen! My God! (*shouts to* AMADEO!) We'll need more of everything—hot water, sheets—

MAN: The station wagon, with five or six more, went round to your back entrance. I'll go and see if I can help. (*Exit to patio. Siren of approaching ambulance is heard.*)

BOB: Thank God! There comes the first ambulance—and a Doctor, I hope. (*Siren stops. Car door slammed. Running feet, and enter* DOCTOR BARROW *by front door.*)

BARROW: I'm Doctor Barrow. Are they all in here?

BOB: Not all here yet, Doctor; but most of them. I'm Bob Gibson. We've done our best in here.

BARROW: (*Kneeling by the girl C.*) Fine!

BOB: This girl looks pretty bad.

DENISE: I've done what I could to stop the bleeding.

BARROW: Good! Let's have a look.

(*Sound of another ambulance as before.*)

BOB: I'll send them to the other entrance; and I'll see if any of the kids out there look really bad. (*Exit by front door.*)

BARROW: Right. I'll be with you in a minute. (*He works at the girl's bandages.*) Are you Mrs. Gibson?

113

DENISE: Yes.

BARROW: You did a good job. She should be all right.

DENISE: I'll go and see what's happening out on the patio.

(Exit to patio. Pause, while BARROW works at the dressings.)

DENISE: *(a scared cry)* Doctor Barrow!

BARROW: Yes?

DENISE: Come quickly, please! It's this boy—

BARROW: Coming, Mrs. Gibson.

(He finishes the dressing, covers the girl, and hurries out to patio. The lights fade to a black-out. Silence for about fifteen seconds. Then siren outside, fading away into the distance. Lights up slowly. The girl has gone. A blood stained sheet lies on the mattress. BOB and BARROW enter slowly from patio.)

BOB: *(Looks at watch.)* Five o'clock! Not much more than an hour since it happened. It seems like ten years.

BARROW: I'll bet it does. Well, Bob, I'll be getting along.

BOB: Thanks for everything, Doctor.

BARROW: It's for me to thank you—and Mrs. Gibson. You did a wonderful job; most of all, by getting the emergency stuff done so quickly. But I'm sorry for what it's done to your house.

BOB: If it helped to save any of those kids, what the hell does the house matter?

BARROW: That's not what everyone would say. Good night, Bob, and God bless you! *(He shakes hands, and goes R.C.)*

BOB: Good night, Doc.

BARROW: *(turning)* Give your wife my very best. She's quite a girl, Bob.

BOB: Yes, she is. I'll tell her.

BARROW: One day I'd like to call on you, and we'll get really acquainted.

BOB: Really acquainted! You mean, with a martini in one hand, and all the trimmings. Sounds strange to say it, but I think I prefer it this way. That is—

BARROW: I know what you mean. Goodbye!

BOB: 'Bye. *(He sees BARROW out, then goes to the telephone and dials.)* Operator, give me the police. Hello, police? This is Bob Gibson, Garnet Road. We—oh, you know about it—yes. Listen, in half an hour two hundred and sixty people will be arriving at my house. Yes, a big party. It's out of the question now, of course. Yes, it's a mess, and—uh-huh. *(pause)* You can do that? Have a

114

patrolman inform them at the end of Garnet Road? That's great. You say it's been on Radio, and TV? Then a lot of the guests will know. Thanks very much for your help. Yes, you're right. Plenty to do here. So long.

(He puts the receiver down slowly, looks off R. towards DE-NISE's *room, then crosses L. to armchair, stopping to pick up the bloodstained sheet, then slowly drops it. He sits down, and covers his head with his hands.* DENISE *enters silently, crosses slowly, and stands watching him. At last he looks up.)*

BOB: Hello, Denise. *(After another pause, she suddenly drops at his feet and puts her head on his knees.)*

DENISE: Bob, I—

BOB: Don't try to talk now, Denise. You're exhausted.

DENISE: There's something I must say, Bob.

BOB: All right, then. Say it, if it helps.

DENISE: *(Kneeling up, and drawing back from him.)* When you ran out of that front door to offer my house to those people, I hated you, Bob. I told you so, and it was true. I hated you. And I hated those children, dead or alive. I just said to myself, why did it have to happen to me? Why destroy what I've sweat blood to build up? And I hated every one of you when you came through the door.

BOB: Even the little girl?

DENISE: Yes, the little girl, too. Oh, I wanted her to live, and I did as good a job as I could bandaging her up; but I hated her, because she was in my house, and because her blood was on my new rug.

BOB: Denise, don't!

DENISE: And then out on the patio, when that little boy, Terry, died, I couldn't stop it, but I tried—God knows, I tried! And I didn't hate him. We always wanted children, and we didn't have them; and I suppose I've shut off that side of me for too long. But I didn't hate him. I knew he mattered. He mattered more than the party, much, much more—more than the rug, the patio, the Band, and—that meant that he really mattered. Oh, Bob!

BOB: Now let me tell you something, Denise. When you were screaming there at the front door, I thought that it was the end for us. I knew that I couldn't stay in a house which means more to my wife than human beings. It's a silly house, anyway.

DENISE: Yes—it's a silly house. *(a long pause)*

BOB: The girl's name is Becky. The driver was her father. He died.

DENISE: Oh, no! *(She breaks down, and buries her head against his knees.)*

115

BOB: I've got their address. Her mother has four other kids. I'm going round in the morning, to see what I can do.

DENISE: Can I come with you, Bob?

BOB: Sure, if—(*a pause*) What about tonight? Do you want to go out and find some dinner?

DENISE: No, Bob. I'd—rather stay here, if you don't mind.

BOB: That's what I'd like, too. It's where we belong tonight.

DENISE: In a minute, I'd like to call Amadeo, and we'll all three have some eggs and coffee in the kitchen. Then I'd like to clean up our home.

BOB: Tonight? You're not too tired?

DENISE: No, I'm not too tired—not for that.

BOB: Funny, you calling it home. Do you know, Denise, till that moment, in my mind, it's always been "the new house"—and was I frightened of it!

DENISE: I know. Inside, I realized that—and resented it! (*She rises and goes C.*) Bob, this house was a craving—for the things life hasn't given us—yet. Bob! I think it's cured. Amadeo! (*She goes back and raises* BOB *from his chair.*) Come on, Bob! How would you like your eggs?

Also suitable for this Sunday: To Enter Into Life Crippled (Gospel B): see 22nd Sunday of the Year End of the World (Epistle C): see First Sunday of Advent: also see *Bible as Drama,* pages 223–283: The Young Church.

19. TRINITY SUNDAY

Finding the Dentist

Bible Reference: General.

Note: This modern parable is intended to provoke discussion and understanding of the doctrine of the Trinity. It is not linked to any particular reading. The meaning is further discussed in the Narrator's introduction below. This introduction can be used on other occasions, when the scene is presented, by adapting it slightly.

Also suitable for: 2nd Sunday of Lent, 2nd Sunday of Easter, 7th Sunday of Easter, 21st Sunday of the Year, Christ the King.

2nd Sunday of Lent: Gospel A, B, and C (Mt 17:1–9, Mk 9:1–9, Lk 9:28–36). The Apostles were on a journey towards the discovery of God, and for the inner circle of three, the Transfiguration was a great step forward. The words, 'This is my Son, the Beloved. Listen to him,' sent them forward on a fresh part of their voyage of discovery.

2nd Sunday of Easter: Gospel A, B, C (John 20:19–31). Of all the Apostles, Thomas had the hardest time finding out the truth about his Master. He was the one who had said, earlier, 'Lord, we do not know where you are going, so how can we know the way?'

7th Sunday of Easter: Gospel A, B, and C (John 17:1–26). In this Priestly Prayer to his Father, Jesus asks that those whom he is leaving in the world may have support and strength in their journey. 'I passed your word on to them.' Now 'I pray for them . . . because they belong to you.'

21st Sunday of the Year: Epistle A (Rom. 11:33–36). The connection here is with the meaning behind the story of Tommy Rowe, rather than with the story itself. He found his way because he had a few clues, but he only knew what those clues revealed to him. In the same way, 'Who could ever know the mind of the Lord? . . . How impossible to penetrate his motives or understand his methods!'

Feast of Christ the King: Epistle A (I Cor. 15:20–26, 28). This reading might be called one of the maps given to us to find our way to understanding God.

117

Scene: Various points on the journey of Tommy Rowe to the Dentist's Office. No props are needed, except a table and chair for the Principal's Office, and Tommy's bicycle. Imagination supplies the rest.

Characters: The PRINCIPAL
The SECRETARY
TOMMY ROWE, *about 10*
GAS STATION ATTENDANT
STEVE COOK
SMALL GIRL
DOCTOR BAKER
NARRATOR

NARRATOR: Today is Trinity Sunday. With Christmas, Good Friday, Easter, Ascension, and Pentecost behind us, we try at this moment in the Church's year to sum up our belief in Almighty God, and to express our praise and worship of His Majesty. No human words can describe Him. But today we remember the phrases in our Creeds, which go back directly to Jesus' own words: 'Baptize them in the name of the Father, and of the Son, and of the Holy Spirit.' God has revealed Himself to us as the Creator, with His infinite power; as the Word and Savior and Redeemer, who humbled Himself to live and die among men; and as the source of inspiration and strength, who answers our prayers, and fills our lives with His presence. This Scene is called 'Finding the Dentist,' and it begins in the Principal's Office at an Elementary School.

(*The* PRINCIPAL *is sitting at his desk, when there is a knock at the door.*)

PRINCIPAL: Come in! (*Enter* SECRETARY.)
SECRETARY: Excuse me, Mr. Jameson. There's a boy outside with a toothache.
PRINCIPAL: You'd better bring him in, Carol. (*She brings* TOMMY *in.*)
SECRETARY: It's Tommy Rowe.
PRINCIPAL: Hello, Tommy! Tooth hurting, is it?
TOMMY: Yes, Sir. A filling came out, and it started to ache.
PRINCIPAL: You don't look too good. We must get you to the Dentist. Shall I call your Mother?
TOMMY: That's the trouble, Sir. My Mom's gone to see my Auntie at Marston, and my Dad's out of town.

PRINCIPAL: I see. And there's nobody else who can take you? How did you get to School?

TOMMY: I rode my bike. I could get to Doctor Baker's, I think.

PRINCIPAL: Where's his Office?

TOMMY: I know it's Diamond Street. I'm not sure of the number. It's only about ten blocks.

PRINCIPAL: I'd take you myself, but I have a meeting coming up. (*He is looking in a Directory.*) Here we are: 4827 Diamond. Listen, Tommy, you ask Mrs. Butler in the Office to draw you a map, and I'll call Doctor Baker and tell him you're coming—we'll say it's an emergency.

TOMMY: Yes, Sir.

PRINCIPAL: Sure you'll be O.K. finding your way?

TOMMY: I'll manage, Sir. (*He goes out.*)

NARRATOR: So Tommy started out on his bike. There was a cold wind, and his tooth kept aching. Perhaps that was why he missed a turning, and found himself on an unfamiliar street. He decided to ask his way at a Gas Station.

(*Enter* TOMMY *with his bike. The* ATTENDANT *is on the other side of the stage.*)

ATTENDANT: Hi, there, young man! What can I do for you?

TOMMY: Which way is Diamond Street?

ATTENDANT: Diamond? What number are you looking for?

TOMMY: 4827. Doctor Baker's.

ATTENDANT: Doc Baker, eh? Oh, I know him. He's often in here for gas. Drives a cream Chevy. Nice fellow. Take the next right, by the Church there, then the second left—that's Warburton. Make a right when you get to Coral, and Diamond leads out of that. Tooth bad?

TOMMY: Pretty bad. Thanks a lot.

ATTENDANT: Doc Baker'll fix you up in no time.

NARRATOR: So Tommy rode away. But he was a little confused still, and at the corner of Warburton and Coral he wasn't quite sure which way to go. He decided to ask a pleasant-looking man, who was getting out of his car.

(*Again* TOMMY *brings his bike in on one side, and* STEVE *is on the other.*)

TOMMY: Excuse me, Sir.

STEVE: Yes?

TOMMY: Could you tell me where Doctor Jones' Office is? 4827 Diamond?

STEVE: I sure can. I know Doc Jones well. See him every week at Rotary, and on the golf course. Straight up that way, and first left. Tell Doc that Steve Cook put you on your way. What's your name?

TOMMY: Tommy Rowe.

STEVE: Well, good luck, Tommy! Doc Jones will make it all right.

NARRATOR: So Tomy came to the 4800 block of Diamond. He still wasn't quite sure which was the right house.

> (*Again* TOMMY *wheels his bike in. The* SMALL GIRL *is playing with a jump rope.*)

TOMMY: Hi!

GIRL: Hi!

TOMMY: Do you know which house is Doctor Baker's?

GIRL: He's my Daddy. He lives here.

TOMMY: Thanks. Can I leave my bike here?

GIRL: Put it there, by the wall. I'll call my Daddy. (*She runs off.* TOMMY *leans his bicycle against a wall. Enter* DOCTOR BAKER.)

BAKER: Hello there, Tommy!

TOMMY: Hello, Sir.

BAKER: Come on in, and I'll see what I can do for you.

NARRATOR: So Tommy found the Dentist. On his journey from School, Tommy found out quite a lot about Doctor Baker. He knew his address. He knew that he was a nice fellow, who drove a cream Chevy, and played golf, and went to Ro—something (this was a little too much for TOMMY to understand). And he knew that he had a daughter with a jump rope. There was much more that he did not know about the Doctor, but this was enough. The Creeds can only tell us some things abut God, to guide us on our way to Him. There is much more that we cannot know. A writer once said that looking at her favorite view was like trying to empty a bathtub with a teaspoon—there was too much beauty to take in. And there is much too much of God's love and power for us to understand. But Trinity Sunday reminds us of some guideposts along the way towards Him.

Also suitable for this Sunday: Honor Your Father (Epistle A): see Third Sunday of Lent: see also *Bible as Drama,* page 52 (OT/A): The Golden Calf, page 196 (general): The Prodigal Son (verse play or musical)

20. ELEVENTH SUNDAY OF THE YEAR

Jonah

Bible Reference: Matthew 9:36–10:8 (Gospel A), Mark 4:26–34 (Gospel B).

Note: This Gospel reading from Matthew contains the words: 'The harvest is rich but the laborers are few, so ask the Lord of the harvest to send laborers to his harvest . . . And as you go, proclaim that the kingdom of heaven is close at hand.' The reading from Mark is also closely akin to the spirit of the book of Jonah: 'A man throws seed on the land . . . the seed is sprouting and growing; how, he does not know.' 'Jonah' has been called 'the most Christian book of the Old Testament,' because of its message of universal love. Like the Book of Ruth, it was written to point out to the Jews the need for generosity towards other nations, in accordance with God's mercy. (See note in JB, page 1257) It is a tender, lovable story, told in parable terms: a reminder that running away from God's appointed task for us may end in sudden and surprising displays of His power, to turn us back. It is refreshing to read Ruth alongside Jonah. They share a charming simplicity and a wide vision.

You can virtually do without props for this play. Keep it moving fast, and do not be afraid of a light, humorous touch where it seems appropriate. Use modern dress.

(To obtain the musical score of this play, see page 7.)

Also suitable for: 3rd Sunday of the Year, Pentecost, 14th, 20th, and 21st Sundays of the Year.

3rd Sunday of the Year: OT/B (Jonah 3:1–5, 10). This is the only reading from the book included in the Cycle. Brought back to shore by the great fish, Jonah is again told by God to 'go to Nineveh . . . and preach to them as I told you to.'

Pentecost: General. 'We hear them preaching in our own language about the marvels of God,' Luke makes the astonished Gentiles of many races say. (Epistle A, B, and C, Acts 2:1–11).

14th Sunday of the Year: Gospel C (Luke 10:1–12, 17–20). The equivalent in Luke to the Gospel reading from Matthew above, Gospel A for the 11th Sunday of the Year.

20th Sunday of the Year: OT, Epistle, and Gospel A (Isaiah 56:1, 6–7; Rom. 11:13–15, 29–32; Matthew 15:21–28). The last eleven chapters of the book of Isaiah come from a writer who believed strongly in the duty of the Jews to preach to other nations. Here he writes about justice and integrity, and about Yahweh's resolve to bring foreigners who love His name to His holy mountain. In the Epistle Paul writes: 'I have been sent to the pagans as their apostle, and I am proud of being sent.' And in Matthew's Gospel story Jesus cannot resist the appeal of a Canaanite woman for her daughter's healing.

21st Sunday of the Year: OT/C (Isaiah 66:18–21). This reading also comes from the final portion of the book of Isaiah. 'I am coming to gather the nations of every language,' Yahweh says.

Scene: See individual scene headings.

Characters: JONAH
JONAH'S WIFE
AMITTAI *and* HANNAH, *son and daughter of Jonah*
SHIP'S CAPTAIN
VOICE OF GOD
KING OF NINEVEH
TRAVEL AGENT
THREE BOOSTERS OF NINEVEH
NARRATOR
CHORUS, *from whom come the sailors and later the Ninevites*

NARRATOR

Hello! I'd like you to meet this family. They're nice people, and they get along well with each other, as families go.

The man of the house, over there, is Pastor Jonah. He has one of the best attended churches here in Pleasantville-by-the-Sea: what you could call a fashionable church. But don't misunderstand me. Jonah may be a trifle too comfortable, and just a bit of a snob, but he works hard, visits his people, both rich and poor, watches over the sick, and preaches a good sermon. That's what he is meant to be doing now—writing his sermon; but he has kept falling asleep. And he's restless. But then, you see, Jonah is a Prophet. Week by week, he denounces things: Red China, foreign aid, long-haired young

122

criminals, too much welfare—he's great on all of those. Most of all the Ninevites. He can't stand Nineveh: it gets under his skin.

Rachel, his wife, is very sweet. It's rough, being married to a minister, with a big congregation, and an even bigger ego. But she loves Jonah; and she puts in a shrewd word of advice every now and then, which stops him from making himself ridiculous.

And the kids? Normal. Odd names, perhaps. This is Amittai. That was his grandfather's name, so he's stuck with it. And this is Hannah. They get a little ribbing at School, of course: preacher's kids, with Bible names. But still, I'd call this a happy family, with not many worries.

As I say, Jonah looks restless. Worried about middle age, do you think? Or his waistline? Or income-tax? Or the women of the church?

Could it be something to do with God? It's not easy, being a Prophet, sometimes. Quite a responsibility. God can step in, and make things awkward.

Let's watch what happens.

(JONAH *and his wife are seated on chairs, the children on the floor playing a game.* JONAH *is dozing over a newspaper, his wife sewing.*)

NARRATOR
You can't keep running away, Jonah;
It makes no difference at all.
You can't keep running away, Jonah;
If you run you'll only fall.
   If you hide your face in another place,
   You will have no peace in your soul.
   Though your course seems set, still you can't forget
   That you must have me as your goal.
You can't keep running away, Jonah;
It's not like Jonah at all.
You can't keep running away, Jonah;
If you run you'll only fall.

(JONAH *wakes with a start, and picks up his paper.*)

WIFE: Is there anything in the paper today, Jonah?
JONAH: Eh? Much the same as usual. Those Ninevites are causing trouble again.
WIFE: Nothing new about that. I wish we had more contact with them. They seem to be so cut off.

JONAH: Cut off! I wish the earth would open and swallow them up, and we might have some peace. Now I must get on with my sermon.

GIRL: What are you going to preach about?

JONAH: The sins of the Ninevites, Hannah.

BOY: You preached about that three weeks ago.

JONAH: And I dare say I shall again next month, Amittai, and the month after. How God can let it happen, I just don't understand. Now quiet, please, all of you. (*He writes.*)

NARRATOR

Jonah was a quiet man;
He lived according to a quiet plan.
He never had the urge to roam,
And he liked to spend his nights at home.
He was a prophet of the Lord,
And loved to preach Jehovah's word;
But he liked the old familiar sights,
And he liked to sleep at home of nights.

CHORUS

But he didn't like those Ninevites.

NARRATOR

No, he didn't like those Ninevites.
But the voice of the Lord said, "Jonah!"
Go preach to the Ninevites!

JONAH: (*Sits up, drops pencil.*) Preach to the Ninevites?

CHORUS ONE: Go preach to the Nine—

CHORUS TWO: Preach to the Nine—

CHORUS THREE: Preach to the Ninevites!

JONAH

If the Lord wants a prophet for that task,
I'm not the prophet that he should ask.
I like to sleep at home of nights,
And I just don't like those Ninevites!

CHORUS

No, he doesn't like those Ninevites!

JONAH

If this is the Lord Jehovah's plan,
I know that I am the wrong kind of man.

I feel so unwilling to obey
That I even should prefer to run away.

CHORUS
But the voice of the Lord said, "Jonah!"

ONE: Go preach to the Nine—
TWO: Preach to the Nine—
THREE: Preach to the Ninevites!
WIFE: Oh, Jonah! Why does God have to send you to Nineveh?
  You're doing so much good here.
CHILDREN: Yes, Father. Everyone says so.

JONAH
(*He rises and prowls about the stage.*)
If God would only cease to interfere,
And let me be what I would like to be!
If God would only leave me here!
I'd be whatever he would ask of me.

CHILDREN
If God would only understand that Father
Has got to keep an eye on us!
If God would only see that he would rather
Be left to do his job without a fuss!

JONAH
I like my work here; I like the life here.

WIFE
I like my home here; I like the shops.

CHILDREN
We like our friends here; we like our School here;

JONAH
And I work so hard it sometimes seems that duty never stops!

WIFE
If God would only be a little kinder!
For now you are the victim of his whim.

CHILDREN
If you could only give him a reminder
Of all the things that you have done for him.

125

JONAH

I'm not a critic; I'm not a groaner;
I'm not a selfish kind of man.
If God could only understand
That Jonah's doing everything he reasonably can.

ALL

If God would only leave us all alone,
To wrestle with the job in hand!
If God would only leave us all alone!
If God would only understand!

(JONAH *picks up a small bag, kisses his wife and children, and hurries away. His wife and children go off.* TRAVEL AGENT, *one of* CHORUS, *puts up a placard: "Trans-World Seaways".*)

JONAH: Give me a ticket, please!

AGENT: Yes, sir. Where for?

JONAH: It doesn't matter. Anywhere far away. I want to leave at once.

AGENT: Far away? Excuse me, sir, which way?

JONAH: It doesn't matter, I tell you. Please hurry!

AGENT: Yes, sir. Let me see. We have the "Swallow" leaving Joppa at noon tomorrow for Tarshish. That's as far as you can go.

JONAH: Joppa: Noon. I'll catch her.

AGENT: Round trip, sir?

JONAH: No! No, not round trip, One way. (*Exit with ticket.*)

NARRATOR: "But Jonah rose up to flee unto Tarshish from the presence of the Lord, and went down to Joppa; and he found a ship going to Tarshish; so he paid the fare thereof and went down into it, to go with them unto Tarshish from the presence of the Lord. But the Lord sent out a great wind into the sea, and there was a mighty tempest in the sea, so that the ship was like to be broken."

(*While these verses are read, the sailors and Captain come on.*)

CHORUS

And the sea wrought, and the storm came,
And the sky burst into lightning flame,
And the sails tore, and the waves leaped—
(*slowly*) But Jonah lay in the ship and slept.

126

NARRATOR

And the Sailors said, If this grows worse
It will show that there's somebody under a curse.
And Jonah heard the Captain say:

NARRATOR: Now God had arranged that a great fish should be there
to swallow Jonah; and he was in the belly of the fish three days
and three nights. Jonah prayed in the belly of the fish, and God
caused the fish to vomit him to the shore.

(JONAH *lies center stage, exhausted.*)

CAPTAIN

Wake up, sleeper! Wake up, and pray!
Wake up, sleeper! Call upon your God!
Pray to him when peril is near!
Wake up, sleeper! Fall upon your knees!
Pray that he may save us from fear!
Pray that Heaven, with its mighty power,
Bring us out of storm and wave!
Wake up, sleeper! Pray that in this hour
God, if he be there, may guard us with his care,
Guard us and be strong to save!

(*The sailors cast lots.*)

FIRST SAILOR: The lot fell on him, Captain.

SECOND SAILOR: He's the one, all right!

CAPTAIN: Tell us who you are! Why should you bring this storm
upon us?

JONAH: I am a prophet, a servant of the true God!

CAPTAIN: A prophet?

JONAH: Cast me into the sea! I know that it is because of me that the
storm is raging!

CAPTAIN: Let us at least try to get you back to harbor safely.

JONAH: No! Cast me into the sea! I have run away from the Lord's
bidding! Cast me into the sea!

(*Sailors take him to the side. We hear a splash, or clash of
cymbals, as he is thrown into the sea. Then silence.*)

CHORUS (*softly*)

You can't keep running away, Jonah!
It makes no difference at all.
You can't keep running away, Jonah!
If you run you'll only fall.
   If you hide your face in another place

127

You will have no peace in your soul.
Though your course seems set, still you can't forget
That you must have me as your goal.

VOICE OF GOD

Jonah, I'm calling you!
Don't run away from me!
Jonah, I'm needing you!
Lift up your eyes and see!
Jonah, the hour is come!
Gird up your loins and go!
Jonah, I'm calling you!
Let not your heart be slow!

NARRATOR

"So Jonah arose, and went unto Nineveh, according to the word of the Lord. Now Nineveh was an exceeding great city of three days' journey. And Jonah began to enter into the city a day's journey, and he cried: Yet forty days, and Nineveh shall be overthrown!"

CHORUS

Jonah went to Nineveh, but he didn't want to go.
Jonah went to Nineveh, but he traveled mighty slow.
Jonah went to Nineveh, when he got back to the beach.
He turned his face to Nineveh, but he didn't want to preach.

(JONAH *has slowly got up during the reading, picked up his bag, and walked off, then returned, and slowly crossed the stage.*)

Jonah preached in Nineveh, but he hoped they wouldn't hear.
He cried aloud in Nineveh, and he filled them all with fear.
He found himself in Nineveh, because he had been sent;
But he didn't want those Ninevites to listen and repent.

(*During the last verse the Chorus of* NINEVITES *come on, and line up at the back of the stage. They bring a small platform for the King, and some signs, such as: 'Nineveh: City in Motion,' 'Assyria, Land of Enchantment,' 'Nineveh, pop. 120,000.' The King comes on, and stands on the platform. At the end of the verse the three* BOOSTERS *march forward, to a drum rhythm. Divide the lines of the recitation between them ad lib. Last verse all together.*)

BOOSTERS

We never have had it so good in the City of Nineveh.
The Chamber of Commerce has plenty to boast of in Nineveh.

128

The Markets are Super, the streets are well lighted;
On Saturdays firework displays are ignited;
There's plenty to make you ecstatic, excited—in Nineveh.

The Schools are a model of modern construction in Nineveh.
The Temples are splendid, the Hospitals spacious in Nineveh.
Downtown there are movies, and strippers, and dancing—
Adult entertainment—alluring, entrancing—
And plenty of credit, and easy financing—in Nineveh.

Though smog is a problem, and crime is increasing, in Nineveh;
Inflation is rampant, and business is stagnant, in Nineveh;
Governmental corruption is rather a pity;
And scandals are rife at the top of the City;
We still like to sing this promotional ditty—for Nineveh.

(JONAH *watches from one side, and, as he walks forward, there is a crash of cymbals and drum.*)

JONAH: Forty days, and Nineveh shall be destroyed!
CROWD: Forty days, and Nineveh shall be destroyed!
VOICE ONE: What was that that the prophet said?
TWO: He said a dreadful thing.
THREE: He said that we should be wiped out!
FOUR: Look! Do you see? the King!

(*The King is gazing in awe at* JONAH.)

JONAH: Forty days, and Nineveh shall be destroyed!
CROWD: Forty days, and Nineveh shall be destroyed!
KING: Let neither man nor beast, herd nor flock, taste anything; let
them not feed, nor drink water; but let man and beast be covered
with sackcloth, and cry mightily unto God. Who can tell if God
will turn and repent, and turn away from his fierce anger, so that
we perish not?

(KING *and* NINEVITES *bow to the ground in silence.* JONAH *sits on one side, near the front.*)

NARRATOR
"And God saw their works, that they turned from their evil way; and
God repented Him of the evil, that He had said that He would do
unto them; and He did it not. But it displeased Jonah exceedingly,
and he was very angry."

JONAH
Take my life away; I don't want to live.

129

I came to curse the Ninevites,
And you tell me to forgive, and you tell me to forgive.
I lived at home and served you, Lord,
The way that seemed the best;
But since you sent me out to preach
I seem to have no rest.
If I could just see what you mean—
I've tried to understand.
How can I love the enemies
Of our own promised land?
So take my life away, I don't want to live.
I came to curse the Ninevites,
And you tell me to forgive, and you tell me to forgive.

NARRATOR

Then said the Lord, "Doest thou well to be angry?
Can't you see that their hearts are turning?
Why do you not rejoice?
Can't you feel that their hearts are burning?
Now that they hear your voice?
Tell them now that the dreadful sentence
Yields to the strength of love.
Pray for them, that their new repentance
Link them to me above."

(*During second verse* KING *and* NINEVITES *kneel facing* JONAH.)

Sing with joy that the voice of warning
Spoke to the hearts of all!
Sing with praise, that a day is dawning,
Blest by a prophet's call!
Turn your thoughts to the way of pity!
Bring your wrath to an end!
Turn in love to this suffering city!
Speak to them as their friend!

JONAH

It's no good, Lord. I can't do more.
I've tried, and done my best.
I pray you, let me lie down here,
And give my spirit rest.

(JONAH *takes no notice of the Ninevites, but lies down.*)

NARRATOR

And God said, "Should not I spare Nineveh, that great city, wherein

130

are more than sixscore thousand persons that cannot discern be-
tween their right hand and their left hand; and also much cattle?"

(*Before the end of this,* JONAH *has risen, gone to the platform,
and stands blessing the kneeling Ninevites, then hurries
downstage.* WIFE *and* CHILDREN *come out from among the
audience to meet him.*)

CHILDREN: Father!

WIFE: Oh, Jonah dear! We've got you back!

JONAH: Yes, I'm back; and I've learned my lesson, I promise you. I
shall never try to run away again.

SON: Did you run away to Nineveh, Father?

JONAH: No, Amittai. I ran away from God, and He rescued me and
sent me to Nineveh. It's too hard to explain all at once; but from
now on we'll try to serve Him together.

JONAH AND FAMILY

I want to serve Him
  Body and soul,
Because I came to Him empty,
  And He made me whole.
I want to give Him
  All that's best of me,
Because I was a prisoner,
  And He set me free.
Is there a gift worth giving
To one who has made me live?
A richer and better living
Is all that I have to give.

CHORUS JOINS IN:
(*Stepping forward to join the family.*)

I want to serve Him
  Body and soul,
Because I came to Him empty,
  And He made me whole.
I want to give Him
  All that's best of me,
Because I was a prisoner,
  And He set me free.

Also suitable for this Sunday: Bible As Drama, **page 68** and page
147.

21. TWELFTH SUNDAY OF THE YEAR

Godparents

Bible Reference: Galatians 3:23–4:7 (incorporating Epistle C)

Note: All children are 'heirs of Christ.' But they must have guardians until they can control their own lives. Ideally, those guardians are their parents. But many things can happen to make children need the help of other guardians, and for this reason the Church has put real responsibility upon godparents.

The duties of a godparent are always important, though they are often taken lightly. Prayer for the godchild, friendship, and concern—these should be automatic, and by no means superficial. Also, the witness shown in the godparent's life should be an important influence for the godchild.

But what happens when there is a crisis involving your godchild? Death of one or more of the parents? Or neglect? Or serious maltreatment? Well let's see.

Also suitable for: 25th and 27th Sundays of the Year.

25th Sunday of the Year: Gospel B (Mark 9:39–37). 'Anyone who welcomes one of these little children in my name, welcomes me.' Churches, as well as individuals, vary considerably in the warmth of welcome which they offer to children. Without such love, how can a Church grow, or feel that it is carrying out Jesus' teaching? This Gospel reading invites us all to search our hearts with respect to our attitude towards children: our own children, our godchildren, and the children, near or far, who need Jesus' influence and love so desperately.

27th Sunday of the Year: Gospel B (Mark 10:2–16). The last verses of this reading have the same message as the Gospel for the 25th Sunday.

Scene: Lorna's living room. It is untidy and run down. She is sitting with a drink in her hand, listening to music on a radio.

Characters: LORNA, *about 30*
PHIL *and* EVIE, *also about 30*

(*The bell rings, and* LORNA *does nothing. It rings again after an interval, and she slowly gets up.*)

LORNA: Oh, shoot! Who'd be visiting me this late? (*She shuffles to the door.*) Who is it?

PHILIP: (*outside*) It's Phil and Evie, Lorna.

LORNA: Oh, God! (*Opens the door.*) You'd better come in, I suppose.

EVIE: (*kissing her*) Hi, Lorna!

PHILIP: We heard that things weren't so good, so we came.

EVIE: To see if there's anything we can do.

LORNA: That's big of you. Suppose I tell you it's none of your damned business?

PHILIP: We'll try to convince you you're wrong. A friend's troubles are a friend's business.

EVIE: Can we sit down?

LORNA: Oh, sure! Sit down! Make yourselves at home, and take no notice of me. I've just had a couple of drinks. Want a drink?

EVIE: No, Laura. Not now.

PHILIP: We heard from your Mother that Jeff has left you, and money is pretty tight. Is that right?

EVIE: We're not trying to be nosey. You'd do the same for me.

LORNA: Good old dependable Evie! Damn you, you shouldn't have come here.

EVIE: But, Lorna—

LORNA: (*shouting*) Do you think I want my friends to see me like this?

PHILIP: No, I understand that. But for us not to come would be worse, wouldn't it?

LORNA: Could anything be worse?

PHILIP: And besides that, there's Tim?

LORNA: (*in tears*) Oh, God! Why can't you leave me alone?

EVIE: Is he asleep, Lorna?

LORNA: (*After a long pause, pulling herself together*) Yes, thank God! I—try to put it off till he's in bed.

EVIE: You're a wonderful Mother to him.

LORNA: Wonderful Mother! Don't try to kid me, Evie! I'm a mess. I worried so much about Jeff—all his lies, and his women, and the money—that I fell apart. And now—I don't know what to do.

PHILIP: For a start, don't be too proud to let us help. We are Tim's godparents, you know.

LORNA: Godparents? What does that have to do with it?

PHILIP: A great deal. Do you know what we promised at his baptism?

LORNA: That was six years ago. You always remember his birthday, but—

EVIE: We promised to see that he was raised to know God, and—

LORNA: So you've come to spy on me, to see if I take him to Church every Sunday!

EVIE: No, Lorna. You know us better than that. We don't know how best to help, but you've been my friend since grade school, and both of us feel a big responsibility as Tim's godparents.

PHILIP: We want you to tell us what we can do for him and you.

EVIE: For example, if you need some time to look for a job—or just to go away and take a rest—without having Tim to worry about, he can always come to us, and share Doug's room.

LORNA: (*after a long pause*) You know, you're really something, you two! You mean it, don't you? (*She bursts into tears.*) Perhaps it isn't such a lousy world after all.

EVIE: Lorna, we feel so badly. We've got everything. We love each other. Phil has a good job. We have our children, our home, our church—

PHILIP: Don't refuse some common-sense help. It isn't charity.

EVIE: For a start, I'm going to make some coffee. Then we'll sit and work out a plan. O.K., Lorna?

LORNA: O.K. You win. (*A pause.*) Godparents! I can't believe it!

Also suitable for this Sunday: The Empire (Epistle B): see 23rd Sunday of the Year; also see *Bible As Drama,* pages 94–100 (OT/A): Jeremiah (Scenes 3 and 4), page 270 (Epistle and Gospel A): Danger at Jerusalem, page 277 (Gospel B): Shipwreck, page 151 (Gospel C): Who Are You, Lord?

22. THIRTEENTH SUNDAY OF THE YEAR

Glad To See You Back

Bible Reference: Mark 5:21–43.

Note: I know that this story is true, because it happened to me in different circumstances. As a Navy Chaplain, in 1942, I was pushing my way through a crowd of men in a ship, and happened to come close to a slight acquaintance, a man whom I knew to have been away on leave. I said these same words to him: 'Glad to see you back'; and next day he came to my cabin, and said very much what Delia said to Marie.

This Gospel reading contains Jesus' words: 'Who touched my clothes?' In a milling crowd the words seemed nonsensical to Peter; but Jesus knew the difference between casual contact and a genuine approach by someone who cared.

Also suitable for: 3rd and 24th Sundays of the Year.

3rd Sunday of the Year: OT/A and Epistle C (Isaiah 9:1–4 and I Cor. 12, 12–30) 'You have made their gladness greater,' Isaiah writes. A few words brought Delia out of darkness into light. They did not solve her problems, but they let light in upon them. In the reading from Paul, we are reminded of the gifts and responsibilities of teachers, among others, to be part of a true community.

24th Sunday of the Year: Gospel C (Luke 15:1–32). The Prodigal Son was dreading his return home. He had every reason to expect coldness and criticism. Instead, he found his Father on the watch for him, running out to greet him and say: 'Glad to see you back.'

Scene: A closely packed crowd of students are waiting in a high school corridor, ready to go into class.

Characters: MARIE EDWARDS *Teachers*
HENRY REED
DELIA PETERSON, *15, a student*
STUDENTS
NARRATOR

135

NARRATOR: (*to one side*) How do you know when the man or woman, boy or girl, who passes you in the street, or sits by you in the bus, is in desperate need of help? Often the need is concealed. All that a caring person can do is try to show courtesy and concern, even in brief, apparently superficial encounters with other people. You are about to see something like this happen in a high school corridor. A teacher, Marie Edwards, is on her way to class. She does not know that she is about to live out a parable told by Saint Mark in these words: 'A man throws seed on the land. Night and day, while he sleeps, when he is awake, the seed is sprouting and growing; how, he does not know . . .' Although the circumstances have been altered, this scene is based on a true incident, which may have saved a man's life.

(*Around a corner, into the crowded corridor, come* MARIE *and* HENRY.)

HENRY: Try to make it by 4:30, Marie.
MARIE: I'll try. Oh. look! How are we ever going to get through?
HENRY: Follow me! O.K., you guys. Let us through, will you?
VOICES: (*simultaneous and overlapping*) Hi, Mr. Reed! . . . We're waiting for Mr. Thompson . . . The door's shut . . . Let Mrs. Edwards through.
MARIE: Thanks, Donna. Hi, Vince! (*She runs into* DELIA.) Hello, Delia! Glad to see you back!
DELIA: Thanks, Mrs. Edwards. (*The door opens, and the students go in, leaving* MARIE *and* HENRY *alone.*)
HENRY: That's better! Who was that kid you were talking to?
MARIE: Delia? I can't remember her last name.
HENRY: She looks kind of lost.
MARIE: I had her in class last year. She's very quiet. See you later, Henry. I must hurry.

(*They go off. Set up a table and two chairs for* MARIE's *office. She sits at the table.*)

NARRATOR: Next morning Marie Edwards was in her room, marking her class's notebooks, when there was a knock at the door.

(*Knock*)

MARIE: Come in! Oh, hi, Delia! Do you want to see me?
DELIA: If you have a minute, Mrs. Edwards.
MARIE: Of course. Sit down, won't you?
DELIA: Thank you. (*A pause.*)

MARIE: What can I do for you?

DELIA: It's—well, I came to thank you for what you did yesterday.

MARIE: What I did? There must be some mistake, Delia. I haven't done anything for you.

DELIA: Oh, yes, you have. In the corridor, when you passed me.

MARIE: I—oh, I remember. But—

DELIA: You remember what you said?

MARIE: I'm not sure. One says such silly, trivial things. Probably just 'Hi!'

DELIA: No. You said you were glad to see me back.

MARIE: (after a pause) Yes, Delia. I believe I did say that.

DELIA: Did you—do you know why I was out of school, Mrs. Edwards.

MARIE: No, Delia. It was pure chance I just remembered you were out at all. What happened to you?

DELIA: It was my sister. Do you mind if I tell you?

MARIE: Of course not—if you would like to.

DELIA: I mean, I'm not in your class, or anything. I don't want to waste your time.

MARIE: I don't think talking like this is ever a waste of time. Tell me!

DELIA: It was my sister. We're twins, you see—or we were. She was always the leader, and—it's hard to explain if you haven't been a twin. She was—well, most of my life. It was almost as if we were inside each other. We fought sometimes, but that didn't matter.

MARIE: I understand. But she didn't come here to school, did she?

DELIA: No. You see, she got sick, when we were in eighth grade. At first they didn't know what it was. Then they found out. Bone cancer. She was thirteen, Mrs. Edwards.

MARIE: Oh, Delia! I'm so sorry.

DELIA: I used to go home and tell her—about everything. I still depended a lot on her. She was—special. (She is crying softly.) I'm sorry, Mrs. Edwards.

MARIE: You don't have to be sorry. You stayed home because she was dying. Is that right?

DELIA: Yes. She died four days ago. The funeral was yesterday.

MARIE: What can I say, Delia dear? I don't think death is any kind of disaster to fear, for a person like her. But it's very hard for you and your family—you especially.

DELIA: I'm not sorry about her dying. It was going to happen anyway, and I don't think at the end it hurt too badly. But it's myself I keep thinking about—and then I feel so mean. It's her I should be

137

caring about—not how I can get along without her.

MARIE: It's only human to think about that, Delia. She is in good hands. You do have a tough battle to fight.

DELIA: Coming back yesterday, I was scared. I wasn't even sure I wanted to go on living. A few of the kids knew about it, but most of them didn't. I felt so lost, Mrs. Edwards. (*She is crying again.*)

MARIE: There's plenty of kleenex. (*She kneels by* DELIA.) Let some of the hurt out, Delia. It helps to cry, sometimes. Do you believe in God?

DELIA: Yes—yes, I do. We don't go to church much. I'm not sure what Mom and Dad believe. But I do—especially now. Only—

MARIE: Let me tell you something. I may be very simple, but I think God meant you to come through that door and talk to me. You see, dear, what I said to you yesterday was mostly sheer chance. Don't be offended if I say this, will you? But I wasn't really glad to see you back. I was saying it, the way you say polite, trivial things. Only He didn't mean it to be trivial. Do you see what I mean?

DELIA: Yes, I can understand that. It was what I needed so much, but you didn't know.

MARIE: Anyway, let's be thankful it happened. You see now I really am glad to see you. And if I can help you, any way, any time, you'll know I'm here.

DELIA: Yes, Mrs. Edwards.

MARIE: We're both due back in class, aren't we? Can you make it, do you think? Or would you rather stay in here for a while. I can tell Mr. Ross.

DELIA: No. It's O.K. I'd like to go. I enjoyed your class last year. You probably didn't realize that. I know I didn't say much. But I did.

MARIE: I'm glad. I didn't know you then. From now on, let's have no barriers. It was a privilege to talk to you, Delia. I mean that. (*Bell*) Now we ought to go. But come back soon!

Also suitable for this Sunday: Baptism (Epistle A): see Baptism of the Lord; Who Is My Neighbor? (Epistle C): see 5th Sunday of the Year (or The Good Samaritan: see 15th Sunday of the Year); also see *Bible As Drama*, page 144 (Gospel B): Women Who Came To Jesus, page 179 (Epistle B): The Talents.

23. FOURTEENTH SUNDAY OF THE YEAR

The Champion

Bible Reference: 2 Cor. 12:7–10 (Epistle B)

Note: Paul writes in this reading: 'My grace is enough for you: my power is at its best in weakness.' Dene Peck had to find this out the hard way. He was every inch a competitor, whose concentration on tennis amounted to a 'graven image.' It unbalanced his life, and endangered his marriage. When a 'thorn in the flesh' appeared in his life, and threatened him with the loss of competitive tennis, he was helpless. It was his wife's strength which saw him through the crisis, or at least pointed toward a way out.

The Bible story most akin to The Champion is that of Samson (Judges 13–16). Try to read the two in conjunction. There are many kinds of strength, and only a well-balanced human being knows clearly his own strengths and weaknesses.

Make the Pecks' living-room the main scene. Use short music bridges to cover scene changes, and train your stage team to set up the subsidiary scenes with simple props quickly assembled. I should add that the parts of Dean and Gilly do require experienced actors. Their scenes together are powerful, but there is a danger of sentimentality spoiling them unless they are skilfully treated.

Also suitable for: 4th Sunday of Lent, 5th Sunday of Lent, 22nd, 25th, and 33rd Sundays of the Year.

4th Sunday of Lent: Epistle C (2 Cor. 5:17–21). Dene needed to become a 'new creation.' The 'standards of the flesh' were no longer applicable. By those standards he had always excelled. Could Gilly lead him to a new set of values?

5th Sunday of Lent: Epistle C (Phil. 3:8–14) is perhaps the Bible passage which Dene needed to read most. 'I have accepted the loss of everything . . . I am no longer trying for perfection by my own efforts . . . I have not yet won, but . . . I forget the past and I strain ahead for what is still to come.'

22nd Sunday of the Year: Epistle A (Romans 12:1–2). In one way, Dene had always offered his body as a sacrifice. He was a truly disciplined man, but a limited man also. Now, if he is to 'know what is good,' he must learn what God means by: 'Let your behavior change, modeled by your new mind.'

25th Sunday of the Year: Epistle A (Phil. 1:20–24, 27). Paul had a struggle to convince himself that it was better to go on 'living in this body.' 'I want to be gone and be with Christ.' Dene has assumed that living in the body is living. The challenge with him will be to find a new dimension.

33rd Sunday of the Year: OT/A (Proverbs 31:10–13, 19–20, 30–31). This famous description of the perfect wife has an old-fashioned ring. Dene needed in Gilly something more than the domestic qualities listed in this reading. He needed, and found, a woman capable of standing up and making decisions important for both of their lives.

Scene: See individual scene headings.

Characters: DENE PECK, *37; champion tennis player*
GILLY PECK, *30; his wife*
BARRY EDMONDS, *25; tennis player*
DOCTOR GEORGE YORK
BILL JAEGER, *accountant*
VINCE VANESSI, *car driver (voice only)*
RADIO ANNOUNCER, *(voice only)*

Scene One

(The dressing room at a tennis club during a national meet. BARRY EDMONDS is half dressed, rubbing cream on his hair and combing it during the first part of the scene.)

ANNOUNCER: *(on radio)* Zarnik to the forehand, Dene Peck deep to the backhand. He's running in. Zarnik a weak return, and Peck puts that away with no mistake. *(applause)* He's playing like a champion today, and it looks as though he has this quarter-final match wrapped up and ready to take home now.
BARRY: Attaboy, Dene!
ANNOUNCER: Peck serves. The first one's a fault, over the sideline. The second's a spinning service. Zarnik returns half-court. Peck a half-volley, Zarnik's chasing it—he lobs, but it's short and the

court's at Peck's mercy. He—(*Oooh from crowd*) Well, well, well! For a man who concentrates like Dene Peck that was a bad miss. Wait a minute! He's bent down, almost as though he had a bad cramp.

BARRY: Oh, no!

ANNOUNCER: No, he's all right. He's going back to serve, and he's got that grim, tough look we all know so well, the look of a man who just won't lose. Now he serves: an ace! (*loud cheers*) And that's match point. Match point to Dene Peck in this quarter-final match of the National Tennis Championship, which he has won three times. Here he is, ready to serve. He serves—that's it! That's the match!

(*Louder cheers.*)

BARRY: Good for Dene! That's the stuff! (*He switches off radio. Whistles as he combs hair. Telephone rings. He answers.*) Hello. Oh, hi, Gilly! Wasn't it great? Yeah, sure I will. He'll be down in a minute. What? Oh, I dunno. Maybe it was a touch of cramp. Made no difference, anyway. To wipe Zarnik up in three sets is really something. Sure, I'll give him the message. Yeah. So long, Gilly. See you. (*He puts down telephone, whistles again, puts on tie.*)

DENE: (*entering from L.*) Hello, Barry!

BARRY: Dene, you old son of a gun! How do you do it? It was great!

DENE: Thanks, Barry. Zarnik was tough in the third set, but he didn't quite make it.

BARRY: You just missed Gilly. She said to congratulate you, and what was all that about cramp?

DENE: Oh, heck, I don't know. I've been having a bit of it lately. Pain in the chest—hurts like hell for a minute, then it's O.K.

BARRY: Well, everyone wonders how you keep going in that heat at 37, Dene.

DENE: A man's the age he lets himself be. Gilly didn't waste much time, did she?

BARRY: You're a lucky man, Dene, to have a wife like Gilly.

DENE: You're telling me. OH! (*He bends over for a few seconds, holding his chest.*)

BARRY: You ought to see a Doctor, Dene.

DENE: I will, when the final's over.

BARRY: That's the stuff. I don't envy Al Brock facing you on Friday; but take care of yourself, Dene.

DENE: I will. It's nothing.

BARRY: Have your shower quick. You look pretty well tired out.
DENE: I'll do that. It'll be good to get home. Drop around if you can, Barry.

(*They go out. We hear sound of cars driven fast, then two cars braking: slight bump, door slammed, and quick steps.*)

VANESSI'S VOICE: What the—you swerved right across into my lane. Are you drunk or something?
DENE'S VOICE: I'm sorry. I had a sudden cramp.
VANESSI: Cramp! You—why, I know your face. Aren't you Dene Peck? I was listening to your match a few minutes ago.
DENE: That's right. I'm sorry, Mr.—
VANESSI: Vanessi. Vince Vanessi. Say, Mr. Peck, aren't you feeling good?
DENE: I'm all right. Just this cramp for a moment.
VANESSI: You'll have to watch out. Sure I can't do anything for you? Call a Doctor, or something?
DENE: No, no. I'm O.K. I'm just sorry it happened. I'll be careful.
VANESSI: Well, no damage done, luckily. But you take care of yourself.

(*After a pause, we see* DENE *making a call from a public booth, which can be imagined.*)

DENE: Doctor York, please—George? It's Dene Peck. Could I drop around tonight? Yeah, just routine, but I'd like to ask you something. Thanks. But it was a rough match today, whatever the scoreboard said. About 8 tonight, then? O.K., George. See you then. (*He makes a second call.*) Hi, Sally. Is Bill in? Dene Peck. I'd appreciate it if you would. (*pause*) Bill? Oh, thanks a lot. Yeah, I'm going fine. Never played better. Look, Bill, have you got a few minutes free tonight? Say about a quarter of nine? That's fine, then. I'll drop by. Sorry to bother you at night, but you know my hours are kind of irregular. O.K.? Then I'll be seeing you.

Scene Two

(*Main stage. The Pecks' living room. The front door is downstage. The entrance from the kitchen is up-stage. There is a couch, and a table near it. A television set and record player downstage R.* GILLY *is going in from the kitchen with a tray of iced tea as the curtain rises. She puts it on the table, straightens the cushions on the couch, and goes to the front door as the noise of a car is heard.*)

142

GILLY: Hi, darling!

DENE: (*entering and kissing her.*) Hello, honey!

GILLY: You made it again.

DENE: Did you have any doubts?

GILLY: No, silly; but it must have been awful in that heat. And you had me worried.

DENE: What do you mean? It was in the bag all the way, even if he is a tough man to beat.

GILLY: No, I mean the commentator talking about you being all doubled up in the last game, and Barry—

DENE: (*angrily*) Why can't they mind their own business? Can't I miss a tennis ball without everybody analyzing it and chewing it—

GILLY: Don't take it so seriously, darling! Here, I've got your iced tea. Sit down and relax. You can't go through two weeks of national tennis without some strain—

DENE: (*tensely*) Strain, strain, strain! God, how I hate that word! You get to be thirty-seven, and they're all waiting for you to drop dead. (*He sits down exhausted.*)

GILLY: Dene! Don't snap my head off, darling. Thank Heavens we have a free evening, and no match tomorrow! Stay at home and put your feet up.

DENE: Yeah, that's right. We have a day to ourselves. Where can I take you, Gilly? A day at the beach? Or a movie? Or maybe dress up and have dinner at Maxie's.

GILLY: Dene Peck, I don't want to go anywhere. (*Sits at his feet.*) Oh, darling. I love you so much!

DENE: That makes two of us. Sorry I got worked up like that.

GILLY: It's all right, darling. I understand. Whatever you may say, it is a strain being out there in front of crowds and TV cameras. And you don't have to be thinking, as soon as you get back here, where I want to go. We have a beautiful home—let's enjoy it. After dinner we'll play some recordings and sit in here.

DENE: I promised I'd drop over and see Bill for a few minutes.

GILLY: Tonight? What a time to worry about Income Tax! Dene, you never give yourself any rest at all. The trouble with you is, you always act as though you were running from the baseline to the net. No, I mean it. You really do.

DENE: I'm sorry, honey. Wait till tomorrow. I'll promise not to stir. A day here, with you, is my idea of heaven.

GILLY: I'm glad, darling. That's how I feel too. And tomorrow you can just read the headlines, instead of making them.

DENE: That's right. (*He suddenly picks her up in his arms.*) Oh, Gilly! You're the thing that matters. Looking after you. I—

GILLY: You what, Dene?

DENE: Oh, nothing. I'm just so glad to be home. Come on, let's drink that iced tea!

(*Lights fade, music bridge.*)

Scene Three

(*Front stage, in two parts. First, we see a couch R.* DENE *is lying on it, and* DOCTOR YORK *is examining him.*)

YORK: Over on your back, Dene. (*pause*) That's it. You say it was only for a few seconds each time?

DENE: That's all. Dizziness, and this tightness in the chest. And I felt my heart sort of thumping pretty hard.

YORK: O.K. Sit up, and put your shirt on.

DENE: Well, what's the matter, Doc?

YORK: Something I've told you would come one day, but you've never listened.

DENE: Does anybody listen?

YORK: Some folks listen so hard they hear three times as much as I tell them. No, Dene, you've got to listen this time. You've come to the end of the road—end of the court, I suppose I should say.

DENE: You mean I'm not fit to play tennis?

YORK: Uh-huh. What happened to you today was not surprising. The thing I admire about you, Dene, is that you've always done more than the body is capable of doing. You just wouldn't lose, and so you've got a row of championships underneath your belt.

DENE: O.K., O.K. So I try to win. Well?

YORK: You race that engine of yours, more than anyone I've ever known; and it's beginning to complain. Only trouble is, a human being doesn't have more than one engine.

DENE: Come on, George! Tell me what I have to do.

YORK: What do tennis players do at your age?

DENE: Go on playing tennis, some of them, and winning.

YORK: Not many. And the few who do are geniuses—Borotra, Rosewall, Gonzalez, for example. But you win on talent and guts, Dene—and I'm telling you that you can't do that any more. It'll kill you.

DENE: Kill me?

144

YORK: Yes, exactly that. These spasms are nervous tension; but your heart's had about all the big strain it can take. It's the same with a diver or an astronaut: championship tennis is a young man's job. Give up, Dene! Keep a sports store, or use your reputation to turn to something else.

DENE: What if I don't have anything else?

YORK: You'll find it. You're not a dumb athlete with no brain. And Gilly will help you.

DENE: Gilly? You mean—sit around and let my wife work for me? No, thanks, George.

YORK: I didn't say that; but Gilly wants to share what you're doing. She can't be on the court with you, but you know she cares about every stroke you play. Well, there are other things in the world besides forehands and backhands, Dene.

DENE: Are there? If you start on the world circuit at seventeen, what else is there at 37—except forehands and backhands?

YORK: Plenty, Dene, plenty. And you've got the right wife to help you see it, thank God! Anyway, my job is to tell you that you've come to the end of big tennis. I mean that.

(*Short music bridge. Then we see* DENE *and* BILL JAEGER *sitting in arm-chairs.*)

DENE: (*accepting drink*) Thanks, Bill. Sorry to bother you so late.

BILL: That's O.K., Dene. Fire away.

DENE: Just how much would I be worth, Bill—I mean, if anything happened to me?

BILL: Well, well! As your accountant I've been trying to get you to concentrate on that question for years. You know the answer: very little.

DENE: You mean, if I—smashed up on the highway, Gilly would be in financial trouble?

BILL: Well, it's relative, isn't it? What I mean is, you and Gilly live on a fairly high standard. Plenty comes in; but you spend it, Dene.

DENE: All of it?

BILL: You don't save much. She puts by a little, but you're no help. I've tried to tell you that.

DENE: Sure, and I wouldn't listen. Too busy winning matches.

BILL: What's the trouble, Dene?

DENE: Oh, car nearly hit me today. Just made me do some thinking, that's all.

BILL: So you came straight to see me, late in the evening after a tough match? Tell you what, I'll check out what you're worth and send you a memo about possible cutting down, and how you might put more aside. And we'll look into your insurance.

DENE: Insurance? You mean, on my life?

BILL: Sure. A great ox like you won't have much trouble with the company. We'll do something about it.

DENE: (slowly) So you'll let me know what I'm worth? Yeah. Yeah, Bill, I'd like to know that. It's about time.

Scene Four

(The Pecks' living room: evening. DENE and GILLY on couch, holding hands. Record finishes after a few seconds.)

DENE: (rising) Don't move, darling. I'll change it.

GILLY: Dene, it's been like a dream today—just us at home!

DENE: I know. We don't do it enough, do we, Gilly?

GILLY: Don't put on any more. Why don't you get to bed? Remember Al Brock's a lot younger than you are.

DENE: Yeah, but I can beat him. He needn't think he can tire me.

GILLY: Well, don't give him the chance.

DENE: That's right. He'll be back in the locker room before he knows what hit him. Want some milk and cookies before bed?

GILLY: I'll fix it.

DENE: Now you sit there, honey. Stay where you are. I want to wait on you.

GILLY: Oh, Dene! All right, I'll sit still.

(He goes out to the kitchen. GILLY sits thoughtfully. Pause.)

GILLY: Is there plenty?

DENE: (from kitchen) Yep. Just coming up. (Pause. He comes to the kitchen door, carrying a tray.) Oh! (Tray crashes to the floor, and he staggers in. Bending over.)

GILLY: (running to him.) Dene! What is it, darling?

DENE: (voice carefully controlled) It's O.K. honey. I guess I tripped on the rug. I'm O.K.

GILLY: You're sure?

DENE: I said so, didn't I? Here, I'll clean this up.

GILLY: No, Dene, you sit down. I'll do it. I—

DENE: (shouting) I'll clean it up, do you hear? I'm not helpless.

GILLY: (after a pause) I'm sorry, Dene. Of course, you do it. I'll fix some more milk.

DENE: Gilly, I'm sorry. I guess I'm all worked up. It'll be over soon. Just two more matches.

GILL: (*laughing*) That's right, darling. Two. That's why you never lose—you never even think about it.

DENE: (*kissing her*) Gilly, you're wonderful! Gilly, I hope I can always make you as happy as we've been today.

GILLY: Just stay around, darling. That's all it takes. And don't think I need to be wrapped up in cotton wool. You've treated me today as though I might break in pieces if someone sneezed in the street.

DENE: I wanted to show you how much I cared for you.

GILLY: I know that, Dene; and I love you for every bit of it; but give me a chance to show it, too. Now, let go of me, and we'll have that milk.

Scene Five

(*Front stage. The dressing room at the club, as before. The radio is on, but the room is empty. Applause heard as lights come up.*)

ANNOUNCER'S VOICE: They're both towelling themselves now, by the Umpire's chair. Dene Peck, holder of the national title, looking very determined. 37, and still winning. And the young Australian, Al Brock, looking very thoughtful, as he well may, because he just hasn't got the answer yet to Dene Peck's great concentration and speed. Now they're getting ready. Brock to serve, to save the set. Peck this end, nearest to us, leading by five games to two in the first set of this semi-final match. Brock serves—a fast one to the backhand—but a great return! (*applause*) A great backhand passing shot by Dene Peck, the kind of stroke that could carry him to another championship title. Now Brock to serve again. He serves fast down the center line, and—wait! What's happened to Dene? What's happened to Dene Peck? (*murmur of crowd*) He's down on the ground, holding his chest, and looks in bad pain. Several of the linesmen are running across. They're waving for the first-aid men. Dene's getting up now—motioning them away. He's picking up his racket, but—Oh! He's down again, on his knees! If this is a cramp it's a bad attack. Young Brock is helping, and they're bringing a stretcher—

(*During the last lines* DOCTOR YORK *has hurried in. He turns off the radio, puts his bag down on a small table, and pulls forward*

147

a chair or couch. He is opening the bag, when DENE *comes in L., leaning on* BARRY EDMONDS.)

YORK: Sit him down here, will you?

BARRY: O.K., Doctor. There, Dene. Easy!

YORK: Keep everyone else out, will you?

BARRY: I will. I'll stand guard just outside. (*He goes out.*)

YORK: Well, you son of a gun, let's have a look at you. Let's see your chest. (DENE *is half lying back, half sitting. He tries to rise.*)

DENE: I've got to—

YORK: Hold it, Dene! I'll do the talking. You answer yes or no. Same thing this time? Dizziness and chest pain?

DENE: Yes.

YORK: 'Mmm. I just hoped you'd get through this week. It wasn't any use insisting that you drop out of the tournament. So I came along to keep an eye on you.

(*Enter* GILLY, *with* BARRY. *She runs to* DENE *and kneels.*)

GILLY: Oh, my poor Dene!

BARRY: Hope I was right to let her in, Doc.

YORK: That's all right. You're the best medicine he has, Gilly.

DENE: Gilly, I—

YORK: Now then, Dene, be quiet! We'll get an ambulance, and all three of us will ride up to the Hospital. I'm happy to say I don't think any real harm has been done today.

GILLY: But—what is it, George?

YORK: No real mystery, Gilly. It's a man of 37 trying to act like a man of 25. He's had enough, Gilly. I told him so earlier in the week.

GILLY: But he's not—seriously sick? Tell me, George! We've a right to know.

YORK: No, Gilly, I don't think he's seriously sick, except perhaps in the head. I admire you as much as any of your fans, Dene, but this can't go on. You'll be as fit as any of us, if you live a quiet, healthy life. Oh, active, too—but not this kind of circus act. It'll be a new kind of life for you, I know; but there's no reason for it not to be a good life—and a long one.

BARRY: (*at the door*) The ambulance is at the door, Doctor.

YORK: O.K., Dene. Let's go. Cheer up! We'll probably have you home by this evening.

Scene Six

(*Main stage. The living room. A car door is closed outside. Then* DENE *and* GILLY *enter. He walks slowly.*)

GILLY: There, darling. You're home!

DENE: Yes.

GILLY: Rosa and I moved the couch over, so that you can easily get sun or shade. Just pull the cord if you get too hot.

DENE: Yes. (*He sits on the couch.*)

GILLY: There are plenty more pillows if you need them.

DENE: (*He sits on couch, face in hands.*) Oh, God, God, God! (*sobbing*)

GILLY: Dene! Dene, my darling, don't! Tell me what it is. Please let me share it. Don't shut me out!

DENE: We've got to face it some time.

GILLY: Face what, Dene? There's nothing we can't face and beat.

DENE: I had one thing to give you, Gilly—my physical fitness. As long as I could win tennis matches, I could give you this house, and travel, clothes, everything. Now it's gone. I'm useless! I don't have anything else. I don't have any money, because I never thought of saving it, and—all I have is gone, Gilly. Everything!

GILLY: All you have? Dene, stop talking nonsense, and listen! You just don't know how wrong you are. I—I don't know quite how to say this, Dene, without it sounding either mean or crazy. And I'm not either of those, am I, darling—except that I am crazy about my husband.

DENE: Go on.

GILLY: I'm not saying it very well, am I? I've often wanted to talk about this, but—well, you weren't an easy person to say it to. You see, darling, all your fitness, and—yes, your strength—they've been a barrier between us.

DENE: A barrier? How?

GILLY: Because you wouldn't let yourself *need* anyone, or anything, Dene—and in a way that included even me. Oh, I know you love me, but—

DENE: But you haven't been happy. Oh, God, Gilly. I can't take—

GILLY: No, no, no! I don't mean that. I love you, Dene, and I know why you had to be strong and independent. It's part of your life. But it made you do things for me which you should never have done.

149

DENE: I wanted to give you everything. I wanted—

GILLY: Dene, I'll tell you my—my prayer for both of us. I want you to need me. You're going to be as strong as ever, my darling, but strong in a new way. And I'll be strong too, because you'll need me to be. Oh, I'm not talking about nursing you while you have to rest—I mean all the years ahead—the wonderful years.

DENE: But what are we going to do, Gilly?

GILLY: I don't know. But I feel happy, Dene—not anxious about that. This time last year we knew exactly what you were going to do: Wimbledon, Paris, Rome, Forest Hills, Davis Cup, Sydney. I got so that I could recite the flight schedules and lists of hotels like things out of a cook book: TWA Flight 758, Grosvenor House, Air France, Alitalia, BOAC, Pan-Am. I'd wake up in a plane, and see mountains or clouds down below me, and I'd have to think hard where we were, and what the next hotel would be, and which meal came next because of the time changes. It's exciting, Dene; and I'm proud of every memory. But I'm not going to live on memories—not for Dene Peck or anyone else.

DENE: (*after a pause*) Do you know what, Gilly?

GILLY: What is it?

DENE: You've got more guts than all the champions I've ever played against. And I never knew you had that kind of guts. I never knew. (*He looks at his watch.*) Hey, I'll tell you something. The final's due to start in three minutes. Let's turn on the TV. Mind you, young Brock has no right to be out there; but I'd like to see how he copes with Bill Farrell.

GILLY: All right, Dene. I'll switch it on. And don't let's waste time arguing about who has courage. Which channel?

(*As she moves to the TV, lights fade.*)

Also suitable for this Sunday: Jonah (Gospel C): see 11th Sunday of the Year, God's Tumbler (Gospel A): see 32nd Sunday of the Year: also see *Bible As Drama,* page 281 (Epistle C): A Prisoner at Rome.

24. FIFTEENTH SUNDAY OF THE YEAR

The Good Samaritan

Bible Reference: Luke 10:25–37 (Gospel C)

Note: 'Who is my neighbor?' (5th Sunday of the Year) is a modern adaptation of this parable. The two plays fit the same Bible readings—though indeed there is no Sunday of the year which would not be enriched by the presentation of this story. Together with the Prodigal Son, it ranks as the best known and best loved of all the parables.

The story explains itself. The respectable passers-by find reasons not to stop and help. The one who stops, and risks danger as well as making a sacrifice of time and money, is a foreigner. More than that, he is a Samaritan. Samaria was once the capital of the Northern Kingdom of the Jews, Israel. When the Assyrians conquered it in the 8th Century B.C., they deliberately left it with a mixed population, by forced migrations—a technique rediscovered in the 20th Century. The Jews despised the Samaritans more than other foreigners, on the principle of 'corruptio optimi pessima,' when the best is spoiled it becomes the worst of all.

Production can be very simple, and I recommend this as a play suitable for children. Fifth and sixth graders could take the main parts, with younger children in the small non-speaking parts of bandits and servants. A simple stage scheme could be: right center, a Rock, made of cardboard boxes. All the travelers walk behind and around this on their journey. At the back, center, is a sign-post: JERUSALEM 15: JERICHO 15, since we are halfway along the road. When we pass to the Inn, the rock and sign are moved, and another sign can be used, stage right: THE HALFWAY HOUSE. Use modern dress and props.

This play is suitable for any season of the Church year.

(To obtain the musical score of this play, see page 7.)

Scene: See individual scene headings.

Characters: THE GOOD SAMARITAN; *his two* SERVANTS
THE MERCHANT; *his two* SERVANTS
THE INNKEEPER; *his two* SERVANTS
A PRIEST
A LEVITE
TWO BANDITS
THREE MODERN "ONLOOKERS"
NARRATOR
CHORUS

(During the opening verses, slides may be projected, representing human needs and suffering. The first should be a Crucifixion or Pieta. Then examples of shipwreck, fire, highway accident, refugees, flood, hurricane. The Crucifixion is shown again to finish the series.)

CHORUS
Is it nothing to you, all ye that pass by?
Is it nothing to you, if the people die?
Can you close your eyes to the grief and pain?
Can you close your minds to the jailer's chain?
    Is it nothing to you?
Is it nothing to you, all ye that pass by?
Is it nothing to you, if the lonely sigh?
Can you close your ears when the hungry call?
Can you close your hearts when the wounded fall?
    Is it nothing to you?

(During the next verse, the MERCHANT *comes in, through the audience or from up-stage L. He looks at the signpost, pulls out a gold watch, and walks around the rock. He must reach the center as the verse ends. Then we hear several shots. He spins around and falls slowly, across the center at the front, clutching his chest. The* SERVANTS *duck behind the rock and drop their bags. Then they run off L., taking no notice of a gesture of appeal from the* MERCHANT. *During the second verse one bandit runs on, looks around, and beckons to the other. They turn the* MERCHANT *over roughly, take the watch and his purse and the bags, and run off R. For the third verse the stage is empty, but for the* MERCHANT.)*

NARRATOR: A Merchant journeyed down the road,
CHORUS: The road to Jericho.

152

NARRATOR:	He took with him a costly load
CHORUS:	To bear to Jericho.
NARRATOR:	He was a man of wealth and pride,
	With Servants walking at his side;
	But thieves and bandits often hide
CHORUS:	This side of Jericho, this side of Jericho.
NARRATOR:	The bandits saw that he was rich,

CHORUS

(Refrain as before.)

This side of Jericho.
They left him bleeding by the ditch,
This side of Jericho.
The Servants dropped their burdens there,
And for his life they gave no care,
And he lay stripped and bruised and bare
This side of Jericho, this side of Jericho.
Unless some kindly passer-by
Will not abide to let him lie,
The stricken Merchant now must die,
This side of Jericho, this side of Jericho.

(As soon as this verse is finished, there is a short drum-roll. In time to the drum, the three onlookers march on, turn together up-stage C., and come forward, stepping over the body. They may be boys or girls, and are smartly dressed, self-satisfied and detached. The verse is spoken, with drumbeat or chords ad lib.)

FIRST:	If a man by the roadside has suffered an assault,
	It's nothing to do with me.
SECOND:	It's risky to help him, and it's probably all his fault:
	It's nothing to do with me.
THIRD:	Why pick on me to stop and lend a helping hand?
FIRST:	Why can't an ostrich hide his head in the sand?
	I tell you, it's nothing to do with me.
ALL:	It's absolutely nothing to do with me.
SECOND:	If the man next door gets drunk and beats his wife
	It's nothing to do with me.
THIRD:	A man (or girl) must be practical in twentieth century life.
	It's nothing to do with me.
FIRST:	Am I my brother's keeper when he gets into a jam?
SECOND:	Can't you see how overworked and put upon I am?

153

SECOND:	I tell you, it's nothing to do with me.
ALL:	It's absolutely nothing to do with me.
THIRD:	If some far-off Africans are fighting all the time
	It's nothing to do with me.
FIRST:	With things as they are, I have to think of every dime.
	It's nothing to do with me.
ALL:	We want to live our lives in peace, and keep them clear of fuss.
	Of course it would be different if disaster threatened us;
	But so far it's nothing to do with me.
	It's absolutely nothing to do with me.

(They march off as they came. In the following verses the PRIEST *and* LEVITE *follow the same route as the* MERCHANT *before. The* PRIEST, *a modern clergyman, makes as if to help the* MERCHANT *when he sees him, but thinks better of it and goes off. The* LEVITE, *dressed as a Rabbi, carries a rolled umbrella. When he sees the* MERCHANT *he drops it, looks around in apprehension, and runs off L.)*

NARRATOR:	A certain Priest came travelling by
CHORUS:	To go to Jericho.
NARRATOR:	He did not want to let him lie,
CHORUS:	This side of Jericho.
NARRATOR:	He wanted that poor man to save,
	And all his wounds to staunch and lave,
	But by himself he was not brave,
CHORUS:	This side of Jericho, this side of Jericho.
NARRATOR:	A Levite next came on his way,
CHORUS:	The way to Jericho.
NARRATOR:	He also would have liked to stay,
CHORUS:	This side of Jericho.
NARRATOR:	He was so frightened of his fate,
	He did not even hesitate.
	He told himself it was too late,
CHORUS:	And made for Jericho, and made for Jericho.
CHORUS:	They passed by on the other side.
	The road was small, and it was not wide,
	And they hurried along with averted gaze,
	'Cause they didn't like those bandits' ways.

They passed by on the other side.
The road was small, and it was not wide,
And when they were too much afraid
It was a Samaritan who gave him aid.

(*The* NARRATOR, *one of the onlookers, comes to the center of the stage, and says these words to the audience. This narration may be edited to suit your own situation.*)

There were other people who passed by on the other side that day. Ed Robinson was on the way to a golf game. He saw what had happened, but he didn't want to be late. The Johnstons were on their way to cocktails at the club. Tom Johnston put on speed to get past quickly. Mary waited until it was too late, and wondered whether they should have stopped. They meant to call the police from the club, but somehow they forgot. Bud Smelzer slowed down, and then lost his nerve and drove by. Frank Sorley nearly stopped to help, but, remembering he was already late for work and would probably get fired if he were even later, took a deep breath and hurried on, looking to neither right nor left.

Maybe you went by. Maybe I did too. We were both in a hurry, I'm sure; and we both had good excuses. The world is full of people who are in a hurry, and they all have excuses—some, maybe, even good *reasons*. Wouldn't it be better if we stopped for those who need our help—the injured, the hungry, the lonely, the unloved? Or if we used our imagination and our compassion, to find out who they are, and what they need?

(*The following verses may be part solo, part chorus, or all solo.*)

There are times when the world seems far too big,
    And your strength seems far too small;
And to fight for the things you value most
    Is to beat at a hard stone wall.
You can't stop war, or crime, or smog,
    Or the strife of race with race:
But close at hand, if you turn your eyes,
    There is pain on a lonely face.

Reach out and touch a lonely person!
Reach out and hold an empty hand!
For every time your love goes out to a lonely person
    It falls like rain on a thirsty land.

155

There are times when you feel that to act alone
   Is a useless thing to do;
For the pain of the world is far too deep
   To be changed by me or you.
But every deed which we honor most
   Goes back to a brave man's choice;
And close at hand, if you stop to hear,
   Is the sound of a lonely voice.

   Reach out and touch someone forsaken!
   Hold in your arms someone unloved!
For every time your love breaks through to a lonely person
   Some little part of human dignity is saved.

There will soon be another billion men
   On the face of the crowded earth;
But the fact of another billion men
   Won't alter one man's worth.
Saint Francis set the world on fire
   When he kissed a leper's cheek—
And so can you, if you turn your eyes,
   Reach out, and touch, and speak!

   Reach out your hand, and feed the hungry!
   Wise men will mock, and call you fool;
But every time your love brings joy to a lonely person
   It spreads like waves on a rippling pool.

CHORUS
   Reach out and touch a lonely person!
   Reach out and hold an empty hand!
For every time your love goes out to a lonely person
   It falls like rain on a thirsty land,
Yes, every time your love goes out to a lonely person
   It falls like rain on a thirsty land.

(*The* SAMARITAN *now comes on up-stage L., with two* SER-
VANTS. *After consulting a map by the signpost, he comes
around the rock. He runs to the* MERCHANT, *gives first aid, and
motions to the* SERVANTS *to pick him up.*)

(*Music bridge. The rock is moved offstage, and the inn sign is
placed upstage R. Meanwhile the* SERVANTS *support the* MER-
CHANT *across to R. The* SAMARITAN *knocks three times, the
drum tapping in time to his mimed gesture.*)

SAMARITAN

Open up the door! Open up the door!
Here is a man in sorest need.
Give him succour, and come with speed!
    Open up the door!
Carry him gently! Carry him gently!
Take him and give him all that is best!
Give him shelter and warmth and rest!
    Carry him gently!
Treat him with kindness! Treat him with kindness!
Call a physician to ease his pain!
Nurse him back to his health again!
    Treat him with kindness!

(*During the first verse, the* INNKEEPER *comes out. He calls the* SERVANTS, *who help to take the* MERCHANT *in during the second verse. During the third, the* SAMARITAN *gives the* INNKEEPER *two large coins. He examines them carefully, takes out a note-book and writes a note. The* PRIEST *and* LEVITE *also come out before the end of the song, and stand L.*)

INNKEEPER
(*Spoken, with chords ad lib.*)

Excuse me, Sir, if I remark
That I am somewhat in the dark.
You are a gentleman, it's clear;
But not, I think, from our Judaea.

Are you perhaps from Galilee?
Or have you come across the sea?
Are you from Sidon or from Tyre?
Excuse me, Sir, if I enquire.

Excuse me, Sir, if I confess
I don't know whom I now address.
Your wounded friend looks like a Jew;
But—you'll excuse me—who are you?

Who is the victim's next-of-kin,
If he's to stay here at my Inn?
And if there is some further fee—
Excuse me, Sir—where will you be?

SAMARITAN: I am a Samaritan, and shall return this way.
INNKEEPER, PRIEST AND LEVITE: (*together*) A Samaritan!

157

PRIEST AND LEVITE
(*say softly*)
We passed by on the other side.
The road was small, and it was not wide;
And when we were too much afraid
It was a Samaritan who gave him aid.

INNKEEPER: Is he your friend, Sir?
SAMARITAN: He was a stranger to me.
INNKEEPER: A stranger?
SAMARITAN: Yes, but he was my neighbor.
PRIEST: A stranger?
LEVITE: And your neighbor?
INNKEEPER: How can that be, Sir?

SAMARITAN
Who is my neighbor?
He whose cry I hear.
Who is my neighbor?
He whose need is near.
He is my neighbor
Who will hear my cry.
He is my neighbor
Who will not pass me by.
Who is my neighbor
In my hour of grief?
He is my neighbor
Who will bring relief.
Go, and do likewise!
Never close your door!
Go, and do likewise!
Seek the sick and poor!
Find out your neighbor!
Serve your God above!
Go, seek your neighbor!
Fill the world with love!

(*Lights fade to blackout. Repeat the slides, adding examples showing the relief of suffering. If you wish, you can also repeat, during the slide show, a verse of the onlookers' recitation, and a verse of "Is it nothing to you?"*)

158

Also suitable for this Sunday: Who Is My Neighbor? (Gospel C): see 5th Sunday of the Year, Baptism (Epistle B): see Baptism of the Lord, The End of the World (Epistle A): see First Sunday of Advent; also see *Bible As Drama,* page 192 (Gospel C): The Good Samaritan (shorter version).

25. TWENTY-SECOND SUNDAY OF THE YEAR

To Enter into Life Crippled

Bible Reference: Matthew 16:21–27 (Gospel A)

Note: In the year 1521, a thirty-year-old Spanish Captain, Iñigo of Loyola, was wounded by a cannon ball at Pamplona. He went to the home of his elder brother, Martin, to recover, and was looked after by Martin's wife, Magdalena. With immense courage, he had his leg broken and reset twice, in order to try to prevent himself from being crippled. Fighting and chivalry were his whole life. Magdalena lent him two books, which proved to be the means of pointing him towards a higher chivalry. He transferred his mighty courage to the disciplined service of God, and became Ignatius Loyola, founder of the Jesuit order.

At this point in his life, Ignatius set himself to follow not man's way, but God's. 'If anyone wants to be a follower of mine, let him renounce himself and take up his cross and follow me.' So he lost one life, and entered upon another.

The Scene is historical, except that Doña Magdalena gave Iñigo the two books some time after the setting of his leg for the last time. I have put the two incidents together for dramatic purposes. The books, and his crippled leg, formed the key to his transformation. (See Mary Purcek, 'The First Jesuit,' chapter III.)

Also suitable for: 9th Sunday of the Year; 2nd Sunday of Easter; 16th and 26th Sundays of the Year.

9th Sunday of the Year: Epistle B (2 Cor. 4:6–11). 'We are only the earthenware jars that hold this treasure . . . We have been . . . knocked down, but never killed; always, wherever we may be, we carry with us in our body the death of Jesus, so that the life of Jesus, too, may always be seen in our body.'

2nd Sunday of Easter: Epistle A (I Peter 1:3–9). The writer is speaking to men and women who have been 'tested and proved like gold,' and tells them that by enduring they will 'have praise and glory and honor.'

16th Sunday of the Year: Epistle C (Col. 1:24–28). Here Paul says that it makes him happy to suffer, and to 'make up all that has still to be undergone by Christ for the sake of his body, the Church.' He adds that 'it is for this I struggle wearily on, helped only by His power driving me irresistibly.'

26th Sunday of the Year: Gospel B (Mark 9:38–43, 45, 47–48). In this reading we find the title of the scene: 'It is better for you to enter into life crippled, than to have two hands and go to hell . . . to enter into life lame, than to have two feet and be thrown into hell.' Could there be a more dramatic commentary on Mark's words than Ignatius' struggle to make his leg fit to carry him back into battle?

Scene: An upper room in the Tower House (*Casa Torre*) at Loyola, furnished with a bed, table and chairs.

Characters: IÑIGO *(Ignatius), aged 30*
               DON MARTÍN, *his brother, about 50*
               DOÑA MAGDALENA, *Martin's wife, about 50*
               DOCTOR LÓPEZ, *a Surgeon*

(MAGDALENA *ushers the* SURGEON *into the room.*)

MAGDALENA: In here, Doctor.
SURGEON: Thank you, Doña Magdalena. A beautiful room.
MAGDALENA: Yes, it is. But I have seen Iñigo suffer so much here, that I have almost forgotten its beauty.
SURGEON: Ah, yes, yes. A tragic case, indeed.
MAGDALENA: Doctor, he will be here in a minute. My husband helps him to walk in the gallery each day. Before they come, let me urge you to try to persuade him against this further torture to his leg.
SURGEON: My dear lady, I am on your side, I assure you. I have no wish to undertake the surgery, for it is my opinion that he will die from the pain. But —
MAGDALENA: Then refuse to do it!
SURGEON: I do not think I can refuse, if it is his express wish.
MAGDALENA: No, I suppose not. I admire his courage so much that it almost reconciles me to his folly. I hear them coming.

(MARTIN *enters, supporting* IÑIGO. *He leads him to the bed.*)

IÑIGO: Ah, Doctor López! I thought you would never come.
MARTÍN: Greetings, Doctor!
SURGEON: Don Martín, Señor Iñigo, my humble respects.

IÑIGO: Well, Doctor, what are we waiting for?

SURGEON: I beg your pardon, Sir, but I think we need to discuss the matter of your leg further.

IÑIGO: Discuss? In heaven's name, what is there to discuss? Look at it, man! One bone overlapping the other, because of those accursed bunglers! How many times does my leg have to be set before I can go back to the Army without hobbling?

MARTÍN: Steady, brother! Try not to be impatient.

IÑIGO: My dear Martín, it's easy for you to say that. You can walk out of this room now, mount your horse, and ride off to battle. While I lie here, useless and helpless, because this Surgeon is too much of a coward to break my leg again, and put the bones back where they belong.

MAGDALENA: You cannot stand the pain, Iñigo. You will kill yourself.

IÑIGO: Is there any point in being alive, if I cannot fight?

MAGDALENA: There are many ways of fighting. The chivalry of the battlefield is not the only path of service.

IÑIGO: For me it is. It is all I know, and all I wish for out of life. So I am ordering you, Surgeon, to break this leg again, and force those bones into place.

SURGEON: You don't know what you are asking. I cannot break the bone, locked where it is. I shall have to saw through flesh and bone, where the broken joint has formed.

MARTÍN: No man can stand that kind of pain, Iñigo. Least of all you, after what you have been through.

IÑIGO: You're wrong, Martín. Suffering becomes a habit. I can stand pain, but I cannot stand the boredom and frustration of lying here, day after day—

MAGDALENA: That reminds me, brother. You asked for books. There are none of the romances which you wanted, but I have brought you these.

IÑIGO: Trying to change the subject, Magdalena? But you are kind. What do we have here? 'The Life of Christ.' Well, I thank you for that.

MAGDALENA: I studied it with Her Majesty, Queen Isabella, when I was her lady-in-waiting.

IÑIGO: You and the Queen are better students than I, but I shall see what I can make of it. And this? "Flos Sanctorum, Lives of the Saints." Really, my dear, you might have spared me that. Lives of soldiers, yes; but to me these saints were milksops, who turned the other cheek because they dared not wield the sword.

MAGDALENA: Then you are very ignorant, Iñigo. If you read, you will find that the true Saints had a courage greater than that of any soldier, and a holy chivalry worth more than all of our tournaments and battles. But I have no right to talk to you about courage. You have too much of it.

IÑIGO: Not too much, but enough, I hope. I will strike a bargain with you. Stop arguing with me about my leg—for I intend to have this good man set it before he leaves this room—and in return I promise to read your book of saints; that is, if I can stay awake to read it. Are you ready, Doctor?

SURGEON: If you insist, Sir, I am ready. I shall have to ask your brother to hold you down; and you, my Lady, to hand me the towels and ointments when I need them.

IÑIGO: No man need hold me down. I am not a baby.

MARTÍN: No, but you are human, Iñigo. Lie back now, if you are determined to go through with this. And may God bless you for your stubborn bravery!

MAGDALENA: Amen to that! It is His strength that must sustain you, Iñigo, not your own alone.

IÑIGO: I know it, sister. And with Him to protect me, and friends like you, I shall live to give thanks for this day. There, Doctor, I am ready.

Note: A NARRATOR may set the Scene by speaking some of the introductory paragraphs. He may also close the Scene with a brief summary, such as: 'Although Iñigo turned unwillingly to the pages of the "Lives of the Saints," he found there a new and greater way of life. From henceforth, he wore the Armor of God, and was one of the greatest soldiers of the Kingdom.'

Also suitable for this Sunday: The Champion (Epistle A): see 14th Sunday of the Year, Honor Your Father (OT/C): see Third Sunday of Lent, Go, Show Yourself (Gospel B): see 6th Sunday of the Year; also see *Bible As Drama,* page 88 (OT/A): Jeremiah: The Prophet at Home, page 149 (Gospel B): Disciples and Critics, page 212 (Gospel C): The Wedding Feast (verse play or musical).

26. TWENTY-THIRD SUNDAY OF THE YEAR

The Empire

Bible Reference: Mark 7:31–37 (Gospel B)

Note: It is hard to think of anyone who needed to hear the word 'Ephphatha' more than Elise Morgan. Her tense, closed life seems to have a chance of being opened up and fulfilled at the end of the play. (See Gospel B, Mark 7:31–37)

The origin of this play was a half-laughing admission by a friend that she used to switch on the radio to hear an announcer say 'goodnight,' and then answered him. Like Dene Peck in 'The Champion,' Elise made herself a graven image—the desk which was a symbol of her security and power. And she had her cat for the emotional side of her life. Take these away, and she is left naked in her loneliness.

Production is not very easy, because of the many Scenes, but it can be contrived with mobile, swift scene changes. If there is enough space, act the scenes in different areas, one for her home, one for the store, one for the office. Then you can leave the basic props unmoved. The hospital bed will have to be carried on for the last scene, which must be central. The cat should be a model. A tape of its voice, or a good imitation, is needed.

Also suitable for: 4th Sunday of Lent; 7th, 12th, 13th, and 18th Sundays of the Year.

4th Sunday of Lent: Epistle C (2 Cor. 5:17–21). It could be that Alex Kandinsky might act as a reconciler, and make a 'new creation' in place of the old, in Elise Morgan. In helping to bring this about, Alex may find his own life, and his wife Tanya's, transformed also.

7th Sunday of the Year: Epistle B (2 Cor. 1:18–22). 'With him it was always Yes.' To learn to say 'Yes' to life, instead of shrinking back from everything outside the mechanics of her work, was Elise's greatest need. You could say that 'Yes' and 'Ephphatha' are two of the most beautiful words in the New Testament.

12th Sunday of the Year: Epistle B (2 Cor. 5:14–17). This reading overlaps the passage already discussed; see 4th Sunday of Lent above.

13th Sunday of the Year: Gospel B (mark 5:21–43). Jesus' answer to those who told him that Jairus' daughter was dead was: 'Do not be afraid: only have faith.' 'I tell you to get up,' he said to her. Alex was the only one available to tell the lonely Elise to get up; but he made the words meaningful by giving her a reason to start living again.

18th Sunday of the Year: Epistle C (Col. 3:1–5, 9–11). This would have been a startling reading for Elise, if she opened a Bible that day in Hospital. 'You have been brought back to true life in Christ . . . You have died . . . You have stripped off your old behavior with your old self, and you have put on a new self.'

Scene: See individual scene headings.

Characters: ELISE MORGAN, *a Business Executive, about 40*
               MR. DRESNER, *her assistant*
               SALLY, *her Secretary*
               MR. ZUCCO, *President of the Plant*
               ALEX KANDINSKY, *a Storekeeper, in his 50's*
               TANYA KANDINSKY, *his wife*
               JANITOR
               RADIO ANNOUNCER, *(voice only)*
               MRS. FERNHOLTZ, *customer in the store*

Scene One

(ELISE's *living room. Very little furniture is needed to suggest the room: an armchair, and table with radio. Music playing very softly.*)

ELISE: *(entering)* Hunter! Come along, boy! Here's your night-cap. Nice warm milk. *(She puts milk down by chair, and picks up cat.)* It's bed-time, Hunter. *(She puts cat down upstage from chair.)* We've had a nice evening, haven't we? Finish your milk. Then up on my lap, and we'll turn the radio louder. There! *(She switches radio up.)* It's time for him to say goodnight. *(Pause while sentimental music finishes. She picks up cat.)*

VOICE ON RADIO: And now this is Con Stobart wishing you all a warm goodnight, and happy dreams. Listen with us again on WGDM tomorrow night; and until then once again, goodnight!

ELISE: Goodnight! *(After a few seconds she switches radio off. Silence.)* Goodnight! *(She sobs softly.)*

Scene Two

(*The Kandinsky store. All that is needed is a table and cash register.* MRS. KANDINSKY *is behind the table,* MRS. FERNHOLTZ *in front.*)

TANYA: 3.65, 75, 4, 5, ten. That's it, Mrs. Fernholtz.
MRS. FERNHOLTZ: Thank you, Mrs. Kandinsky. I'll be seeing you. Goodbye.
TANYA: Goodbye. Come back soon!

(MRS. FERNHOLTZ *goes out R.*) Alex!

ALEX: (*off stage L.*) Coming, Tanya.
TANYA: Time for you to go.
ALEX: (*entering L.*) Yes—yes, it's time.
TANYA: Oh, Alex! You've got to persuade them not to take our furniture away.
ALEX: I'll try, Tanya. I'll try. But you know they don't run a charity. They're hard people.
TANYA: Miss Morgan will help. She's been in our store to buy things for the cat. She'll help us, I know she will.
ALEX: Tanya, we can only hope for the best.
TANYA: Yes, Alex, I know. But, oh God, don't let them take it all away! I don't know what we should do if all our furniture went.
ALEX: (*kissing her*) Well, I'll be going, Tanya. Keep hoping—and try not to worry too much.

Scene Three

(ELISE'*s office. Desk and two chairs.* DRESNER *is standing by the desk.*)

DRESNER: Sally.
SALLY: (*entering L.*) Yes, Mr. Dresner?
DRESNER: Miss Morgan will be here in a minute. I need that report.
SALLY: This is it.
DRESNER: Thanks, Sally. She should be pleased. It's quite a triumph for her idea.
SALLY: Pleased? Will you know it if she is? She never shows anything.
DRESNER: No, you're right. She's a machine. And yet—
SALLY: That sounds hard, and she isn't hard. Or is she? It frightens me—all that ability and charm, and yet you never even see the real person.

166

DRESNER: I know it. I've worked for her for four years, and watched her make this place an empire. She's dedicated, and she's brilliant—and I like and respect her. But as for personal life—

SALLY: I know. This desk scares me. You'd think she was married to it, the way she fusses over it. Everything in place, and nobody but she can touch it. It's a kind of symbol.

DRESNER: The throne room of the empire. Yes.

SALLY: (*as buzzer sounds*) Here she comes. Tom always gives me the signal from the front hall. I'll be next door if you need me.

(*She goes out.* DRESNER *glances through report. Enter* ELISE.)

DRESNER: Good morning, Miss Morgan.

ELISE: Good morning, Mr. Dresner. Is Mr. Zucco back yet?

DRESNER: No. He called to say that he would be here in a few minutes. Sounded pretty pleased about something.

ELISE: I want to look over the report on the mail order scheme before he comes in.

DRESNER: This is it. I thought you'd need it early. You're going to be pleasantly surprised.

ELISE: I doubt it. I believed in the scheme all along. This just bears out what I predicted.

DRESNER: It sure does. You got it through. Zucco and the Board were pretty sceptical.

ELISE: It's my business to know our market. I've spent twenty years here, and I should know what I'm doing. That will be all, Mr. Dresner. I must read this report.

SALLY: (*entering*) Excuse me, Miss Morgan. Mr. Dresner, you're wanted out here, if you can spare a minute.

DRESNER: Coming. (*He goes out.* ELISE *sits at desk and reads. After a pause, buzzer sounds on desk.*)

ELISE: Yes?

DRESNER'S VOICE: Miss Morgan, there's a man here asking to see you. His name's Kandinsky. He's very anxious to talk to you personally.

ELISE: Kandinsky? What's it all about?

DRESNER: I'll come in and tell you, shall I?

ELISE: Now? Oh, I suppose so. (*She switches off buzzer with an impatient gesture.*)

DRESNER: (*entering*) Kandinsky keeps that small store on Drummond and 8th.

ELISE: Oh, yes. I remember. Well, if he must come in, let's get it over.

DRESNER: Miss Morgan—

167

ELISE: Yes?

DRESNER: This man, Kandinsky—he says he knows you well by sight. Apparently you walk past the store—

ELISE: That has nothing to do with our business.

DRESNER: No, I know. But that's why he specially wanted to see you. It's the usual story; they're behind on their payments. He and his wife are real nice people, Miss Morgan. They're always helping somebody in the neighborhood.

ELISE: Yes, Mr. Dresner, I'm sure they are; but could we run this business if we stopped to listen to every sob story?

DRESNER: No, but—it *is* tough on some of these people.

ELISE: They ought to think of that before they enter into commitments they can't carry through.

DRESNER: Yes. I suppose you're right. I'll send him away.

ELISE: I will deal with it myself. Send him in.

DRESNER: What's the use, if—

ELISE: Mr. Dresner, will you please stop wasting time and send Mr. Kandinsky in here?

DRESNER: Just as you say, Miss Morgan. (*opens door*) This way, Mr. Kandinsky. Miss Morgan can see you now. (*Enter* KANDINSKY. *Exit* DRESNER.)

ELISE: Sit down, Mr. Kandinsky.

ALEX: Thank you, Miss Morgan. I sure do appreciate—

ELISE: I'm afraid I have to tell you that you have come on a vain errand. I'm sure you understand that we can't run a business like this unless we stick strictly to the terms of the contract.

ALEX: Yes, yes, I understand. But I promised my wife—

ELISE: We have fifty thousand clients making payments on furniture.

ALEX: Fifty thousand. Yes. But you see, Miss Morgan, it's the store. It's not for ourselves. We have clients too. You come in yourself, once in a while. And we need those tables and chairs—

ELISE: Mr. Kandinsky, that is, literally, your business. We have ours, and it isn't a charity. If I hadn't learned that twenty years ago, I wouldn't be here now.

ALEX: You worked here twenty years?

ELISE: Yes, I have; but that has nothing to do with—

ALEX: No, no. But most days I see you come by our store, on the sidewalk in Drummond; and when I get the notice, that you take our things back if we can't make the payment, I think, "She knows my store—sometimes she buys a magazine, or food for the cat, or something—maybe I can ask her for a little time."

ELISE: I'm sorry, Mr. Kandinsky. The answer is No. Good morning. (*She walks to door.* KANDINSKY *follows slowly.* SALLY *is at the door.*)

SALLY: Oh, Miss Morgan. I came to tell you that Mr. Zucco is on his way up.

ALEX: I'll be going along. Thanks, Miss Morgan—for seeing me. (*He goes out.*)

(ELISE *walks to desk thoughtfully, and picks up report. Enter* ZUCCO.)

ZUCCO: Hi, Miss Morgan. I've got news for you.

ELISE: Shall I come through to your office?

ZUCCO: No, no. Sit down. Let's talk here.

ELISE: It sounds like something good. Is it about the mail order program?

ZUCCO: No. Oh, I knew about that. You've proved us wrong— shown that you were the smart one who knew what was good for us, and put a million and a half on the profits for next year, at a guess. But I've got something bigger to tell you.

ELISE: Bigger?

ZUCCO: Sure. May be a shock, but it's big all right. I've sold the plant.

ELISE: (*after pause*) You've—what?

ZUCCO: Sold the plant. Lock, stock and barrel. Oh, it's a wonderful deal, and opens up the way for something in a different class altogether—for you too, Miss Morgan.

ELISE: You mean—this Office—my job—

ZUCCO: What's so special about this place? You'll get a bonus equal to what you're worth—and that's a lot! And then you can either come in with me, wherever I go, or move to any firm, anywhere, and name your own price.

ELISE: My price—yes. (*She sits back, eyes closed.*)

ZUCCO: Here, Miss Morgan. Are you all right? I didn't think—I'll get you some water.

ELISE: It's quite all right, Mr. Zucco. I congratulate you on the deal. It is—something of a shock; but please don't worry about me. I shall be quite all right.

ZUCCO: I must run and make sure the word percolates. Wanted you to be the first to know. See you later.

ELISE: Thank you. Goodbye. (*Exit* ZUCCO. ELISE *sits back, eyes closed. Soon, gets up. She stands at desk, still and silent. Then she presses buzzer. Enter* SALLY.)

169

SALLY: Yes, Miss Morgan?

ELISE: Sally, I'm going home now. Will you ask Mr. Dresner to come in here for a minute?

SALLY: Yes, Miss Morgan.

ELISE: Sally—

SALLY: (*turning by door*) Yes, Miss Morgan?

ELISE: You have learned your job well, Sally. I—I'm grateful for all your help.

SALLY: (*surprised*) Thank you, Miss Morgan. I like to work for you. (*pause*) I'll fetch Mr. Dresner. See you in the morning, Miss Morgan.

(*Again* ELISE *stands still by her desk. Then* DRESNER *enters.*)

ELISE: Mr. Dresner, I'm just going home. I've put everything in order in my office.

DRESNER: Yes. It's been a big shock to all of us, I know. But especially you. Would you like me to drive you home?

ELISE: I've walked home every evening for twenty years. I think I can manage, thank you. This note is for Mr. Zucco. Leave it on his desk. He'll be here in the morning.

DRESNER: I will.

ELISE: Then I think that's everything. Goodbye, Mr. Dresner.

DRESNER: Goodnight, Miss Morgan. Don't—

ELISE: Don't what?

DRESNER: Oh, nothing. I like this place, too. But—well, it's a logical move that Zucco's made, and—after all, it isn't places that matter, but people.

ELISE: People. Yes, of course. Good-night!

(*Exit* ELISE. DRESNER *picks up note. Stands at desk.*)

Scene Four

(*Front stage.* KANDINSKY's *store: as before.*)

TANYA: Alex! Come here. There she is, on her way home.

ALEX: (*entering*) Miss Morgan? Already? Must be something wrong. She never leaves the office early.

TANYA: Alex, now is your chance. You've got to go and ask her again—at home. She may feel different at home.

ALEX: It won't do any good, Tanya.

TANYA: Maybe it would, outside that office.

ALEX: (*sighing*) I guess it's worth a try. I'll go—soon as I finish putting these cans on the shelves.

Scene Five

(ELISE's *living room. Darkness. Sound of latch-key. She enters and switches on table lamp.*)

ELISE: Hunter! Hello, Hunter! There you are—my only friend. (*Sits on armchair.*) Your bowl's empty. I'll fetch you some milk. (*Goes into darkened area of stage, and returns with bowl and glass. Puts it by chair, and sits.*) There you are, Hunter—and something for your mistress to drink too. I need it, Hunter. They've taken away my life. They expect me to begin all over again. (*Pause. She begins to sob.*) And I can't, Hunter. I can't. I can't do it. We were all right here. I could bear it, with you—and the office. Oh, God! It isn't fair. He didn't even ask me. And I can't go on. (*pause*) We're going away, Hunter. It won't hurt you, I don't think; and I want you to come with me. (*Walks to dark part of stage, carrying cat.*) Look, we can just lie here, with this cushion under my head, and we'll go to sleep. When the radio announcer says good-night, we won't be here. Goodbye, Hunter! I want to go to sleep now. I'm so tired. (*A sob. Then silence. Pause of half a minute. Then play on tape sounds of cat mewing R. and scratching door. Footsteps, doorbell and knock. Pause.*)
ALEX: (*offstage*) Hi, pussycat in there! Where's your mistress? (*Bell repeated, and knocking. Furious scratching.*) Quiet, pussycat! You'll scratch the paint. What's the trouble? You want to get out? (*hard knock*) Miss Morgan! (*Repeat knock and bell.*) Miss Morgan!
JANITOR: (*also offstage*) Hey, you! What's going on? Who are you?
ALEX: Do you live here?
JANITOR: I'm the janitor.
ALEX: I think there's trouble in Miss Morgan's apartment. (*Noise of cat scratching and mewing.*)
JANITOR: Miss Morgan? She just came in. Wait a minute. Do you smell gas?
ALEX: Yes—yes, I think I do. Quick! Something's wrong.

(*Sound of keys. They burst in.*)

JANITOR: Oh, God! She's killed herself.
ALEX: Call a doctor and an ambulance, quick! (*Exit* JANITOR. ALEX

runs to ELISE, *and drags her to the door.*) Merciful God! Don't let it be too late! (*by door*) You did your best, puss. Poor Miss Morgan. Pray God it isn't too late!

Scene Six

(ELISE'*s office. The telephone rings and* SALLY *answers.*)

SALLY: Hello! Yes, this is Global Furnishings. Mr. Zucco isn't here. I see. Yes, I can connect you with Mr. Dresner. Just one moment. (*Enter* DRESNER.) Oh, Mr. Dresner. It's Grace Hospital. They asked for Mr. Zucco, but—

DRESNER: The hospital? What on earth—(*at telephone*) Hello! Yes, Mr. Dresner, Miss Morgan's assistant. What?! (*pause*) Oh, my God, no! She's—Yes. Yes, of course. Just a minute. (*to* SALLY) It's Miss Morgan. She went straight home and tried to commit suicide. Turned on the gas.

SALLY: Oh, no! She—

DRESNER: They say she's going to come through. Someone found her. They want her next-of-kin. Can you get the card?

SALLY: Yes. (*She goes out.*)

DRESNER: (*on telephone*) We'll have it in just a moment. I never heard her talk about her family, but we must have the information filed. (SALLY *re-enters.*) Here it comes. Well, Sally, what's the answer?

SALLY: (*Voice only just under control.*) It says: "Next-of-kin: NONE. Please contact the Manager, Fidelity State Bank, in case of emergency." Oh, dear God, she had nobody! Don't you see? Nobody. I wish I'd known—

Scene Seven

(*A hospital room.* ELISE *in bed. Table with lamp and telephone, and a chair. She is motionless, lying down, as* ALEX *enters.*)

ALEX: Miss Morgan? Are you awake?

ELISE: (*No movement. Flat voice.*) Yes, I'm awake.

ALEX: It's me. Kandinsky.

ELISE: (*slowly*) Kandinsky. Yes, I remember. (ALEX *sits by bed.*)

ALEX: I don't want to disturb you, Miss Morgan; but I thought you'd like to know about your cat.

ELISE: Poor Hunter! (*sobbing*)

ALEX: No, no. He's O.K., Miss Morgan. He's with Tanya—that's my wife—and me.

ELISE: You've got Hunter?

ALEX: Sure, we've got him, and he's fine. You're not to worry about him. He's O.K.

ELISE: Thank you, Mr. Kandinsky. It was kind of you to care for him, and to come here and tell me.

ALEX: His name's Hunter?

ELISE: Yes. Hunter.

ALEX: You know he saved your life?

ELISE: Hunter saved—my life? I don't understand.

ALEX: Well, you see, I was outside your door, and I hear him scratching and whining; and suddenly I know something's wrong in there. So the janitor and me—we open the door.

ELISE: So *you* saved me.

ALEX: No, no. I just happened to be there. Hunter saved you.

ELISE: Mr. Kandinsky, why were you outside my door?

ALEX: Oh, we don't talk about that now. It's time for me to go.

ELISE: I must know.

ALEX: I tell you, it doesn't matter. I better go. I'll come back later. (*He rises.*)

ELISE: I think I understand. You followed me home last night, didn't you? To ask about the payment again? And you heard Hunter, and that—saved my life. (*She tries to sit up.*)

ALEX: Miss Morgan. What are you trying to do? You can't sit up.

ELISE: Oh, yes, I—(*She falls back.*) I—guess you're right. I'm not as strong as I thought. Mr. Kandinsky, hand me that telephone, please.

ALEX: You shouldn't be—

ELISE: Please! What time is it? 9:30. Mr. Dresner should be there. Operator, give me OR 6-3000, please. Yes. (*pause*) Mr. Dresner, please. Mr. Dresner? This is Miss Morgan. Yes, thank you. I can't talk about that now. I want you to do something for me. Pull Kandinsky out of the file, will you? I'm sending a check to cover his account—

ALEX: You—no, no!

ELISE: Well, that would be nice, if you want to come and see me. And Sally. Please thank her for me. I'll give you the check when you come. But, Mr. Dresner, don't let anyone take away Kandinsky's things. Thank you. Will you hang it up for me, Mr. Kandinsky?

ALEX: But, Miss Morgan, I don't want—

173

ELISE: You don't want payment for saving my life. I know that. And I'm not doing it for you. I did it for myself.

ALEX: I don't get it, Miss Morgan.

ELISE: Then I'll try to explain it to you. A long time ago, I loved a man. He—well, it wasn't pleasant; and I let it hurt me far too much. I just shut love out of my life—made sure that it wasn't going to hurt me anymore. So I made my work my whole life. Oh, it could have been worse. It was good work; and I had Hunter. But, yesterday—well, there was nothing to fall back on, nothing to live for.

ALEX: I'm sorry you had trouble, Miss Morgan; but—

ELISE: Let me finish, please. This morning, when I first knew that I was alive I just cried, because I wasn't dead. But I think you've changed that, Mr. Kandinsky. I'm not very sure of anything yet, but I think you did something. You make me feel as though I had run away—which is true, I know. You make me want to find the warm things again, the things that matter. If the world is like that, I want to start again, and I want to start by giving—not paying, giving. Do you see?

ALEX: (*after a pause.*) You know something, Miss Morgan? I've been figuring that now you pay for my furniture, a whole lot of what's in my store belongs to you.

ELISE: But, I tell you, I—

ALEX: O.K., O.K. So you gave it to me and Tanya. That's good, Miss Morgan. We need it, and we'll take it. But that means I got a right to share something too. My wife and I, we talked this over. We want to help you—take care of you till you're on your feet again. You need someone to visit—to run errands. So you just tell us what you need—please. We want to do it.

ELISE: (*after a pause*) Let me think about it. I have to get my mind clear before I even know what I need. But, Alex—thank you— you and your wife—from the bottom of my heart. I know you are making the offer with your heart, and nothing else matters. You're making me see that.

ALEX: You better rest now, Miss Morgan.

ELISE: I will.

ALEX: And when you're ready to go home, you give me a call. I'll bring some groceries around to your place—things you'll be needing. That makes sense, doesn't it?

ELISE: Yes. Yes, it makes sense. You make a lot of sense, Alex Kandinsky. Now it's up to me to learn something about living.

Also suitable for this Sunday: The Perfect House (Epistle B): see Fifth Sunday of Easter: Who Is My Neighbor? (Epistle A): see Fifth Sunday of the Year (or The Good Samaritan; see 15th Sunday of the Year); also see *Bible As Drama,* page 212 (Epistle B), The Wedding Feast (verse play or musical), page 73 (OT/C): Solomon: The New King, page 281 (Epistle C): A Prisoner at Rome, page 187 (Gospel C): The Rich Farmer.

27. TWENTY-FIFTH SUNDAY OF THE YEAR

The Crafty Steward

Bible Reference: Luke 16:1–13 (Gospel C)

Note: This is the most startling of Jesus' parables. Its ending is totally unexpected. The listeners would expect the Steward to be punished, like the selfish and dishonest servant in Gospel A of the 24th Sunday of the Year (see below). But instead of that he is congratulated on being so smart! 'The Master' is of course a worldly Boss, not God. It seems that Jesus is urging the 'good' people of this world not to leave all the enthusiasm and energy to the 'bad' people. Be as wholehearted in serving God as Jack Steward was in serving his own interests. The slovenly Chorus of Church-goers may be a cruel parody, but then this is not a gentle or kindly parable. These Chorus members should either wear sloppy Choir robes or ill-fitting 'Sunday best.'

A large cast is involved. The key is quick flexibility. Some chairs are needed, for the Chorus; a Lectern or Podium; a small desk, to be placed in the center for Jack Steward's scenes; and two Altars, for the Cross and Golden Calf. All characters should wear modern dress. Make the debtors caricatures.

(To obtain the musical score of this play see page 7.)

Also suitable for: 20th, 24th, and 26th Sundays of the Year.

20th Sunday of the Year: Epistle B (Eph. 5:15–20). 'This may be a wicked age, but your lives should redeem it . . . do not be thoughtless.' Paul often talks to the Church members about faith, and spiritual qualities, not so often about effective action, and intelligence. There is an earthy quality about this passage.

24th Sunday of the Year: Gospel A (Mt. 18:21–35). This is the conventional parable, in contrast to the paradoxical 'Crafty Steward' story. Mean dishonesty is followed by severe punishment. The lesson is quite different in the two parables: one is about mercy being our duty, the other about efficiency being an essential part of our faith.

176

26th Sunday of the Year: OT/B (Numbers 11:25–29). The withering reply of Moses is similar in spirit to the surprising twist of Jesus' parable. Joshua was expecting Moses to be horrified that Eldad and Medad were daring to prophesy. Instead, Moses says in effect, 'Why cannot some of our religious leaders take a leaf out of their book, and do better?' Sloyan compares Lincoln's famous reply, when he was told that General Grant drank heavily: that he wished a case of the same brand of whiskey could be sent to all of his Generals.

Scene: See individual scene headings.

Characters: MOSES
AARON
SATAN
VOICE OF GOD
MINISTER
JACK STEWARD, *manager of a Ranch for Mr. Lord*
MR. LORD, *his boss*
VERA, *Jack's girl friend*
MR. GALETTI ⎫
MRS. SCHEER ⎬ *debtors of Mr. Lord*
MR. GOMEZ ⎭
MISS MACPHERSON
TWO COMMENTATORS, *a young man and woman*
NARRATOR
CHORUS, *part of which also forms the* CONGREGATION

(MOSES *kneels in the center of an empty stage.*)

CHORUS
God spoke to Moses long ago,
God spoke to Moses long ago,
God spoke to Moses long ago,
  Tell the people of Israel,
  The people of Israel,
  To serve me with their might.

God spoke to Moses long ago,
God spoke to Moses long ago,
God spoke to Moses long ago,
  If they follow me truly,

Follow me truly,
They are precious in my sight.

VOICE OF GOD
(from a distance, offstage)

Tell them to have no other Gods but me, Moses. Tell them that my love is with them, and underneath are the everlasting arms; but they must make no graven image, and must love me with heart and soul and mind.

MOSES

I will tell them, Lord. It will be hard to follow you sometimes, but I will tell them. Lord, if we fail—

VOICE

If you fail, come back to me in penitence, and I will give you strength. But do not compromise with evil, and with other Gods.

MOSES *(he recites)*

I will do my utmost, Lord.
Preserve me, O God; for in thee have I put my trust.
O my soul, thou hast said unto the Lord,
"Thou art my God; I have no good like unto thee."
But they that run after another God shall have great trouble.
I have set the Lord always before me;
for He is on my right hand, therefore I shall not fall.

(MOSES *goes off.* AARON *is sitting at desk writing.*)

SATAN: *(entering L.)* Good morning, Aaron.

AARON: *(looking up)* I beg your pardon. Who—I don't think I know you.

SATAN: My name is Satan.

AARON: Satan? Why, you—

SATAN: Not so fast, Aaron! Before you condemn me so hastily, let me tell you why I have come. I have been watching with admiration all that you are doing for your people.

AARON: It is not I who lead our people, but Moses, my brother.

SATAN: Exactly. And Moses is a great man, a very great man—in some ways too great a man, Aaron.

AARON: Too great? How can that be true?

SATAN: Too great for ordinary people to keep up with him. That is where your wisdom and your gifts come in. Moses goes up to Sinai and talks with God. He has the limelight. But you have your finger on the pulse of the ordinary man, Aaron.

AARON: Yes, that may be true.

SATAN: It is true. And that is why I want to give you some advice and help. This is going to be a critical moment for mankind, and you are called to be the moderating influence. Moses will come down from Sinai, after having seen a great vision. But religion, like everything else, must be practical; and Moses is not practical. If what he tells the people is far beyond their reach, what is its use?

AARON: I see that risk; but what do you want me to do?

SATAN: See that the people keep their feet on the ground, when he comes with his head still in the clouds! See that they mix common sense with his ideals. It is going to depend on you.

AARON: But—if you are right, how shall I go about it?

SATAN: Compromise is the key; intelligent, sensible compromise. Keep them in touch with reality! Now I suggest that it would be a good idea, for a start, to collect all the gold that the people possess, rings, ornaments and so on, and make a Golden Calf . . .
(SATAN *and* AARON *go off.*)

NARRATOR: Aaron did what Satan told,

CHORUS: Build that Golden Calf!

NARRATOR: Gathered all the people's gold,

CHORUS: Build that Golden Calf!

NARRATOR: Gathered bracelets, gathered rings,
Gathered all their golden things,
Sang the songs a pagan sings,

CHORUS: Build that Golden Calf!

NARRATOR: Moses' anger then was grim,

CHORUS: Break that Golden Calf!

NARRATOR: Bitter words they heard from him,

CHORUS: Break that Golden Calf!

NARRATOR: "Lord Jehovah gave us birth;
All your gold is nothing worth.
Tread that Calf down in the earth!"

CHORUS: Break that Golden Calf!

(*The commentators are seen at one side of the stage.*)

SHE: I'm confused. I thought this was about the Unjust Steward. I can't remember the story very well, but at least I know it didn't have Moses in it.

HE: No, you're right. But I think they're all part of the same situation.

179

SHE: Well, I don't understand it yet.

HE: The parable of the Unjust Steward is about the most surprising story that Jesus ever told; but the clue comes at the end, when he says, "The children of this world are wiser than the children of light."

SHE: What does that mean?

HE: That people who are out for worldly ends are more whole-hearted than most so-called religious people. It's not always true. Some religious people are as whole-hearted as they could possibly be. But I think Jesus must have been suffering from some pious and ineffective people, and wanted to wake them up with this story. The moral is; bad men try really hard to gain their ends— why don't the people who call themselves good try equally hard? Must the good be soft, while the bad have all the guts?

SHE: I see that, yes. But what about Moses and Aaron?

HE: It looked as though Satan was trying to soften up Aaron, so that he wouldn't be in danger of serving God too hard.

SHE: Here they come again! It looks like a modern Church.

(Church scene. MINISTER and AARON are at The Lectern. Congregation seated opposite them, holding hymnals. At the back are a cross, right, and a golden calf, left.)

SATAN: *(downstage L.C.)* Yes, it is a Church. You may be surprised at the Hymn they are singing; but I have managed to persuade them that honest compromise is better than hypocrisy. The Church is called "The Temple of Christ and the Golden Calf." Perhaps some of you out there would care to join, that is, if you don't already belong.

(The congregation rise and sing. If the numbers are small, the whole hymn should be sung by all. SATAN beats time from L.)

RIGHT SIDE: We are the children of light,

LEFT SIDE: And we worship the Lord with part of our might.

RIGHT: We come to Church, and we pray and sing,

LEFT: And we half believe in everything.

RIGHT: We half believe in God above,

LEFT: And we practise half of Christian love.

RIGHT: We believe in half of the Christian creed,

LEFT: We believe in half of the things we read.

RIGHT: On Sunday it seems a high ideal,

LEFT: But on Wednesday it doesn't seem quite real.

ALL: We follow Christ, just half and half;
But we also keep an eye on the Golden Calf. AMEN.

(During the last two lines, they bow to the two symbols.)

MINISTER: Will you please all be seated? It is a great privilege for
me to introduce our visiting preacher, Aaron. I know that you
have heard something of his work, and of course you all know that
he is the brother of the great Moses. I am sure that he has a
message to give us of a truly practical kind, and I am delighted to
call upon him to speak to us. Aaron!

AARON: May the words of my mouth, and the meditations of my
heart, be always acceptable in thy sight, O Lord, my strength and
my redeemer! My friends, it is I who am privileged to be speaking
to you, a typical, decent, normal congregation of Christian people.
And what I want to say to you today is this. I am a great admirer of
my brother Moses. I know no man whose touch with God is so
close and deep. What disturbs me about him is this: will he, by
giving us such high ideals that we cannot keep them, frighten most
of us away from religion altogether? Or else, shall we turn into
hypocrites, pretending one set of ideals and living by quite differ-
ent standards? That was why I persuaded my people to make the
Golden Calf, when Moses was up on Mount Sinai. I feel that we
preachers must realize that we are dealing with human beings, not
angels. The Golden Calf represents an honest compromise be-
tween God and Mammon; and if you are shocked by that idea, ask
yourselves whether in fact it is not the kind of common-sense
religion by which you are yourself living.

It's all very well for Moses,
As he stands on Sinai hill.
It's all very well for Moses;
He has an iron will.
But for people who aren't like Moses,
The standards are too high.
So half and half, with a Golden Calf,
   I divide my loyalty.

CHORUS

It's all very well for Moses,
Conversing with the Lord.
It's all very well for Moses;
It's a thing he can afford.
But for lesser folk than Moses—

181

Which means, for you and me—
We must recognize that compromise
Must be religion's key.

(*The congregation repeats: "We are the children of light . . ." and files out.* MOSES *enters, and kneels.*)

MOSES: Lord, I have come back to pray to you. It's a long climb up here, but I need to be as near to you as I can be. Lord, you saw what was happening down there. I could hardly believe it, when I saw what Aaron had done. My own brother! And to build an idol, a Golden Calf, just when we were trying to find our way to you as our one true God! And you saw what I did. I'm afraid I saw red, Lord; and we destroyed it so that you would never have known it existed. But since then, Lord, I've been thinking. Aaron isn't a bad man, I know that. His point of view is that it's better to have most of the people half-way on your side than to have a very few who go all the way in loving and serving you. Which do you want, Lord? Do you want me to rewrite the Ten Commandments? You know: "Serve God, but only within reason. Honor your father and mother, as long as they are reasonable and agree with your point of view. Don't kill, or steal, or commit adultery, unless things become too difficult." Lord, even up here it's hard to see it all clearly. But you did speak to me clearly before. And until I know that you have changed your mind I shall stick to what you said then. Most people are going to say that it's hopelessly unpractical; and it's going to be a tough time, Lord. Please be with me, and don't let them water down your word with compromises! (*He recites.*) I will lift up mine eyes unto the hills, from whence cometh my help. My help cometh even from the Lord, who hath made heaven and earth.

(MOSES *goes off.* JACK *and* VERA *come in.* JACK *sits at his office desk. On it are two telephones.* VERA *sits on the edge of the desk, polishing her nails.*)

JACK: (*on telephone*) Mrs. Hawkins? Yes, this is Jack Steward. You can't what? You can't pay your rent this month? Well, Mrs. Hawkins, you know, that's really your problem, isn't it, not mine? Arrange something? Well, yes, I dare say we could talk it over. But there's no getting away from the fact that Mr. Lord must have his money. Yes, call up here in the morning; about eleven will do fine. I'll see you then, Mrs. Hawkins. *(Puts down telephone.)*

VERA: Who was that, honey?

JACK: Old Mrs. Hawkins? Oh, she lives in one of the cottages west of the Ranch.

VERA: And she can't pay.

JACK: With a little persuasion she'll pay. Maybe I shall have to lend her some of the money, for a consideration.

VERA: What would the Boss say to that?

JACK: What can he say? He spends his time in New York and Florida and Europe, and leaves this place to me. And I reckon I do a good job for him. If I make a bit on the side, there's nothing so wrong in that. It won't be long now before we can take that honeymoon trip to Mexico City.

VERA: Sounds good to me. What does the Boss do, Jack?

JACK: Better not enquire too closely. He's one of those big wheeler-dealer financiers, with interests everywhere, some of them shady, I imagine. *(Telephone rings. He picks it up.)* Hello! Yes, this is Jack Steward. Put it through. Who? Yes, sir. Yes, of course. Come right on over! I wasn't expecting—why, yes, certainly it's convenient. I'll be seeing you then, Mr. Lord. *(He puts telephone down.)* It's Mr. Lord—arrived unexpectedly. He's on his way over. Listen, honey, you wait in there. You might meet him if you go out now. Keep out of the way, and I'll cope with him. Hurry!

(She goes off L. JACK *tidies desk. Then enter* MR. LORD.)*

JACK: Why, hello there, Mr. Lord! Good to see you. This is a great surprise.

LORD: I expect it is. You weren't expecting to see me, were you?

JACK: No, sir; but you're very welcome.

LORD: Welcome! I wonder!

JACK: What do you mean, sir?

LORD: I'll tell you what I mean. You think I live a long way off, and so you reckon that I don't know what goes on down here on the ranch. Well, maybe my ears are sharper than you thought, Jack Steward. I've come to find out the truth.

JACK: I have no idea what all this is about, Mr. Lord.

LORD: You don't? Well, reports have reached me that you're taking too much into your own hands, in more ways than one—robbing me right and left, and wasting my money.

JACK: Robbing you and wasting your money? I'd be interested to know who told you that!

LORD: Never you mind who told me! I want to be fair, and I'll give you a chance to prove that everything's straight. You've got till ten tomorrow morning. Then I'm going through the accounts; and they'd better be in order, or you're fired! Is that understood?

(JACK *remains at the desk. The commentators come on at one side.*)

SHE: I should think he deserved it, wouldn't you?

HE: Maybe. I'm sure that's how Jesus' hearers expected it to end.

SHE: You mean, that he was caught, thrown into prison and punished?

HE: That's the obvious ending, isn't it? Pay the uttermost farthing, weeping and gnashing of teeth, and all that.

SHE: But it doesn't end that way in this story?

HE: Far from it! Here come the lights again. Let's watch!

(VERA *enters, and stands near* JACK.)

VERA: That sounded pretty bad, Jack.

JACK: I'll say it's bad! If I lose this job, he'll make it very nearly impossible for me to get another. I'm ruined!

VERA: What are you going to do?

JACK: We're going to fight, Vera! I've got to think. If he fires me, I have only two choices: to dig as a hired laborer, or to beg. Just think of that! I'll do anything, anything, to avoid it! We have until ten o'clock tomorrow morning. All right! If that's the way he wants it, he can have it. Where's that list?

VERA: List of what?

JACK: The Boss's debtors. Here it is! We'll begin with these four. You take Mrs. Scheer and Miss Macpherson. Use that telephone. Tell them to come here—and quick! (*They speak alternately on the telephones.*) Mr. Galetti? come at once.

VERA: Hurry on over, Mrs. Scheer!

JACK: Mr. Gomez, come along quick!

VERA: Miss Macpherson, we want you here!

(*Enter* GALETTI, MRS. SCHEER, GOMEZ *and* MISS MACPHERSON.)

VERA: Sit down, Mr. Galetti. All of you, please sit down.

GALETTI: What's it all about, Mr. Steward?

SCHEER: Yes, Mr. Steward. Tell us! I don't understand.

184

JACK: You'll know in a minute, all of you. Now, Mr. Galetti, I have your account with Mr. Lord here. (GALETTI *goes to the desk. The others are sitting on the chairs.*) Do you remember how much you owe him?

GALETTI: A hundred measures of oil, Mr. Steward. It's a big burden.

JACK: Well now, Mr. Galetti, you know that you owe Mr. Lord a hundred measures of oil, and I know it; but Mr. Lord doesn't know it, Mr. Galetti. And if I were to take a pen and alter that figure to—what shall we say?—fifty? It could be a secret between the two of us, couldn't it?

GALETTI: Fifty! Gee! You'd do that for me, Mr. Steward?

JACK: I'm doing it at this moment, Mr. Galetti. There! You see? I have no great reason to love Mr. Lord. The difference between fifty and a hundred matters to you, but it isn't going to hurt him. And perhaps one day you can do something for me.

GALETTI: I sure will, Mr. Steward! Only fifty! What a load off my mind!

(GALETTI *returns to his chair.* VERA *crosses to desk.*)

VERA: Mrs. Scheer has a problem too, Jack.

JACK: Well, I'm hopeful that we can tackle all these good people's problems helpfully.

SCHEER: (*remaining seated*) It's all that wheat, Mr. Steward. You know how it is. Times have been bad, and I owe a hundred measures.

JACK: A hundred measures of wheat? Hm, that's more difficult. He can do some checking. But suppose we change that figure to— eighty?

SCHEER: That sure would be a great help, Mr. Steward.

JACK: And you, Mr. Gomez?

GOMEZ: It's the rent on my place, see. (*He hurries across to desk.*) I do my best, but the arrears—

JACK: The arrears amount to a thousand dollars. Is that right?

GOMEZ: A thousand or a little over. Gee! It's a lot of money.

JACK: Something tells me that seven hundred would be a more satisfactory figure, Mr. Gomez. There! Not a bad piece of forgery!

GOMEZ: (*returning to chair*) Wow!

JACK: Now, Miss Macpherson; a loan, wasn't it?

MACPHERSON: That's right, Mr. Steward; and the interest adds up so. I owe Mr. Lord about five thousand dollars.

JACK: Five thousand? That's funny. Come here, Miss Macpherson!

(*She goes to the desk.*) I thought for a moment that figure was a three, not a five. You see? I could swear it's a three now.

MACPHERSON: Oh, thank you, Mr. Steward! You don't know what it will mean!

JACK: Glad to do it for an old friend, Miss Macpherson. We're all old friends and neighbors, aren't we? Anything we can do to help each other—

GALETTI: We'll sure be glad to help you, Mr. Steward.

GOMEZ: Yes, sir! Anything you need—

JACK: I'll remember that, Mr. Gomez. I certainly will remember what you said. Now, I'll be asking all of you to get along home. I've work to do here, getting everything straight.

(*They all say goodbye, and go out.* VERA *escorts them, then returns to desk.*)

VERA: Gee, Jackie, aren't you taking a big risk?

JACK: Risk of what? He's out to ruin me, isn't he? Well, I'm fighting him. I've got to look after you and me, and if he suffers that's just too bad. Now, let's get down to these account books!

(*Sound of organ from a distance. Then voices reciting "We Are The Children Of Light . . . " offstage.*)

VERA: What's that noise?

JACK: The soppy chant? That's the Church over the road. The do-gooders having their social hour. I'll bet they'd have a shock, if they knew what we were doing!

VERA: If they ever work as hard for their God as we're working now, I reckon religion will take a sharp turn upwards.

JACK: It sure will—if it ever happens. Hand me that ledger, honey!

VERA: Listen!

CHORUS: (*offstage*) Fight the good fight with all your might! (*Sung to a familiar tune.*)

JACK: (*speaking*) That's no use to me, you children of light!

CHORUS: Cast care aside, lean on thy guide!

JACK: I must help myself. The Lord won't provide!

CHORUS: Lay hold on life, and it shall be—

JACK: (*shouting*) Oh, nuts! You sing half-heartedly.

(*The organ continues softly while* JACK *and* VERA *recite.*)

JACK: I must fight my fight with all of my might.
Those people in there half believe in right!

VERA: When a crisis comes, and things look tight,

186

You can give up hope for the children of light!

JACK: They can bleat away about faith and prayer,
But the children of darkness really care!

VERA: And there's nothing to make the Devil laugh
Like the children of light, with their "half and half"!

JACK: There! That's the best I can do. And if I'm fired, we'll see how Mr. Galetti and the rest can help. Cheer up, darling! We'll have that honeymoon trip yet!

(*They go off.* SATAN *appears on one side.*)

SATAN: On the whole I'm well satisfied with the way things are working out. I have Moses really worried, Aaron preaching compromise, the people in Church listening to him and bowing to the Golden Calf; and everything's going well here on the ranch. Mr. Lord is being as mean as he can, and Jack Steward is forging the accounts. And not one of those pillars of respectability objected to the help he offered them. Ah, well! I can usually rely on my followers working a good deal harder than His. (*He points upwards.*) Yes, I think the situation is turning out very nicely!

(*He goes off. After a pause,* MOSES *comes on.*)

MOSES: Lord, did you hear all that?

VOICE OF GOD: Yes, Moses. I heard.

MOSES: It's terrible to hear that man Jack and his girl treating your Church with contempt, and Satan crowing over us!

VOICE: I know, Moses. And you can't help feeling, can you, that he is partly right. Is that what is troubling you?

MOSES: Yes, Lord. Those people in Church—from their singing they didn't sound like very good witnesses for you, did they?

VOICE: No, Moses. They are not bad people, but they are weak. I am afraid that you didn't put an end to compromise when you stamped out that Golden Calf.

MOSES: Must it always be like this, Lord? Will good men always be half-hearted?

VOICE: They rise above it sometimes. But I wish that some of them, who sit and doze in their comfortable seats in Church, would take some lessons from Mr. Lord and Jack Steward. I can't help admiring Jack and that girl Vera.

(NARRATOR *repeats the first verse of "God spoke to* MOSES *long ago."* MOSES *goes out. Office scene:* LORD *sits at the desk:* JACK *stands by him.*)

187

LORD: Hm. It all looks plausible enough.

JACK: Thank you, Mr. Lord.

LORD: But then I should expect that. What I want to know is the truth behind all these figures.

JACK: The truth is, sir, that this ranch has been making a big profit ever since you put me in charge of it.

LORD: Yes, and I expect you've made a big profit as well. Hello! What's this?

JACK: Which, Mr. Lord?

LORD: Mr. Galetti. With all that family to feed, only fifty measures of oil? It sounds very little.

JACK: It's all there in the books.

LORD: So I see. And Miss Macpherson. She wrote to me in Florida. I thought she mentioned five thousand, not three. Wait a minute! That 3—very clever! Very clever indeed! And others like it, I have no doubt. Let's have another look at Galetti. Aha! I've got it now! Just how many forged entries are there in this book, Mr. Steward?

JACK: None that you can prove. You left me here to run this ranch, and I've done my job. You can fire me if you like, but you can't pin any forgeries on me.

LORD: *(laughing)* You know, Jack, I underestimated you. Sit down and let's fix ourselves a drink!

JACK: I don't get it, Mr. Lord.

LORD: You don't? Fix me a Scotch on the rocks, and I'll explain.

JACK: Why, certainly, Mr. Lord. Just a moment.

(*While* JACK *fetches drinks from offstage,* LORD *looks at the ledger.* JACK *returns.*)

LORD: That's better, Jack. Cheers!

JACK: Cheers, sir!

LORD: See here, Jack. I left you to run this ranch, because I had big deals to look after, and—other things. I was too busy to run it myself. Right?

JACK: That's right, sir.

LORD: My business is growing, Jack, and it's getting tougher. I need some tough men to help me, too. So I decided to pay you a surprise visit, and find out what kind of a job you were really doing.

JACK: Well, the books are in order. You can't prove anything against me!

LORD: *(laughing)* On the contrary, Jack—I've proved that you're the kind of man I need. You're smart, and you're doing a great job. Those forgeries—that was quick thinking, and clever, too.

JACK: You mean—you don't want to fire me?

LORD: Fire you? How about moving to New York? Whatever you're making here, I'll double it. But you must be prepared to take responsibility, and the going will be rough and dirty. How about it?

JACK: You bet I'll go to New York! I can hardly believe it.

LORD: Just you wait, Jack! Together we can do wonders—sky's the limit!

JACK: Vera! Come in here! Mr. Lord, I want you to meet the girl I'm going to marry. Vera, this is the Boss.

VERA: I've heard a lot about you, Mr. Lord.

JACK: Vera helped me fix the books up yesterday.

LORD: Well! Is that so? Then you'll be a valuable member of our partnership in crime.

JACK: I've been promoted, Vera! What do you think about that? I was all ready to be fired, and I've been promoted!

LORD: Congratulations, both of you! Vera, get yourself a drink!

(She gets herself a drink.)

(While the CHORUS *recites the next verses, the three on stage continue to act.* JACK *gets the bottle, and fills their drinks.* VERA *flirts with* MR. LORD, *and they are all cheerful and slightly drunk. They point out entries in the ledger, and laugh over them. Half-way through the song* SATAN *appears at one side. He watches the rest of the scene with obvious amusement.)*

CHORUS *(sings)*
So Mr. Lord commended Jack Steward,
Because he was crooked and smart.
He could plan a crime in double-quick time,
And he made deceit an art.

And if you were only like Jack Steward,
And I were only like Mr. Lord,
We should fight God's fight with the whole of our might,
With the Spirit as our sword.

And if you were only like Jack Steward,
And I were only like Mr. Lord,
We should serve God's ends more than Satan's friends,
With a strong and glad accord.

189

Yes, Mr. Lord promoted Jack Steward,
Because he was crooked and smart.
When it came to lies, he was shrewd and wise,
Never slack or faint of heart.

So which of us can fight Jack Steward?
And which of us can beat Mr. Lord?
If the Christians dream, while the bad men scheme,
Then the Cross will be ignored.

(The congregation shuffle on with hymnals. SATAN *comes across and conducts them as they cross the stage. The three at the desk watch them derisively.)*

CHORUS *(sings)*
We are the children of light,
And we worship the Lord with part of our might.
We come to Church, and we pray and sing,
And we half believe in everything.
We half believe in a God above,
And we practise half of Christian love . . .

(They go off downstage. Their voices trail away. SATAN *and the others on stage raise their glasses and drink to them.)*

Also suitable for this Sunday: The Champion, The Rosebush; also see *Bible As Drama,* page 187; The Rich Farmer.

28. TWENTY-NINTH SUNDAY OF THE YEAR

Turning the World Upside Down

Bible Reference: I Thess. 1:1–5 (Epistle A)

Note: The story on which this scene is based is told in Acts 17:1–10, which does not occur in the lectionary. However, Paul's first letter to the church in Thessalonica is very close to the events recorded in the story.

Nowhere did the first church members require greater courage than in this Macedonian city. Paul came to it from Philippi, on his second missionary journey. He remembered with admiration and affection the friendship and fortitude of the first Christians there. His thankfulness for their steafast faith is plainly genuine and heartfelt (verse 2; compare 2 Thess. 1:3). In this scene we see a raid being made on a Christian home, as Luke describes it. A mob has been hired to support the Jews, who are outraged at the defection of some of their number to the new sect. Presumably Luke was an eyewitness.

The names in this scene are made up, except for Paul, Silas and Jason; but the details are implied in the Bible story.

Also suitable for: 30th and 31st Sundays of the Year, Epistle A: I Thess. 1:5–10 and 2:7–9, 13. See notes above.

Scene: A simple living room in Thessalonica, in the home of Jason and Arete.

Characters: JASON
ARETE, *his wife (pronounced A-re-tay)*
PHORMIO, *their son, 16*
PAUL
SILAS
SOSIPATER ⎫
XANTHE: ⎬ *Jewish Christians*
LYSIPPUS ⎭

JULIA
ANTIPHON } *Gentile Christians*

PAMPHILUS, *Leaders of the Synagogue*
TITIUS, *Roman official*

(*In the simple home of* JASON *and* ARETE *eight people are seated: the Christians listed above, except for* SOSIPATER. *They are singing a hymn.*)

ALL SING: Jesus, my Lord, my God, my all,
Hear me, blest Savior, when I call;
Hear me, and from thy dwelling-place
Pour down the riches of thy grace!
Jesus, my Lord, I thee adore;
O make me love thee more and more!

(*As the hymn finishes,* SOSIPATER *enters.*)

JASON: Welcome, Sosipater! Come and join us!

SOSIPATER: Thank you, Jason.

PAUL: We need you. We were just going to discuss the next steps in organizing the Church, before Silas and I go on our way.

SOSIPATER: Before we begin, I think you ought to know that there is something going on out in the street.

ARETE: Outside our house?

SOSIPATER: Yes. Or at least that is what it looked like. Some young men are standing out there, the other side of the road—a rough-looking bunch. They jeered at me as I turned towards your door.

LYSIPPUS: Did you recognize any of them?

SOSIPATER: No. I got the impression they were waiting for some-one.

JASON: Phormio, take a look outside, first the back, then the street entrance. Then stay at the window of the store, and let us know at once if you see anyone come near the door.

PHORMIO: I will, Father. (*He goes out.*)

JASON: If he gives us the warning, Paul, you and Silas are to leave at once by the back way, as we agreed.

PAUL: We will, Jason. Now let us quickly finish our business. Silas, you have a report to give?

SILAS: I have worked with Lysippus and Sosipater to make a list of all who have made their commitment to the Lord. Sosipater, you can speak for the Jewish community.

SOSIPATER: Yes. Nine families have joined us, God be praised! It

has caused bitter hatred in our synagogue, as you know—
especially since we began to hold our meetings with our Gentile
brothers and sisters.

SILAS: We know it, from what Paul and I have seen in other cities.

JASON: Still, we firmly believe that we have a strong enough nu-
cleus of our people to make our Church secure.

PAUL: I believe that also. Three Sabbaths in the synagogue! So
much has happened in this short time.

XANTHE: May we speak?

SILAS: Of course, Xanthe! I was going to ask Lysippus to speak
next, and tell us about the response among the Gentiles.

LYSIPPUS: (*laughing*) I think I know how Xanthe feels. I was grow-
ing uncomfortable at all of you talking about "our Church," and
your "strong nucleus."

XANTHE: That's right. It sounded as if we had no part to play,
except to make up the numbers.

SILAS: But you know that we do not feel that! Paul and I have
always gone to the Synagogue first, because we have felt it to be
right—

PAUL: We take the Messiah to those who should be ready to wel-
come him. But in God's eyes all are equally precious.

SOSIPATER: You need not have any fear that when Paul has left
us the Jewish families will look down on you, Xanthe. How could
we go on alone? We all need each other desperately.

PAUL: You could put it like this. The Jews have special responsibil-
ities in our Churches. They need to interpret the Eucharist, and
the Law, and the Scriptures—all of which you would find it hard
to understand and accept without them. They are the cement
of the Church. But they have no special privileges.

XANTHE: We understand, Paul. Jesus means far too much to us
for us to waste time on party jealousy and strife.

PAUL: One thing which never ceases to amaze me is the courage
and leadership which women are giving, wherever I go. It is the
same here: women like Julia, from among the Jews, and you and
your friends who were Gentiles, Xanthe. There are so many of
you, standing firm as rock. I see a great future—

(PHORMIO *hurries in.*)

JASON: What is it, son?

PHORMIO: I don't like it. The crowd has grown. And there's a group
with torches coming down the street. I heard people shouting your
name, Paul, and Jason's.

JULIA: God be with us! Come quickly, Paul!

ARETE: This way.

JASON: Send us news, Paul; and we will get a message to you.

PAUL: God bless you all!

SILAS: Goodbye, friends!

(PAUL, SILAS *and* JULIA *go out of a back door.*)

JASON: Sit down again, all of you.

ARETE: We aren't breaking any law. Surely they can't—

(PHORMIO *enters again.*)

PHORMIO: Antiphon and Pamphilus are coming to the door.

JASON: Then it is the Synagogue leaders.

PHORMIO: There's another man with them; and a crowd of thirty or forty—(*A loud knock on the outer door.*)

SOSIPATER: Let me go! Trust in the Lord, all of you!

(*He returns, with* ANTIPHON, PAMPHILUS *and* TITIUS.)

ANTIPHON: This is the house, Officer.

PAMPHILUS: And this man is Jason. He is one of them.

JASON: May I ask why you have come here?

TITIUS: You are Jason?

JASON: Yes.

TITIUS: And which of these men is Paul?

LYSIPPUS: Paul is not here. He was with us earlier, but he left.

ANTIPHON: Where did he go?

JASON: Just a minute! Antiphon, I know that you and Pamphilus bear us much ill will. I am very sorry for it. But this is a Roman city. We are not breaking any law—

PAMPHILUS: That is for the magistrates to decide. Is it loyalty to Caesar to preach publicly that Jesus is a King?

ANTIPHON: Wherever you go, you turn the world upside down, you Christians. We are going to see to it that here at least justice is done, and decent citizens protected.

LYSIPPUS: Officer, what do you want with us?

ANTIPHON: That man is a Gentile! This is what you have come to, Jason—eating and drinking with unclean scum!

TITIUS: That's enough, Sir. I want to know what is really going on here. We have had complaints about you, Jason—

JASON: Of course! From these men, the Jewish leaders. I know that they hate us, but that is no proof that we are disloyal. Have you a warrant to arrest us?

194

TITIUS: Nobody is talking about arresting you. I have to ask you all to come to headquarters for questioning.

JASON: And leave that mob to ransack our home?

TITIUS: No. Before we leave here, Antiphon, I want you to see to it that all these men are dispersed. We aren't having any mob violence in this city!

SOSIPATER: You talk about what we have come to, Antiphon, because we treat all men as equals. Is it worthy of you to incite a crowd of undesirables to threaten us?

PAMPHILUS: Just you wait, Sosipater! This is only the beginning.

TITIUS: Go out there, both of you, please, and get rid of them. As for you, Jason, since Paul is not here we shall hold you responsible for any charges brought against the Christians. You will have every chance to answer for yourselves. Now, let us go!

ARETE: You don't want our son? He is only a boy.

TITIUS: No. He can stay here and look after the house.

JASON: Don't worry, Phormio! We shall be back soon.

PHORMIO: I know you will, Father. Take care of Mother. And God go with you all!

TITIUS: Follow me, the rest of you!

Also suitable for this Sunday: Camels for the Ark (OT/B): see First Sunday After Christmas, Glad to See You Back (Epistle C): see 13th Sunday of the Year; also see *Bible As Drama,* Page 113 (OT/A): The End of the Exile, page 150 and 260 (Gospel A); Disciples and Critics and Corinth, page 257 (Epistle C): Frustration at Athens, Page 182-4 (Gospel C); The Widow and the Judge and Out of Town Guests.

29. THIRTY-SECOND SUNDAY OF THE YEAR

God's Tumbler

Bible Reference: Mark 12:38–44 (Gospel B)

Note: The widow at the Temple treasury 'put in everything she possessed, all she had to live on.' This was what the Abbot saw the Tumbler doing, when he danced. And in the Abbot's judgment the Tumbler, like the widow, put more in than others who would certainly have assumed that they were contributing more—like Brother Eldred. The Tumbler found it hard to give himself to God, but once he learned what it was that God wanted, he discovered fulfillment and happiness.

This play is based on a medieval French story, 'Le Jongleur de Dieu.' The names and details are imaginary.

One of the depressing things about a modern industrialized society is the lack of joy in so much of the work which needs to be done. The lesson of joyful, whole-hearted self-offering should shine through this play. All of us need to give ourselves, to God and to our neighbors, if we are to be fully ourselves.

The main production problem is the Tumbler's dancing. If you can find a dancer able to play the part, other problems will easily fall into place. The dancer need not also be a singer. Another actor can sing the songs.

The crowd in the opening scene wears modern dress; the Tumbler, leotards with a touch of bright color. The Monks could wear black cassocks rather than habits. The Crypt scene is the only hard one to present. With sophisticated lighting, you could act the final scene with a second actor, dressed like the Tumbler, lying 'dead' on the Altar steps, while he himself dances to the Altar, and is received by two angels, recognizable as Pierre and Louis.

(To obtain the musical score of this play, see page 7.)

Also suitable for: Epiphany; 7th, 11th, and 14th Sundays of the Year.

Epiphany: Gospel A/B/C (Matthew 2:1–12). 'They offered him gifts.' Wherever words like this occur, the Tumbler's story is appropriate. As Paul said, 'There is a variety of gifts but always the same Spirit; there are all sorts of service to be done, but always to the same Lord.'

7th Sunday of the Year: Gospel C (Luke 6:27–38). The lesson of this reading is very simple, but very profound. 'Give, and there will be gifts for you: a full measure, pressed down, shaken together, and running over, will be poured into your lap.' I imagine that in the final days of his life the Tumbler loved this passage more than almost any other in the Bible. He was living it.

11th Sunday of the Year: Epistle C (Galatians 2:16, 19–21). 'Now I can live for God . . . The life I now live in this body I live in faith.' Our play is about the Tumbler's discovery of this joyful piece of truth.

14th Sunday of the Year: Gospel A (Matthew 11:25–30). When the Tumbler heard the call of the bells he was a sick and weary man. He needed the words: 'Come to me, all you who labor and are overburdened, and I will give you rest.'

Scene: See individual scene headings.

Characters: THE TUMBLER
PIERRE ⎱ *his boy servants*
LOUIS ⎰
BROTHER ALBAN
THE ABBOT OF CLAIRVAUX
BROTHER ELDRED
TWO LORDS
TWO LADIES
VOICE OF GOD
NARRATOR
CHORUS OF PEASANTS, *and of* MONKS

(*A village square in France. On three sides, stands or sits a crowd of all ages and stations in life. The verses of the opening song are spoken by the* NARRATOR, *the crowd joining in the* REFRAIN, *while the* TUMBLER *dances.*)

NARRATOR: Once a wonderful Tumbler
               Used to journey through France.
               All the people came when they heard his name,
               And their feet began to dance.
REFRAIN: Dancing, Dancing, till the end of the day.

197

NARRATOR:	All the people of France began to dance
	When the Tumbler came their way.
	He was slender and graceful,
	He was nimble and gay;
	And all day long there was dance and song
	When the Tumbler came to stay.
REFRAIN:	Dancing, Dancing, in the markets of France.
	All the people came when they heard his name,
	And their feet began to dance.
NARRATOR:	But the Tumbler was weary;
	There was pain in his heart.
	While the crowds went mad he was tired and sad,
	And he longed to rest apart.
REFRAIN:	Dancing, Dancing, till the end of the day.
	Though his feet danced quick he was tired and sick,
	And you might have heard him pray:
TUMBLER:	O give me peace!
	O God, give me peace!
	My soul is weary, O give me rest and peace!

(*At the end of the dance he bows repeatedly, while the crowd cheers him loudly. He is very tired, and moves as though in a dream. The two servants take round caps, into which people put money. Then all go off, except* TWO LORDS *and* LADIES, *who say to him:*)

FIRST LORD:	Tumbler, come to my house!
	Come with me and dine!
FIRST LADY:	You shall eat from golden plates
	All that's rich and fine.
SECOND LORD:	Tumbler, come to my house!
	You shall have the best.
SECOND LADY:	You are worn and weary.
	Come with me and rest!

THE SAME FOUR (*one line each*):

You shall have linen and satin and silk,
Butter and honey and cheeses and milk.
You shall have silver and gold as well.
Servants will come when you touch a bell.

TUMBLER: I thank you, my Ladies, and you, my Lords. I thank you from my heart. But my dancing has made me weary, and I would

198

rest alone. My servants will see to my wants. I bid you goodnight, and I thank you for your kindness.

(They depart, saying, "Goodnight, TUMBLER! *Goodnight!* PIERRE *and* LOUIS *return R., as he sits down, exhausted.)*

PIERRE: Master, are you sick?

LOUIS: Master, you look pale!

TUMBLER: Never mind, Pierre! Never mind, Louis! I shall recover when I have sat and rested. Yet in truth it is not my limbs only that are tired, but my heart and my spirit.

PIERRE: Shall we go to the Inn, and see that your supper is ready?

LOUIS: Shall we prepare wine for you, Master?

TUMBLER: Yes, yes. See that everything is ready. Another Inn, another supper, another bed. Perhaps I should have gone with one of the fine Lords or Ladies, and lain between silken sheets, with servants to give me hot baths and pour my wine.

PIERRE: We shall look after you, Master.

TUMBLER: I know it, I know it. How many Inns have we slept in, you and I? How many times have I danced since winter? Well, never mind! I am rich, I am famous throughout France! But in truth I love none of it, except that I love to dance, and to set the feet of Lords and peasants dancing. And even of that I grow weary, and long for peace.

LOUIS: Come to the Inn, Master!

TUMBLER: Yes, I will come. *(The bells have begun to ring softly.)* Stop! What bells are those? I saw an Abbey as we rode by, but we travel so far and so fast that half the time I do not know where we are.

PIERRE: This is Clairvaux, and those are the Abbey bells.

TUMBLER: Clairvaux! I have heard of it. The good Bernard was Abbot there. Clairvaux! The bells have a sweet tone.

PIERRE: Will you come now, Master?

TUMBLER: Go to the Inn, both of you! I want to listen to the bells. Perhaps I shall walk to the Abbey while the sun is setting.

LOUIS: Yes, Master. I will take the money bag.

PIERRE: It is heavy tonight.

TUMBLER: Yes, take it, my sons. I wish that my heart would grow lighter when the bag grows heavier! But enough of that: go to the Inn!

BOTH: Yes, Master.

(They go out, and he sits and listens to the bells.)

CHORUS (*offstage*)
The Bells are ringing to call you home.
The Bells are ringing, and bid you come.
They say that pain can cease,
That you may find release,
That there is rest and peace
If you will hear.
The Bells are ringing, to speak to you.
The night is falling, and rest is due.
From all the fever and labour and fear
The Bells are calling, if you will hear.

(*The* TUMBLER *walks off towards the sound. After a music bridge, he comes on and knocks at the monastery door.* BROTHER ALBAN *comes out.*)

ALBAN: Good evening, Sir, and welcome!
TUMBLER: Greetings, Father!
ALBAN: No, no. Not Father. I am only a lay brother, Sir, whose task is to watch the door and help strangers.
TUMBLER: You give welcome to all who come?
ALBAN: All but rogues; and sometimes they are welcome too. But come in, Sir! You look tired. Abbot Benedict would scold me if he knew that you were standing out in the darkness.

Yes, everyone may enter,
To wash and rest and feed.
So come inside, for the door is wide
For a man in need.
And I am here to welcome
The stranger at the gate.
I should think it shame if you called my name
And I made you wait.

You are no casual beggar,
You are no wandering tramp,
With clothes so fine, and shoes that shine,
You bear a rich man's stamp.
We ask no prying questions;
We take you as you come.
You may work or pray, you may sleep all day,
You may speak or be dumb.

Now sit there, and I will tell the Abbot that we have a guest. For indeed you must not stir from here tonight.

200

TUMBLER: I have a lodging at the Inn, and my serving boys—

ALBAN: Your serving boys may fend for themselves until morning. Hot milk or mulled wine is what you need, and a square meal.

(The chanting of "Remember, O Lord" has begun off stage.)

TUMBLER: What is that chanting?

ALBAN: It is some of the brethren on the way through the cloister to the Chapel. Make yourself at home, and listen till I come.

(We hear the CHORUS *chant: "Remember, O Lord, what thou hast wrought in us, and not what we deserve; and, as thou hast called us to thy service, make us worthy of our calling." Then the chanting fades away. The* TUMBLER *sits with his head buried in his hands.)*

TUMBLER: "Make me worthy of my calling"! O God, I have no calling, but to dance and tumble. How useless I am, with all my fame and finery! O for peace of heart, for peace of heart!

NARRATOR: The Tumbler was made welcome by the Abbot, first as a guest and then as a novice. He sent for his Servants, gave them a generous portion of his money, and delivered the rest to Abbot Benedict. He said a loving farewell to Pierre and Louis, who went away sorrowful, for they had loved their Master well. France soon forgot the Tumbler, and he for his part began to try to learn to be a good Monk—a task which he did not find easy.

(In the workroom, the TUMBLER *is working clumsily at a carpenter's bench. He makes a false blow with his hammer, and the wood falls to the ground. The* ABBOT *stops at his table.)*

ABBOT: It seems that your hands are not as deft as your feet, Brother Tumbler. Let me see this work that you have done.

TUMBLER: I have tried hard, Father Abbot, but it is bad work, and I know it.

ABBOT: There at least you are right. In the garden, you dug up Father Juniper's asparagus when you were trying to sow cabbages. In the kitchen, you upset a skillet over Brother Matthew, and broke four earthenware dishes. You can neither read nor write, so that the manuscript room is hardly the place for you. In truth, Brother, I am at a loss to know just how you can best serve Almighty God.

TUMBLER: *(to himself)* I can dance.

ABBOT: What was that?

TUMBLER: I am sorry, Father. I was thinking far-off thoughts. I will try harder at the work, and perhaps God will give me grace to become a passable gardener or carpenter even yet.

(*A bell tolls for the next half minute.*)

ABBOT: There is the bell for Vespers. Go and prepare yourself; and do not worry too much about your bruised thumbs or bad work! As long as nobody has to depend on eating your cabbages, or use this box (which may the good Lord forbid!) God will watch your heart rather than your hands.

(*The bell stops tolling. The* TUMBLER *moves slowly to kneel in front of the altar.*)

NARRATOR: But the Tumbler did not go to Vespers. Instead he waited in the Cloister until the rest had gone to the Chapel, and then stole down to the Crypt, where there was a Chapel of Our Lady. He prayed long at the Altar steps, and as he prayed he seemed to hear music. His whole body began to tingle, and his feet itched to dance.

TUMBLER: O God! What use am I? It is as the Abbot said. I can do nothing right, and I am sick. Yet here I feel at home, and near to you. Can I do nothing to serve you.

VOICE OF GOD: You can dance. (*The* TUMBLER *looks up, astonished.*) One gift I gave you, Tumbler, which no other man in France shares; and that gift you sacrificed to serve me here. I have often watched you dance on village greens and in city squares. Dance for me now, and do me service!

(*Music sounds, first softly, then louder. Choose music appropriate for the* TUMBLER's *dance.*)

TUMBLER: Whose was that voice? And what is this music? Pierre! Louis! Is that you?

VOICE OF PIERRE: (*from behind the Altar.*) Dance, Master! It was God who called you.

VOICE OF LOUIS: Dance for Him, and for the Virgin Mary, Master!

(*As though in a trance, the* TUMBLER *slowly takes off his habit, and begins to dance, at first hesitantly, then with more and more fluency. When the dance finishes, he kneels.*)

TUMBLER:　　　　I can give you dancing,
　　　　　　　　I can dance and sing.
　　　　　　　　I can tumble and leap and turn;
　　　　　　　　That is all I bring.
　　　　　　　　Only by my dancing

I can play my part.
All my love is here in my feet;
I'm dancing with my heart.
There's no gift of hand or head that I am fit to bring.
There's no work that I can do to serve my God and
King.
I can give you dancing,
I can dance and sing.
I can tumble and leap and turn;
That is all I bring.

(*He has a fit of coughing and seems to be in pain.*)

NARRATOR: So every day the Tumbler slipped away into the Crypt
and danced. But at length one of the brothers, Eldred, noticed his
absence.

(*The* TUMBLER *is still kneeling at the Altar.* ELDRED *enters
stealthily, and hides in the shadows.*)

NARRATOR: Eldred was not a bad or vindictive man; but Monks are
very much like other men, and perhaps he envied the Tumbler his
former fame in the outside world, or despised his clumsiness in the
work of the Abbey. At all events, consumed by curiosity, he
noted one evening where the Tumbler lurked in the Cloister; and
he too slipped away in the shadows, and followed him. He saw
him dance, but he did not hear the music, because his ears were
not attuned to it.

(*The music comes up again gradually, and the* TUMBLER *rises,
and again begins slowly to dance. After the climax of the dance
he falls, coughing, then lies still.* ELDRED *hurries to the side of
the stage, and speaks the next verse.*)

ELDRED: Its disgusting, it's disgusting,
          All his posturing and lusting!
      Bowing to the Altar like the Devil at his prayers!
        He's revolting, he's revolting,
          With his juddering and jolting!
    Somersaulting openly upon the Altar stairs!
        It's disgusting, quite disgusting—

(*The* ABBOT *enters, and* ELDRED *breaks off.*)

ABBOT: What is the matter, Brother Eldred? You look angry and
upset.

ELDRED: It is nothing, Father Abbot. I—

ABBOT: Nothing! I am sorry that you can look so deeply and sadly moved by nothing. When there is anger in a man's heart, especially if he be a monk, better to let it out and so draw its sting.

ELDRED: Indeed, Father, you are right. But when it means causing harm to a fellow brother—

ABBOT: I see. *(He pauses.)* Even so, you had better let me be the judge of that. Such harm also may best be cured by the open light of truth. What has made you so full of indignation, Brother?

ELDRED: Truly, Father, it is a sight which I have just seen, and which I little thought ever to see in a house of God.

(We see him talking and gesticulating, as they walk away together.)

NARRATOR: And so Brother Eldred told the Abbot; and the Abbot, who was a good and wise man, said little, but made Eldred promise, on his oath of obedience, to say nothing of what he had seen. And then the Abbot went away, and prayed.

(The ABBOT *enters, and kneels.)*

ABBOT: O God, show me what is right for your servant and our brother, the Tumbler! You have taught us that as monks we should do unto you true and laudable service; and no one could want to carry out your bidding more than he does. Yet all that he can do well is to dance; and I have never read nor heard that to turn somersaults is to pray; though to be sure King David danced before your Altar. O Lord, you know that the Tumbler is not long for this world, being grievously sick, and that he is a good man, generous of heart. Teach me what I should do . . .

NARRATOR: In the morning the Abbot awoke, knowing what he should do. All that day he went about his duties, and the hours of the monastic life passed as usual in work and worship, in the eating of meals and in the brief period of relaxation. When the time for Vespers came, the Abbot went to the Chapel in the Crypt, hid himself, and watched.

(The TUMBLER *is still kneeling, and the* ABBOT *slips in and hides. The dance is repeated, shorter and wilder, as though the* TUMBLER *has to drive himself to finish it. He falls suddenly, in a paroxysm of coughing, while the music is at its height. It ceases abruptly. The* ABBOT *runs forward to kneel by him.)*

TUMBLER: O, Father Abbot, I— *(He starts up.)*

ABBOT: Do not be afraid, my son!

TUMBLER: But I am afraid. You saw me?

ABBOT: Yes, I saw you dance.

TUMBLER: I have sinned, Father, and I know that now I shall not be able to stay here. I have abused your goodness; for night after night I have come here and danced. But I swear that I did it because I was hungry and thirsty to do God service, and to give him thanks.

ABBOT: Which is what you have done, my son.

TUMBLER: You mean that you—

ABBOT: I mean that when I watched you my heart was more full of thankfulness than it has been for many a year, perhaps more than it has ever been. And full of humility also.

TUMBLER: But—I don't understand. You don't want to send me away? You can punish me in some other way?

ABBOT: I am not going to send you away. I do not think that either you or I will live much longer in this world. I am old, and you are sick. I hope that we shall make our pilgrimage together, and proud should I be to come to my Lord with such a friend beside me! But I enjoin upon you one thing, on your vow of obedience. Each day you must dance here alone; for it is your service to him who gave you such grace and strength. Do not overtax yourself, but dance to give thanks. That is your carpentry, your gardening, your reading and writing, yes, and your cooking and your prayer. Our walls will rejoice with the pulse of your dancing, for it too is sacred.

(During the final narration, the ABBOT *and* TUMBLER *remain still.)*

NARRATOR: So he danced every day. And it came about that one night, as he danced, he seemed to see his servants again, welcoming him; and his mother and father, whom he dearly loved; and a great crowd that watched and took pleasure in his dancing—but it was a crowd of Angels, not of peasants. And the music was the music of a heavenly choir. Had you been there, you would have seen the Tumbler stumble, fall and rise no more. For in that hour his body was shed away. But his spirit danced out of earthly life, and danced right through the gates of Heaven, which lay open before him. And on the other side the trumpets sounded for him, in the rhythm and joy of his dancing, and the Angels rejoiced, as men on earth had rejoiced, at his grace and beauty.

CHORUS: Dancing, dancing, up to Heaven so high!
            All the trumpets rang, all the Angels sang,
                When the Tumbler's feet danced by!

30. FEAST OF CHRIST THE KING

Martin the Cobbler

Bible Reference: Matthew 25:31–46 (Gospel A)

Note: This play is included in 'Christmas Is Coming' (see page 9). See the notes given there. It makes a beautiful presentation by itself. This reading forms part of Martin's own Bible reading in the play.
See also: Corpus Christi, 31st Sunday of the Year.

Corpus Christi: Epistle and Gospel A: (I Corinthians 10:16–17, John 6:51–59). The sharing of the cup and the loaf brings Martin close to God, after he had for a long time felt far away from him.
31st Sunday of the Year: Gospel A (Matthew 23:1–12). This links up with Martin's soliloquy about the Pharisee, as well as with his reflections in taking to Stepanich, where he quotes the verse: 'The greatest among you must be your servant.'

Also suitable for this Sunday: Take-Over (OT/A): see Fourth Sunday of Easter, Finding the Dentist (Epistle A): see Trinity, The Empire (Epistle C): see 23rd Sunday of the Year: also see *Bible As Drama,* page 237 and 238 (OT/B and Epistle B); The Stoning of Stephen and The Conversion of Saul, page 151 (Gospel C): Who Are You, Lord?

DRAMA CALENDAR

You should feel free to adapt the use of the plays to your needs. The schedules suggested here are for your guidance only.

With a company of ten to twenty actors and actresses, some with previous experience, you could consider a three year program on these lines:

YEAR A

ADVENT: *CHRISTMAS IS COMING* (6 adults, 5 young and chorus)
JOSEPH AND MARY (2 adults or young)

CHRISTMAS to EPIPHANY: *THE INNKEEPER* (6 adults or young)
THE ROAD TO BETHLEHEM (3 adults)
THE GOOD SAMARITAN (large cast, young)

EPIPHANY and LENT: *GODPARENTS* (3 adults)
WHO IS MY NEIGHBOR? (13 adults or high school)
THE CHAMPION (7 adults)

PASSION and EASTER: Use *THE BIBLE AS DRAMA:* "Scenes from the life of Jesus" and "Good Friday."

EASTER to PENTECOST: *THE PERFECT HOUSE* (6 adults and some young)
JONAH (large cast and chorus)
GOD'S TUMBLER (large cast and chorus)

SUNDAYS AFTER PENTECOST: *GLAD TO SEE YOU BACK* (2 adults and some high school)
FINDING THE DENTIST (5 adults, 2 young)
TO ENTER INTO LIFE CRIPPLED (4 adults)

207

CAMELS FOR THE ARK (5 adults, 1 young)
TURNING THE WORLD UPSIDE DOWN (12 adults)
TAKEOVER (5 adults)
GO, SHOW YOURSELF (9 adults, 2 young)

YEAR B

ADVENT: *THE END OF THE WORLD* (4 adults)
GRANNY IS COMING FOR CHRISTMAS (2 adults, 2 high school)

CHRISTMAS TO EPIPHANY: *CAMELS FOR THE ARK*
BAPTISM (3 adults)
THREE WISE MEN (3 adults)

EPIPHANY and LENT: *TO ENTER INTO LIFE CRIPPLED*
GO, SHOW YOURSELF
HONOR YOUR FATHER (8 adults)

PASSION and EASTER: *see Year A*

EASTER to PENTECOST: *TURNING THE WORLD UPSIDE DOWN*
FINDING THE DENTIST
MARTIN THE COBBLER (5 adults, 1 young)

SUNDAYS AFTER PENTECOST: *THE CRAFTY STEWARD* (large cast of adults)
THE PERFECT HOUSE
THE EMPIRE (9 adults)
THE ROSEBUSH (3 adults, 2 young)
GOD'S TUMBLER
CANA OF GALILEE (6 adults)

YEAR C

ADVENT: *JOHN THE BAPTIST* (8 adults and crowd)
JOSEPH AND MARY (2 adults or young)

208

CHRISTMAS TO EPIPHANY: *THE ANIMAL WHO DIDN'T*
TALK (5 young)
THREE WISE MEN

EPIPHANY and LENT: *CANA OF GALILEE*
THE ROSEBUSH
THE GOOD SAMARITAN
THE CHAMPION

PASSION and EASTER: *see Year A*

EASTER to PENTECOST: *TAKEOVER*
BAPTISM
GLAD TO SEE YOU BACK

SUNDAYS AFTER PENTECOST: *THE EMPIRE*
HONOR YOUR FATHER
THE CRAFTY STEWARD
WHO IS MY NEIGHBOR?
GODPARENTS
JONAH

For a company of beginners, who prefer to undertake short scenes, this schedule is suggested:

ADVENT: (Any of the following): *CHRISTMAS IS COMING*
THE END OF THE WORLD
GRANNY IS COMING FOR
CHRISTMAS
JOHN THE BAPTIST
JOSEPH AND MARY

CHRISTMAS to EPIPHANY: *THE INNKEEPER*
THE ANIMAL THAT DIDN'T
SPEAK
THE ROAD TO BETHLEHEM
BAPTISM

EPIPHANY AND LENT: *GODPARENTS*
CANA OF GALILEE
HONOR YOUR FATHER

PASSION AND EASTER: *Use* THE BIBLE AS DRAMA
("Scenes from the life of Jesus" and
"Good Friday")

209